How We Got
to the Moment
That Just Passed

How We Got to the Moment That Just Passed

a brief history
to help you prepare
for what's next

THOMAS LINCOLN

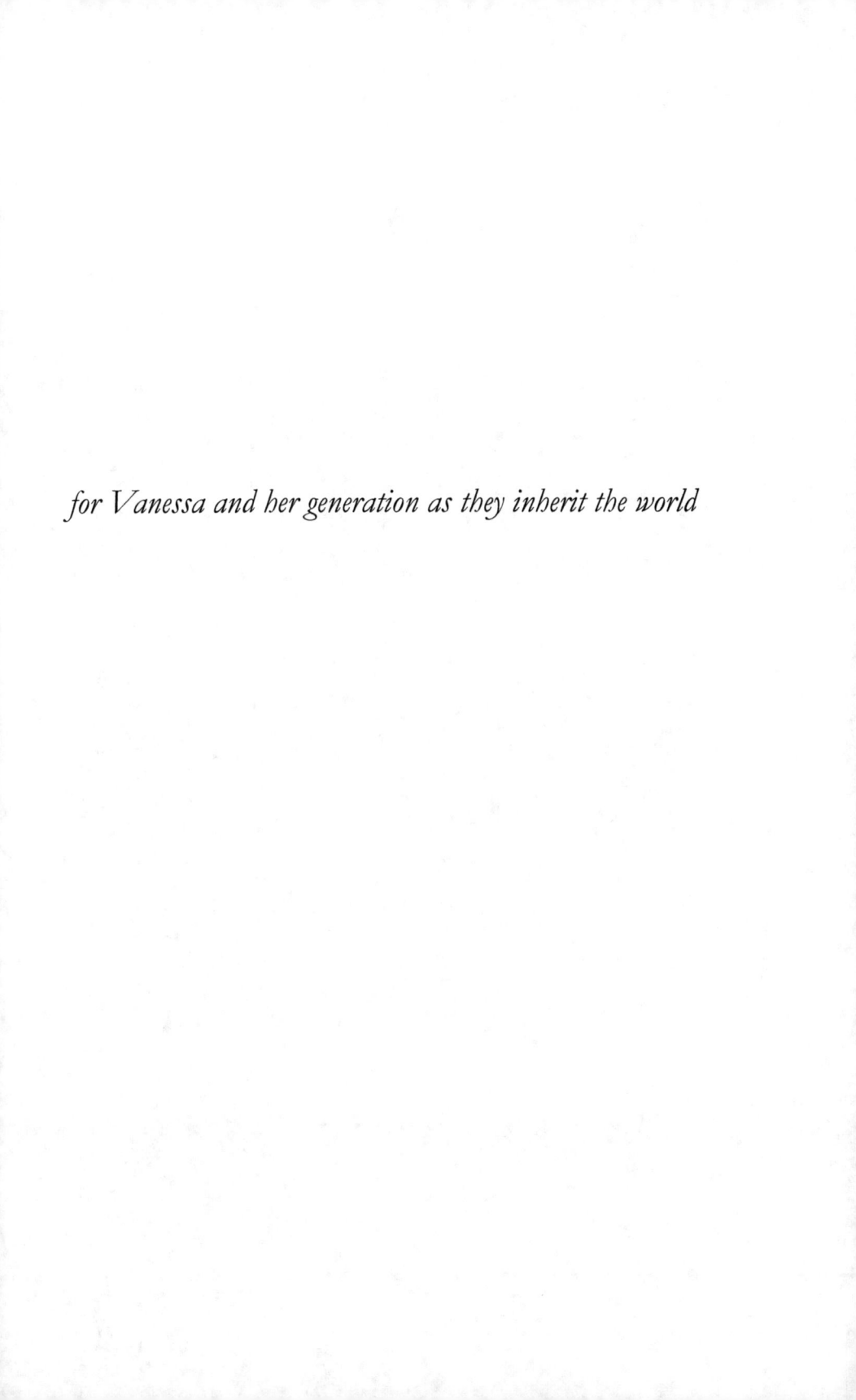

for Vanessa and her generation as they inherit the world

TABLE OF CONTENTS

PROLOGUE

How History Teaches Us That the Future Will **Not** Be Like the Past

Let me be up front about this: I'm not a scholar; I'm a retired high school teacher. I've had to learn a lot of history, and I've had to make it accessible enough and engaging enough to keep a high school student from drifting off. I'm going to include pictures. But I'm not going to include footnotes or even end notes. You'll have to trust me.

I realize that's a lot to ask these days, in a world full of mis- and (worse) disinformation. And it isn't generally a good thing for a high school teacher to say; I should be preaching cross-checking your sources.

But, though learning to cross-check sources (and how) is important for young people, it is not the most important thing to impart when teaching history. The most important thing is to *challenge perspectives*. History should not nibble away at you as an amalgam of details uncovered by disparate experts. It should jolt you to attention like a splash in the face and make you see the world from a different angle.

I want this to be a history that is accessible to everyone, but it isn't going to be history for dummies. My goal is *clarity*, not simplicity. Not simply stripped-down history, *distilled* history. And I need to do it in as few words as possible because the clock is ticking. You'll soon see why.

From the start of Chapter 1, this book follows a pretty straightforward narrative. The "I" that is talking to you now disappears once this prologue is through. But first I'm going to describe how I began my 9th grade world history classes...

We teachers like to give our students some structure by heading our lessons with "guiding questions" (GQs). The one for this intro lesson is the very unoriginal "Why do we study history?"

In my opinion, the absolute *worst* answer to this GQ is "So we can learn from the mistakes of the past." Could there be any more boring a way to begin 180 class days of learning about world history? Oh boy, we get to study a bunch of old screw-ups just so we won't screw those things up again.

1

Is that all history can do for us? Teach us what to watch for when it comes around again? No! I don't even think it's true. Who says our future is going to be anything like our past?

A knowledge of history gives us a far greater power than a bagful of old mistakes. History, when viewed from a broad perspective, can tell us what is *about* to happen that has *never happened before*! How cool is that?

Let me *show* you:

I've turned the classroom walls into a blank timeline. But it's a timeline without any dates. Instead, there are class periods. It says "Start of 1st period" just clockwise from the door. A ways further clockwise is "Start of 2nd period." A ways past "Start of 4th period" comes "Start of LUNCH," etc. through all seven periods. School lets out as we come back to the door.

I've seeded our timeline with two significant *events, inventions,* or *persons* of world history. By the start of 1st period, I've taped up a card that says "Rise of first civilizations." (Tricky word, I know; we'll come back to that at the end of Chapter 1.) At the end of 7th period, I've taped up another card that says "the iPhone."

Now it's the students' turn. Each is handed a similar card as they come in the door, with their own significant *event, invention,* or *person.* Their job is to tape it anywhere on any of the four walls. They should do this as quickly as possible, according to their gut, not according to what's on the wall already, what their buddy thinks, or, well, their iPhone. Then they sit down.

Once everyone is seated, I invite everyone to take a minute to look around and see where things ended up. Then the floor is open to point out things that don't look right. For example, someone has placed the American Revolution in 3rd period, but gunpowder doesn't show up until after lunch. The person who commented on this gets to rearrange the events in question.

We spend quite a bit of time at this, with more and more discrepancies identified, until things are reasonably close to the correct order, which would be:

1. the wheel

2. the Egyptian pyramids

3. Moses

4. Buddha

5. Socrates

6. the Great Wall

7. Jesus

8. paper

9. the Fall of Rome

10. Muhammad

11. gunpowder

12. movable-type printing

13. Columbus

14. the first factory

15. the American Revolution

16. railroads

17. Napoleon

18. the electric motor

19. the telephone

20. widescale electric lighting

21. the Eiffel Tower

22. the gas-powered car

23. the radio

24. the airplane

25. plastic

26. television

27. Hitler

28. the computer

29. the atomic bomb

30. the moon landing

31. the PC

32. the Internet

But even if we were 100% perfect with the chronology, as above, we would still have a long way to go to get things placed properly. At the moment, they are fairly evenly distributed.

Then someone makes the astute observation that Jesus and Columbus are too close together, with the former near the end of 2nd period and the latter still before lunch. I have already promised the class that precise dates will rarely have importance in this course, but already they have reared their head. Most are thinking "Jesus = year 0" and when was Columbus again? Many don't remember, since he rightly isn't lionized in elementary school anymore, but his impact on world history is *huge*, so I don't mind reminding them that he sailed the ocean blue in... 1492. So that means there should be 1,492 years between him and Jesus, which only leaves roughly 520-odd years for all of lunch and 5th through 7th periods. That can't be right!

Invariably, this is when I finally get asked the date of the first civilizations. I tell them 4000 BCE. It's close enough, and it makes calculating easy: Each of the seven class periods covers 800 years, with 400 for lunch, between 4th and 5th periods.

Now we've really upset things, and it takes an ad hoc committee of the more enthusiastic students, eventually stumbling over each other as they cram into the six feet of wall that comprises the second half of 7th period, the more exacting of the bunch with phones out, calculating, fine-tuning the arrangement until we have the results you see on the facing page. ⎯⎯⎯⎯⎯⎯⎯⎯⎯⎯⎯➤

I have had the picture below up on the screen at the front of the class the whole time. Now I finally draw attention to it:

I tell the class it is a special telescope that can look back in time. Like an ordinary telescope, it condenses perspective; it is hard to compare the distance between the viewer and the foreground to the distance between the foreground and the background. We have established that the pyramid in the background was erected far back in 2nd period. Where does the foreground belong in our timeline? In other words, when was the photograph taken?

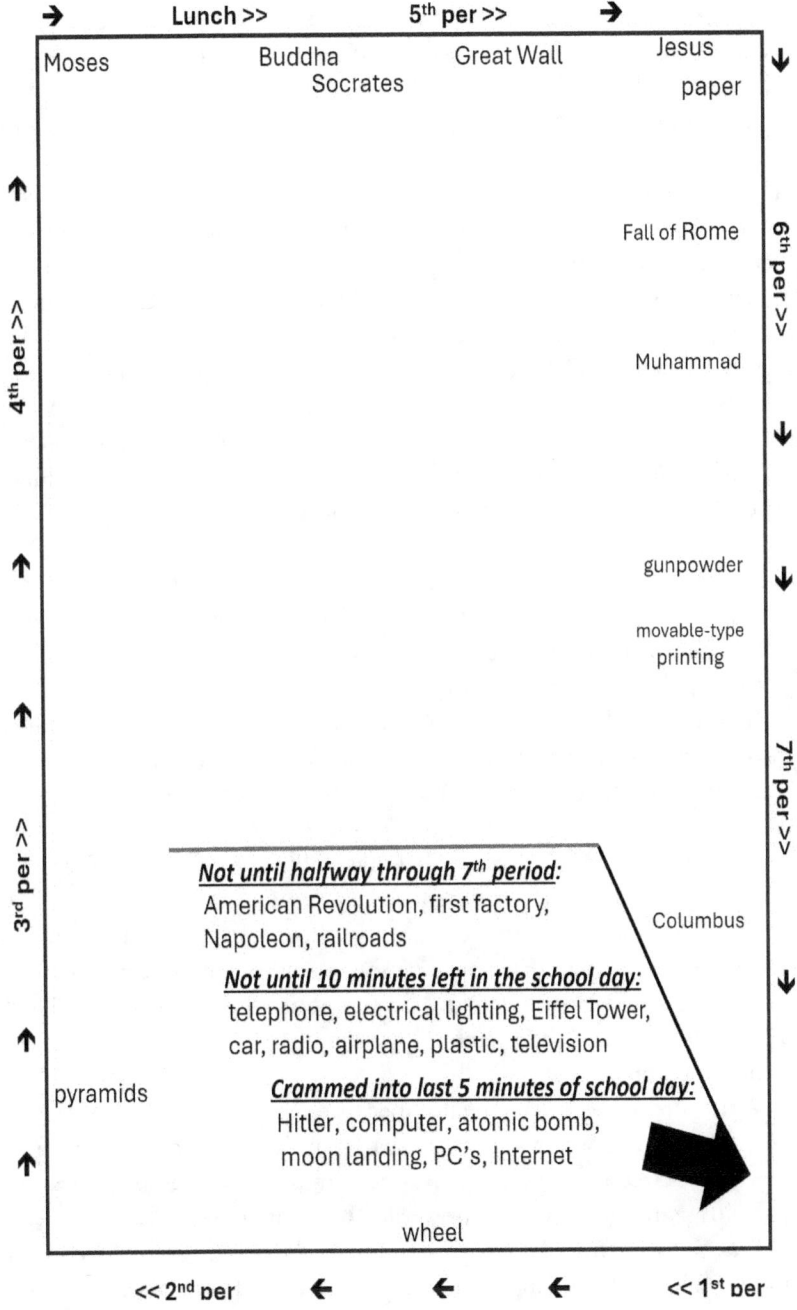

We didn't put up a card for the first photograph, but as no one can remember any photos of the American Revolution, it's certain that the foreground belongs somewhere in the second half of 7th period. This is quite revealing to many 9th graders, who tend to consider men with mutton-chop sideburns and women with funny hats and full-length dresses to be just about as ancient as the pyramids. Now they can begin to appreciate that the pyramids were just as ancient to the Victorians in the photo as they are to the Gen-Z'ers in the room.

The more important understanding to glean is that human history does not move at a constant pace. It did for a long while. But then—from a big picture perspective, fairly recently—it sped up.

Which brings us to why: Why did it suddenly speed up? We turn our attention to that point on the timeline (check out the prior page again).

Someone suggests Columbus, but that is debunked quickly; there is too big of a gap. Someone says the American Revolution (the influence of American exceptionalism is alive and well). Soon after that, someone gives the correct answer: There on the wall, virtually in tandem with the American Revolution, is the cause of a much more impactful revolution: *the first factory*. It is the *Industrial Revolution* that speeds up our history.

So how do we use this high-level view of history to get an idea of what is going to happen in the future that has never happened before? For that, we need to zoom *in* on one point in our timeline to flesh out a little more detail: the point represented by the above photograph...

If you look closely, you will see two very different types of people. The men with the considerable facial hair and the women in the funny hats seem quite out of place in the Egyptian desert, but there are two guides in turbans, as well. The former group—we'll call them the tourists—are Europeans; the guides are of course native Egyptians. The picture belongs about ten minutes before the end of the school day, around the time the Eiffel Tower was built. It was taken in what is often referred to as the Era of New Imperialism. An era of new empires. A time when a small group of European nations—and two non-European nations, the United States and Japan—subjugated the entire remaining world. This was possible because the industrial technology they had acquired gave them much better ships and guns.

I use the broad term "subjugate" because, unlike with empires in earlier times, the lands taken over were kept apart from the ruling country. Sometimes they were ruled directly as colonies. At other times, they were only economically overrun, with native governments powerless to do anything about it.

Here's the important part: The secret of industrial technology remained guarded within the small "club" of imperialist nations. Although the *products* of industry were introduced to the subjugated peoples (for instance, those Europeans would build the Suez Canal through Egypt and sail their steamships through it), the

6

factories, and the technology within them, were not. *None of the native people became industrial producers themselves.* And nearly all of them lived a much poorer lifestyle than the people who lived in the imperialist nations.

Time passes. Two world wars are fought. Finally, with only a little over three minutes left in our school day, an explosion of decolonization around the world puts an end to the Imperialist Era, and industrialization begins to spread through what becomes known as the "developing world."

This is an entirely new development in the history of the world—*begun scantly three minutes ago by this scale!* What do you think is going to happen next?

Will this explosion in new development be a positive or a negative? Will the growth of the world's economy support the growing population equally? Will the spread of industrialization buoy all boats and lift much of the world out of poverty? Or will there be new winners... to be offset by new losers? What about natural resources? Will there be enough to share? Or will the ex-imperialists' share have to diminish as the ex-colonies' share increases? Will this lead to conflict?

There is much to speculate, but there is one thing to be absolutely sure of...

In 1896, at the height of the Era of New Imperialism, with industry limited to the few imperialist nations mentioned above, a Nobel prize-winning Swedish chemist named Svante Arrhenius made a prediction. He said that the burning of fossil fuels (like coal and petroleum) that was driving the Industrial Revolution would raise the temperature of the planet in "a few centuries"—*or sooner if consumption increased.*

Our timeline shows us the one thing that is clearly going to happen next: Rapid decolonization leading to a new surge in industrialized development is going to *send consumption through the roof.*

If you look at the following graph, you can see why:

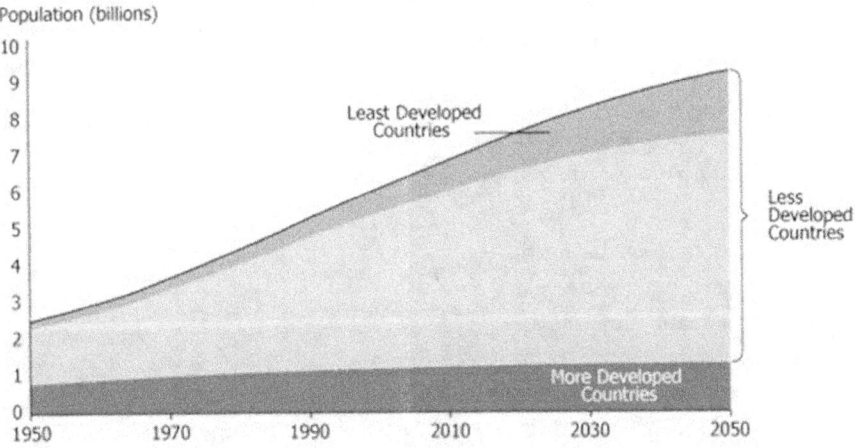

Carl Haub, "World Population Trends 2012," Population Reference Bureau, June 18, 2012, www.prb.org/resources/world-population-trends-2012/. Reproduced by permission. All rights reserved.

The populations of the former imperialist countries (More Developed Countries) have been relatively stable in recent years and are predicted to remain so. It is the growth of the developing world (Less Developed Countries) that has driven us past nine billion people. It is all those billions that are going to be the new consumers. And that growth in consumption is going to raise the temperature of the planet far sooner than Arrhenius anticipated.

Few people are aware that science first predicted human-caused global warming more than 125 years ago. But it takes more than a knowledge of science to predict just how soon this phenomenon will become a threat to the very survival of humankind—it takes a knowledge of history.

Because they have historically monopolized industry, the More Developed Countries, despite being quite a small slice of the world's population, have almost exclusively driven the increase in global temperatures. Only a few years prior to this writing, they were contributing 30 times more global warming-inducing carbon to the atmosphere *than all the rest of the world combined.* Already that is changing, as the Less Developed Countries become more developed, themselves.

At the point in history when I set down these words, the average American emits more than 15 tons of carbon into the atmosphere annually. The goal of the Less Developed Countries is to achieve the American lifestyle. So let's project this American "carbon footprint" onto one of them as an example: India.

In 2022, the 11 leading carbon-emitting nations added more than 25 billion metric tons to the atmosphere.

The average Indian's carbon footprint is only about 2 tons per person. But since India's population is rapidly approaching 1.5 billion, it already emits 56% of what the United States emits. And while an American is born every 16 seconds, an Indian is born every *second.*

Now let's project that population increase out to the year 2050 and assume that India has achieved its modernization goals and that most of its people have a lifestyle similar to that of Americans.

By this time, India alone

2022	Total carbon emissions (millions of metric tons)	Carbon emissions per person (metric tons)
China	11,397	8.0
USA	5,057	15.5
India	2,830	2.0
Russia	1,652	11.5
Japan	1,054	8.6
Indonesia	729	2.7
Iran	691	8.0
Germany	666	8.0
S. Arabia	663	17.9
S. Korea	601	11.8
Canada	548	13.7
	25,888	

will be emitting nearly 26 billion tons of carbon to the atmosphere—more than the leading 11 carbon-emitting countries do today, in total.

And that's just one Less Developed Country. There are 180 more.

2050	Projected millions of metric tons by 2050	Carbon emissions per person (metric tons)
India	25,963	15.5

Scientists are alarmed by the radically steep increase in atmospheric carbon and other greenhouse gases that has occurred since the Industrial Revolution. Now, a second historical landmark –the spread of that revolution to the world's underprivileged masses—is about to bend that curve even more vertically.

So, in sum, if you have followed the science you will already be concerned about climate change. But if you follow the history you will be extremely concerned about the looming climate *crisis*.

Those who fixate on identifying repetitive patterns within the narrow band of modern history are like researchers who make claims without a large enough sample size. Without removing oneself much farther from the bounds of the present, it is natural to feel that we have evolved to here—as if all history of any consequence is over now, as if history is only the past and explains only the present. In this view, capitalism, democracy, and a lone superpower USA are the culmination of a natural order. That is human naïveté. If we step back for a broader view, we learn that history's arc extends well into the future and that we are a point in constant motion, rocketing along it with ever-increasing speed.

◇◇◇

How we got ourselves to this point in time is a long story, but the rate we are hurtling into the future necessitates that I keep it brief. Much of what you expect to find in these pages may have been left out altogether. Impact on our present world has been my sole criteria in making choices. How did we get to the present state of inequality in the world today? What allowed those More Developed Countries to be the first to industrialize? How did sub-Saharan Africa become so poor and racked by conflict? How did areas of the Middle East become so radicalized by religion? What caused the great cultural differences between East and West? How did our political differences develop? These are some of the questions I hope will become clearer by the end of these pages.

In Chapter 1, we zoom out for an even broader view. Two extremely important technological advancements predate the 4000 BCE mark, where I placed the first civilizations: farming and writing.

9

A prerequisite to writing would, of course, be speaking. If we were to create a school-day timeline with a card representing the first evidence of "speaking" at the start of 1st period, then farming would not occur until near the end of 6th period. Writing and the development of early civilizations would occur early in 7th period. Everything else, even the pyramids, would be crammed into the remaining minutes of the day.

We could have started here, and I would be asking the same question: Why? What made history speed up? And you would look to that spot in the timeline, and you would point to farming as the cause.

There have been two great revolutions in human history. The Industrial Revolution was the second. The Agricultural Revolution was at least as impactful.

CHAPTER ONE

Cast Out From Paradise: The First of the Two Great Revolutions of Human History
(~9000-~1500 BCE)

The story of Adam and Eve doesn't come along until about 200,000 years after the rise of homo sapiens, but it's a good place to start. Anything earlier is more the purview of anthropologists than historians. The story is not uniquely Judeo-Christian; there are similarities in the ancient stories of the Mesopotamians, and even in those of the Mesoamericans.

Humans began to farm as early as 9000 BCE in multiple locations around the world. As you can see below, Mesoamerica, Mesopotamia, India, China, and New Guinea seem to have been the earliest, followed by the Andes and the Amazon, along the southern edge of the Sahara, and in Ethiopia.

farming

[9000-7000 BC]
[7000-5000 BC]
[5000-3000 BC]
[3000-1000 BC]

Middle Yellow River Valley & Yangtze River Valley

Eastern US

Mesopotamia

Sahel

Mesoamerica

India

West Africa

Ethiopia

Andes & Amazonia

New Guinea

In the beginning, before actual "civilized" city-states began to form, engaging in agriculture was highly unrewarding. Compared to the beginning of industry—where only the factory workers suffered while owners became fabulously rich, life

11

got better and better for a rising middle class, and the downside of climate change wouldn't become an issue for more than a century—the Agricultural Revolution seemed like a failure for all from the get-go.

One might think that settling down and farming would be a relief after having to chase around after your dinner, but in fact adopting agriculture caused average life spans to *decrease* by 27%. Skeletons of Greek and Turkish hunter-gatherers are taller than those found in agricultural sites—so much taller that their modern, living descendants *have never caught up!*

The main reason for this was diet. Until wider-ranging trade routes developed, farmers were typically limited to only a couple of crops that were native to their area. Vegetarians today know how to combine their foods to ensure they are consuming a full complement of amino acids, but that wasn't possible for early farmers. The greater variety of the hunter-gatherer diet was superior.

Farming by hand was a hard life. For women, being subjected to constant pregnancies, something that isn't possible for always-migrating herders and hunter-gatherers, was an added drain. Diseases, also, spread much more rampantly among settled communities of farmers.

It's a good bet that it was women who began this revolution. We now know that settlement led to farming, not the other way around. While the menfolk were more likely to range farther from the settlement to track game, women, more expert at gathering, may have more closely observed the behavior of plants through the seasons and thus began to experiment with seeds. Matriarchy, too, was much more common in pre-agricultural societies, so many a woman may have led her tribe down the farming path. It was probably not long after farming began that a story spread about a woman receiving some bad advice from a devious snake and dragging her male mate into it.

And yet, despite harder, shorter lives, the adoption of farming inexorably spread. Though diets were less than optimal, farming still produced a *food surplus* (the produce of one farmer can feed more than his or her own family). More pregnancies increased populations. Larger populations overwhelmed the neighbors and took away their herding and hunting grounds.

Farther on in the book of Genesis comes the story of Adam and Eve's sons, Cain and Abel. Abel, the good guy in this story, is a herder. Cain, the farmer, murders him.

Archaeologists surmise that people first developed sophisticated speech at least 50,000 years ago. That's because they have unearthed skulls from around that time that are the earliest to show a significant development in the palate, the part of the mouth that helps form different sounds. The oldest evidence of writing that we have unearthed is from about 8,000 years ago. So why did it take so long to write things down? One reason is that people who could not rely on writing had what we would consider to be super-human memories; they could recite whole book-length legends.

It took more than 40,000 years(!) to write down speech. Why?

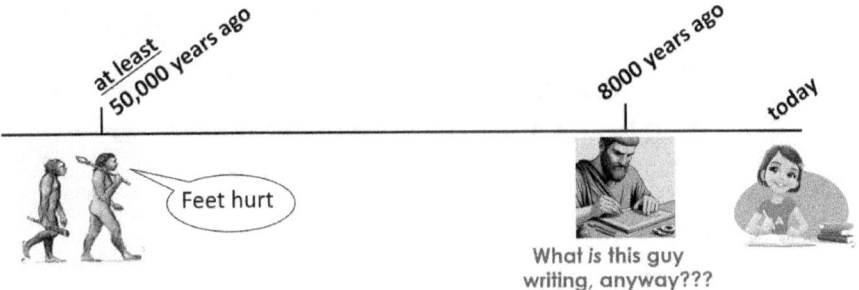

What *is* this guy writing, anyway???

As Plato said, "Necessity is the mother of invention." So what would be so hard to remember that even someone with a phenomenal memory would have *the need* to write it down?

Go to IMDb or Rotten Tomatoes and read a synopsis of any film or TV show. Without looking back through it, try explaining it to someone else. It probably won't be hard to get across the gist. Then go to Market Insider and try to memorize the current prices of the 30 stocks in the Dow Jones. It may be hard to remember the stocks alone, to say nothing of the prices. The oldest excavated samples of writing (in symbols on dried clay tablets) are not epic tales; they are numbered lists. They are lists of stored food.

Thus the invention of farming was a direct cause of the invention of writing. And yet farming didn't *always* cause writing. Though farming developed independently in several areas around the world, and it is hard to pin down exactly which was first, writing clearly began first in Mesopotamia (present-day Iraq). It appeared soon after in India (where it had likely spread), hundreds of years later in China, and *thousands* of years later in Mesoamerica.

A possible explanation for this is simply that the better you were at farming, the bigger your food stores, and the sooner you needed to keep track of them. Which begs the question: Why were the people of Mesopotamia so good at farming?

The map below shows the wildlife that inhabited the various regions of the world. There is something very special about the four animals that are circled...

The cow, the horse, the donkey, and the water buffalo are the only animals that humans have ever been able to teach to pull a plow. In Mesopotamia, oxen-pulled plows made farming exponentially more efficient. Eventually, the water buffalo did the same for farmers on the other side of Asia. But in the Americas, southern Africa and Australia, farmers continued to toil away by hand.

Large food surpluses lead to a specialization of labor. In contrast to earlier communities where everyone pitched in to some degree with food procurement, now there could be administrators, traders, builders, accountants, and scribes...

Gets to keep 2 bags wheat + 1 bag lentils

12 bags wheat + 9 bags lentils go to these guys

(FOOD SURPLUS)

Reading and writing were the basis of all learning and thus all technological advancement. It was the presence of bovids like cattle and water buffalo that led to efficient farming, which led to the early invention of writing, which led Eurasia to become the cradle of "civilization."

Living near tamable plow-pulling animals was not the only advantage of being born in Eurasia. All four of the above animals could also carry trade goods, as could camels, Asian elephants (but not African ones), and yaks. Camels could traverse the desert. Horses could move with great speed. Camels, horses, and Asian elephants could all be mounted by soldiers.

Carrying trade goods was especially important because where trade went, ideas followed. Eurasians not only had a wide choice of beasts of burden, but they also lived on a continent that was situated to facilitate a trade superhighway (it would one day be dubbed the Silk Road). Because Eurasia stretches along an east/west axis, one could hypothetically travel 7,000 miles between Spain and the east coast of China, all while remaining in relatively similar climate zones. That meant agricultural produce could be carried hundreds of miles and the seeds of that produce planted in a climate where they could germinate. As a trade benefit, this meant Eurasian societies could more rapidly diversify their agricultural diets. But, more importantly, as an *ideas* benefit, it meant that advancements like writing and the wheel could rapidly spread, as well.

North African societies could also tie in to this wider community, but those farther south (where there were no tamable beasts) could not. The only other tamable animals in the world that are capable of carrying loads are llamas and alpacas, both native to the Andes region of South America. But the people of the Andes were separated from the people of Mesoamerica by jungle and a narrow isthmus, and, since the Americas were situated on a north/south axis, a journey between these regions passed through several rapidly-changing climate zones.

Clearly then, geography is destiny.

Continuing the Garden of Eden metaphor through to the present point in time, this world that humanity fashioned was all contained in the apple of knowledge, and few would still question Eve's decision to bite into it. But the downsides of "civilization" also still remain. Food surpluses were the world's first significant *items of value*. And items of value are the poison latent in the apple, because where there are items of value there will be those who aspire to power in order to control more of those items for themselves. So efficient farming leads not only to writing and learning and progress, but also to the inequality of social division, including poverty and slavery. Women, too, lost status from the start of this revolution that they likely initiated, as patriarchy became the norm. In this sense, over the course of history, there have been more losers than winners as a result of biting the apple.

Many are hesitant to apply the word "civilization" to the world wrought by the Agricultural Revolution. The word gets contrasted with "barbaric," making it seem clearly superior and discounting all other lifestyles. Alternative societies that once populated the majority of the planet and still exist in scattered pockets deserve respect. Perhaps theirs is a better way; perhaps we will even return to it one day. Nevertheless, the scope of this narrative will focus only on those who are part of a direct line of causation to the present status of humankind. For that reason, the next four chapters will address only Eurasia and the parts of Africa near to it. We won't be returning to Paradise.

CHAPTER TWO

What Doesn't Kill You Makes You Stronger:
Human Thought Leaps Forward
...in Four Distinctive Ways
(~1500 BCE-325 CE)

"Civilization," such as it is, had four initial geographical centers spread across Asia and North Africa. These were all along great rivers: the Nile in Egypt, the Tigris and Euphrates in Mesopotamia, the Indus and Ganges in Pakistan and India, and the Huang He (Yellow) in China.

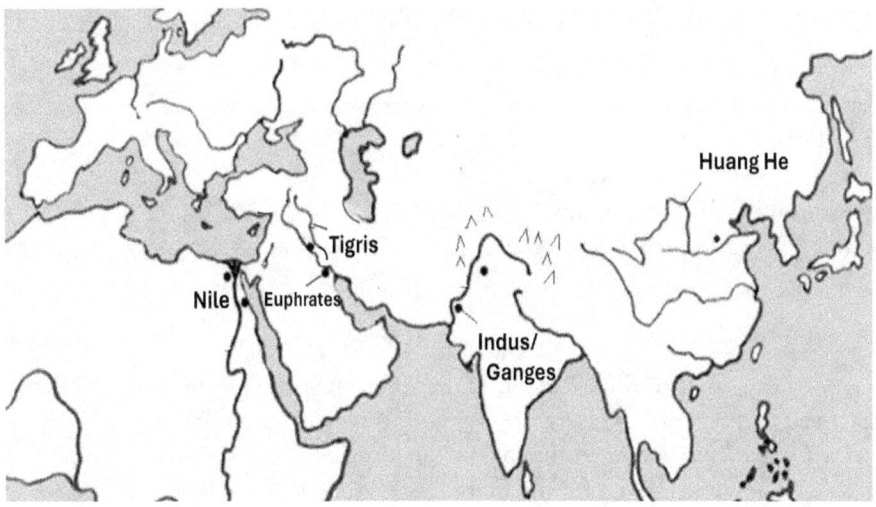

Agriculture, at this time, was still highly dependent on the whims of nature. The nature of people, meanwhile, was shaped by their environment. For example, in Egypt, the Nile River flooded like clockwork after the fall harvest was in, spreading a rich layer of silt to make the ground exceptionally fertile. In Mesopotamia, the Tigris and Euphrates rivers were not so cooperative. Violent storms would often strike late in the spring, destroying the planting that had just been completed. Since early agriculturalists, awed by nature, attributed their farming results to "the gods," in the case of Egypt these were very beneficent gods. Mesopotamian gods were... not nearly so nice.

If one had to choose which of these environments to be born into in ancient times, Egypt would be the clear winner. However, one of the most recurrent maxims of world history is "What doesn't kill you makes you stronger." It was the more rigorously challenged Mesopotamians who were the earliest to write, had the first number system, and invented the wheel.

On a larger scale, this maxim would soon apply to Eurasia as a whole. Sometime after 1500 BCE, Eurasia experienced a drought more severe than anything since the Ice Age. (We know quite a bit about the climate of the past from analyzing cores drilled deep into the ground and studying pollens trapped in levels of depth that can be correlated to specific time periods via carbon dating.) For a period of years, there were no regular monsoons to bring moisture north from the Indian Ocean. Crops failed across all of the great civilizations.

Desperate people began migrating in search of better conditions. These migrants overwhelmed already-suffering civilizations.

Yet all across Eurasia, in the wake of destabilization, an awakening of new ways of thinking propelled civilization forward again, such that historians have named the period the Axial Age. As in, the whole world turned on its axis, and everyone saw the light...

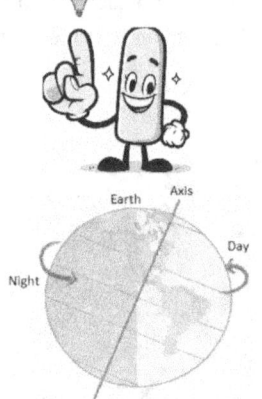

...At once.
It was the birth of modern thinking.

As they shouldered the burden of reestablishing civilization, people became less awed by the power of the natural world. Whereas before they put full faith in their priests, who conducted the mysterious rituals that tried to appease the gods of nature, now they began for the first time to individually practice *critical thinking*. Whereas before they felt that the direction of their lives was beyond their control, they now began for the first time to conceptualize *free will*.

Free will and critical thinking tend to take different thinkers in different directions; therefore this universal shift was also the beginning of significant divergence in the worldviews developed in separate regions across Eurasia:

- China, farthest from the others, would develop a distinct secular society.
- India would become the most separated by social leveling, but the most tolerant in their spirituality.
- From Iran to the eastern Mediterranean, the Middle East would form a very different spiritual culture from India.

18

- The Greeks, late to the game, would form a very different socio-political-based culture from China.

In each case, the result was a distinctive lens that continued to guide the perceptions, thoughts, and actions of a multitude of people in the moment that just passed.

Chinese culture remained remarkably durable from the very beginnings of its civilization until communism shook it up in the mid-20th century, and even since that time, the major aspects of the culture have proved impossible to erase. Much of this is due to the influence of one man: the great Axial Age thinker, Kong Fu-zi (or Confucius, as he is known to Westerners), though there were key pillars of the culture already in place at his time, which we should go over first.

Imperial China lasted at least 3,500 years (from ~1600 BCE or earlier to 1912 CE). This was not without interruption, but it was all within an accepted framework of successive dynasties. Thus you will always hear periods in Chinese history as belonging to one or another dynasty. Below is a chronological list of the major ones. The names are spelled alphabetically in Pinyin, which has several phonetic discrepancies with English. Where those are significant, the phonetic pronunciation is given in parentheses. Otherwise, just pronounce the a's like a British person would (Shang = Shahng):

Shang
Zhou (Joe)
Qin (Chin)
Han
Sui (Sway)
Tang
Song (Soong)
Yuan (Ou-en)
Ming
Qing (Ching)

The reason the dynasty framework worked so well was because of a concept that seems to have been invented by the Zhou when they wrested control away from the Shang. It is called the Mandate of Heaven. It says that every emperor is given a mandate to rule China... virtuously (in a way that is best for China, not just for the emperor or his family). The mandate is given by "Heaven," and as long

19

as the emperor has it, he must be obeyed. But if he should fail Heaven by not ruling virtuously, then Heaven will take the mandate away and give it to the next usurper of the throne. Which works out rather nicely for any usurper looking for instant loyalty.

The Chinese did not consider Heaven to be a *place* where a god lives; it was more like a formless whatever-rules-the-workings-of-the-world—a sort of collective fate. A keen awareness of every *individual's* fortune, along with the ability to influence fortune with things like lucky numbers and symbols or the practice of *feng shui*, was another pillar of Chinese culture that predated the Axial Age. Feng shui (pronounced "fung shway") and its emphasis on precise physical placement was so important that it, rather than any navigation need, was what would lead to the early invention of the compass during the Han Dynasty.

Confucius lived during the later Zhou Dynasty, as it was entering a period of long, slow decline. He believed in the Mandate of Heaven and encouraged people to obey their emperor. He also had some words of advice for the emperor:

> Govern the people by regulations and laws and keep order among them by punishments [and] they will flee from you and lose all self-respect. Lead them with virtue and regulate them by the rules of propriety, and they will keep their self-respect and come to you of their own accord.

Those "rules of propriety" are key. To Confucius, this meant:
- Following the rules of social etiquette, which were to be sincere and polite, and to have good manners
- Showing the highest respect at all times to your parents, elders, and teachers
- Always practicing this: "What you do not want yourself, do not do to others" (Sound familiar?)
- Working and studying hard
- Being thankful and *humble*

The last two give an accurate impression of the true Confucianist: Work and study dillegently in order to reach your fullest potential. But always remain humble.

Confucius said one's personal goal should be to become *junzi*, the ideal man:

> The *junzi* calls attention to the good points in others; he does not call attention to their defects. The small man does just the reverse.

> The demands that a *junzi* makes are upon himself. Those that a small man makes are upon others.

> The *junzi* is concerned with rightness. The small man is concerned with profit.

> The *junzi* does not mind failing to get recognition; he is too busy doing the things that *entitle* him to recognition.

Unfortunately, when Confucius spoke of the "ideal man," he really did mean ideal *man*. Of women specifically, he had little to say except, "Woman's greatest duty is to produce a son."

Confucianists are focused on advancing themselves in society, but only through their own head-down dedication and never at the expense of others. Society—a well-ordered society—is all-important. Harmony is more important than individualism. An emphasis on dutiful subjects showing respect for an emperor who is the embodiment of moral authority fits handily with the Mandate of Heaven, completing a strong base for an empire to last 3,000 years.

And this code for living properly outlasts the empire and spreads to the surrounding areas influenced by China throughout history. We see it today in East Asian schools, with the respect shown to teachers and administrators and with the pressure placed upon oneself to achieve the highest test score. We see it in the deference shown to others, in the absence of drawing attention to one's achievements, even downplaying them, like the impeccable gourmet cook who apologizes that her food may be "too salty." We see it in CEOs who publicly apologize or even give up their position (or worse) when they learn that their company's actions have harmed society. And we see it when an undemocratic government finds wide acceptance among "mainland" Chinese because effective rule (resulting in economic success and public order) is prized even more than absolute freedom.

To Confucius, society required all of our focus in this life. He had no use for the spiritual, for speculation on gods or the nature of the universe, or on the afterlife:

> Before you have learned to serve human beings, how can you serve spirits?
> When you do not yet know life, how can you know about death?

But there was another Axial Age thinker whose influence began to spread in the later Zhou Dynasty, and whose focus was quite different...

Lao-zi was the originator of Taoism (also spelled Daoism). With its emphasis on spiritualism, positive self-reflection, and communing with nature, Taoism seems almost the antithesis of Confucianism. This is only fitting, as it is the philosophy  that gave birth to this popular symbol, which represents the *yin* (dark, the moon, earth and water, passiveness) and the *yang* (light, the sun, wind and fire, action), equal opposites flowing seamlessly together to form a perfect whole.

The one constant between Confucianism and Taoism is harmony. The Tao, which cannot be called anything or categorized, is eternal and flows through all things. It preserves universal harmony.

Lao-zi lived in China's far west, where the influence of nomadic herders was strong and the social sphere that influenced Confucius was more distant. Rather than strive to be *junzi*, Lao-zi professed striving to be happy: to achieve an inner peace through reflection and to express this outwardly as tolerance for others.

This is a way of thinking that can be very comforting when times are hard and when society's demands are distant or society itself breaks down. It will have its day in the history of China before very long, but for now we will move farther west, and farther into the realm of spirituality, as we follow the drought-driven migrations south into India...

The most respected members of many pre-Axial Age communities were the priests, who are supposed to be in direct communiqué with the gods who control the community's fate. In ancient India, this would have been quite the time-consuming task, as there were hundreds of gods to keep track of.

Priests were born into their elevated position because it was believed their souls were the most *pure*. They ate only pure unadulterated food, where purity was also maintained in its preparation. For instance, if someone less pure crushed seeds into the oil that was used to cook your food, you would become spiritually polluted by eating it.

This concept of degrees of purity of soul and pollution by those who were less pure was *so* important that a formal social structure with levels was created to make it easier to keep track of the people you should avoid. Today, this is known as the caste system. As much as the legal system has tried to eliminate it, it still persists in India, and it even remains a problem with Indian immigrants to the United States; in Seattle, an anti-discrimination law has recently made caste a protected class.

"Caste" is a word that won't come along until the Portuguese enter Indian history around 1500 CE. Ancient Indians called it *jati*.

Priests, as you see, were even higher on the scale than rulers. Though social leveling was found in all civilizations, this was an especially strict form, as each level took great care to not even associate with any below them. Rulers and warriors

Jati = a hierarchy of purity

BRAHMIN (Priests)
|
KSHATRIYA (Rulers & Warriors)
|
VAISYA (Farmers & Traders)
|
SUDRA (Workers & Servants)

avoided farmers and traders, who in turn avoided workers and servants.

By the 20th century, there would be hundreds of castes in Indian society. The lowest of the low became known as "the Untouchables" (meaning just the slightest touch from one will spiritually pollute you). In fact, the Untouchables were seen as so low as to not even be considered a caste at all. It is where we get the word "outcast."

Religion served as the great pacifier, keeping the lower levels content. It was said that if you followed your *dharma*, your duty to live a life without complaint that is true to your *jati*, then you would have positive *karma* and therefore be reincarnated to spend your next life one level higher.

But then comes the Axial Age, and Indians begin to question the assumption that life is beyond their control. As in, maybe these priests don't have a corner on the god market after all.

The ancient religious texts known as the *Vedas*, are extended at this time by the addition of the *Upanishads*, which mold the ancient religion into modern Hinduism. Spirituality becomes more personalized. Now, via meditation and other practices, everyone can find their own way to *moksha*, liberation from the cycle of reincarnation and finding oneness with God.

Note also the replacement of "gods" with "God." Hinduism is no longer polytheistic. It is said that there are 330 million gods in Hinduism, but in fact there is only one. The others are avatars. Lao-zi, who lived on the other side of the Himalayas as the last of the Upanishads were being written, would call them "mere human constructs." They are there to help people find their way to the one true God. But this is not the monotheism that will develop in Western Asia, where we will go next. Rather, it is *monism*, the belief that God is everywhere and every*thing*.

And every*one*. Hindus refer to this as the greater Self (with a capital 'S') that is at the center of your self (lesser 's'). There is a section of the Upanishads where a father discusses the nature of God with his son. It goes generally like this:

> FATHER: Bring me a banyan fruit.
> SON: Here it is, sir.
> FATHER: Cut it up.
> SON: I've cut it up, sir.
> FATHER: What do you see there?
> SON: These quite tiny seeds.
> FATHER: Now take one of them and cut it up.
> SON: I've cut it up, sir.
> FATHER: What do you see there?
> SON: Nothing.

FATHER: This finest essence here, son, that you can't even see...
Look how on account of that finest essence this huge banyan tree
stands here. Believe me, my son: The finest essence here...
That constitutes the Self of this whole world. That is the Self.
Thou art That.

To become one with God, then, requires searching within. This requires dedicated meditation. Finding God is said to be a long and arduous journey, although a joyful one that may be pursued in your own way.

Hinduism considers the visible world to be a veil that covers true reality and must ultimately be shed to reach your goal. Some individuals called *ascetics* go to extremes in an attempt to shed the veil, standing for days on end, even while sleeping, or going to sleep every night on a bed of nails. In this way, they teach themselves to ignore the false reality of the world.

None of this puts a dent in the caste system, which remains as rigid as ever. But sometime in the 5th century BCE, Siddhartha Gautama, who will become revered as "the Buddha," begins to use meditation to achieve liberation from reincarnation in a similar but subtly different way. He trains his mind to overcome *desire* in order to achieve what he calls *nirvana*, a personal peace that is secular and, importantly, can be achieved by anyone, in any lifetime. There is no differentiation by caste.

Buddhism will have an uneven history in India, reaching a height of popularity under the emperor Ashoka in the 3rd century BCE but then fading from its native land. Instead, it will pass north of the Himalayas to the lands of the pastoral peoples where Taoism arose, then travel on the trade routes to China.

Hinduism, Taoism and Buddhism are examples of *mysticism*. Each focuses on a separate reality from the world of the basic senses. Each involves searching for that true reality; they do not profess to know that truth. This contrasts sharply with the strict monotheism that arises at the same time to the west, where *belief* and the sureness of *faith* will be foremost...

The book of Exodus, in the Jewish Torah and the Christian Bible, tells of how Moses led the Hebrews (the ancestors of the Jews) out of Egyptian captivity, supposedly around 1250 BCE. Reaching the Sinai desert, Moses is given the Ten Commandments by God, the first of which states, "I am the Lord, thy God. Thou shall have no other gods before Me." This is often claimed to be the beginning of monotheism, the belief in a single god. But we must separate history from religious tradition and, from the historical record, the dates don't add up.

There were indeed Hebrews in captivity in Egypt around this time, but most of the Hebrews lived in Canaan (location of present-day Israel) and, from archaeological records, we can see that until at least 700 BCE, they were polytheistic, worshipping multiple gods in the form of idols.

The book of Exodus, itself, was not written until the 7th century BCE, 550 years after the events it describes. It is definitely the product of Axial Age thinking. But was it drawing on a tradition that began with a small group of Hebrews who came out of Egypt hundreds of years before? Or did monotheism come much later to Canaan than the Torah and Bible would have us believe?

We do know that monotheism existed in the Middle East as early as 1000 BCE, but it was 2,000 miles east of Canaan, in Persia (present-day Iran). A Persian named Zoroaster was the founder of Zoroastrianism, in all likelihood the oldest monotheist religion. Some go so far as to argue that it was Zoroastrian Persians who brought news of the one true God to the people of Canaan. But with everyone all across Eurasia beginning to see the light during the same few centuries, it could just be another example of great minds thinking alike, with Moses and Zoroaster both converting people to faith in one God.

One thing for certain, though, is that Zoroaster was the most successful in spreading this word to greater numbers of followers. Zoroastrianism would become the biggest religion in the Middle East and remain so for hundreds of years, being eventually supplanted by Islam.

Zoroastrianism and Judaism were both born of the Axial Age. They challenged the priests and their idols, and they asserted that individuals had free will to choose between good and evil. Granted, it may not have seemed like much of a choice because choosing to do evil was certain to result in your soul going to Hell. There also was much certainty about the one true God. This was quite the opposite of the mystics' ongoing *search* for God.

The earthly outcome of a choice to be good was not always so certain. The Jewish story of Job (pronounced with a long 'o') illustrates God's relationship with humanity. In summary, Job is a devoted elder who keeps all God's commandments and gives to the poor. Suddenly, he loses all his goods, watches his sons and daughters die, and experiences great personal pain and disease. Job cries out, "Why me, oh Lord? Why am I suffering when I have done no wrong?"

The Lord speaks to Job "out of the whirlwind," demanding to know, "Were you there when I laid the foundations of the earth?!"

Experiencing the majesty of the Lord, Job is filled with awe. Realizing the Lord has purposes that he, a mere mortal, cannot begin to fathom, Job falls down in absolute devotion.

In other words, God has a plan that is beyond our understanding. God is unbelievably awesome (in the old-fashioned, shake-in-your-boots-before-awesomeness meaning of the word). But God is good. And since God is good, it does no good to question God, no matter how illogical God's plan may seem to puny humans.

But to the people of the Middle East, whether Jew or Zoroastrian, though God's awesomeness may have been on full display in the form of a burning bush, a booming voice, or an angry, thunderstruck sky, the nature of God is just as formless as the Tao or the monist Hindu's Self. To the north, in Greece, it was vastly different...

The pantheon of Greek gods were not only human in form; they were very human in nature, as well. No awesomeness here. Greek gods partied, fooled around, and cheated in other ways, too. Except for living on Mt. Olympus, riding chariots in the sky, and hurling the occasional thunderbolt, they practically *were* human, even coming down to walk among the mortals from time to time.

Greeks didn't worry about morality or going to Hell. They were tolerant of each others' faults, and of the less-than-godly acts of their gods, to whom they assigned those same faults.

Though the word is used differently today, you might call the Greek worldview "humanism." Greeks were all about being human. They were proud of looking like the gods, prouder still of being endowed with the godlike quality of *reason,* being able to use their logical minds to figure things out.

The center of Greek Axial Age thinking was the city-state of Athens, where, from the 5th century BCE, the *sophists* became active. These thinkers not only speculated on the nature of the physical world; they also, like Confucius, were very interested in social conduct. Plato's *The Republic,* written as a dialogue with his teacher, Socrates, discusses how just and virtuous governance creates a happy society.

The teachings of the sophists, however, contradicted Confucianism in that they prided themselves on having a society that featured a rich diversity of ideas, as opposed to one steeped in tradition. Athenians in their so-called Golden Age (480–404 BCE) were highly political—in a good way. Their famous leader Pericles had this to say: "We do not say that a man who takes no interest in politics is a man who minds his own business; we say that he has no business here at all."

This is the antithesis of polarization: He wants to hear what you have to say. If it is different than his own opinion, so much the better. No wonder they were the cradle of true democracy! (Of course there were those groups that didn't even have a vote: women, laborers, immigrants, the usual riffraff...)

Ultimately, whereas the Greeks and the Chinese, at their separate ends of Eurasia, were both focused on creating a just and virtuous society, the Chinese went about it with humility and propriety; meanwhile, the Greeks prized their godlike figures and minds and reveled in a good argument.

Politically, the Greeks were a collection of independent city-states. Threatened by the mighty Persian Empire to their east, they formed a confederacy for a time that was led by Athens but could never get it together to form an actual union. Nautical Greek traders spread their culture westward to Sicily and the Italian Peninsula, where it influenced a group called the Etruscans. There was this one colony of the Etruscans by the name of Rome that broke away, and the rest, as they say, is history. The small Roman kingdom became a republic and then a great empire that encircled the Mediterranean (the Romans just called it "Our Sea"), including Egypt and Judea (formerly Canaan).

Meanwhile, far to the East, the broken warring pieces of the former Zhou Dynasty were united by one who would become known as Qin Shi Huangdi. His family name Qin, remember, is pronounced "Chin," as in Chin...a. The *Shi Huangdi* part means "first emperor." Yes, he proudly called himself "First Emperor of China."

Eschewing humility was not the only way that the first emperor turned his back on Confucianism. He governed by laws and kept order by punishments—rather harsh ones, like the time he had each limb of an offender tied to a separate horse, then had all the horses whipped at the same time to bolt off, one north, one south, one east, one west.

Aside from the naming of the world's longest-lasting empire (and the nation that followed it) and the laying of the first foundation of the Great Wall, Qin and his dynasty have little bearing on the moment that just passed. Unless you consider their negative example to have been the thing that solidified Confucianism as China's cultural compass. The Qin Dynasty was a one-hit wonder. After Qin Shi Huangdi's death (likely hastened by his ingesting mercury in an attempt to

27

attain immortality), his successor was rapidly overthrown, and the imminently more successful Han Dynasty followed.

Embracing Confucianism wholeheartedly, the Han instituted a program of civil service examinations based on the master's teachings that would ultimately have great importance in the fate of the entire world (as relayed in Chapter 5). It was a grueling process with several rounds to advance through in order to be considered for a position of status in the government. Candidates were under enormous pressure because the future status of their families depended on their performance. And you know how Confucianists feel obligated to their families. Suicide was common among those who failed.

We have reached what is known as the Classical Age. It was a time when Eurasia was balanced by two great empires at either end, connected by the fabled Silk Road, stretching from its terminus in the west of Han China through the Central Asian market towns of Tashkent and Samarkand, then across the Kushan Empire and Persia to connect with the eastern reaches of the Roman Empire.

On the foundations of strong, distinctive cultures, these two great empires would become great builders and conquerors and political administrators. But it was the thinkers who came before them that were the influencers who formed their foundations and whose impact is felt to the present day, which is why they—and not the Han and Roman emperors, warriors, or statesmen—are the stars of this narrative.

But although we are through describing the birth of Greco-Roman culture, we haven't yet described the full picture of what will become "Western" culture. For that is more of a blend of two of the above mindsets: the Greek "humanists" and the Middle Eastern monotheists.

Which may seem a little like a blending of oil and water...

THESE GUYS ? *Dionysus taking a cup*

Moses awed by God
BLEND WITH THESE GUYS ??

Yes, they do.

28

◇◇◇

Sometime around the year 36 CE in Jerusalem, the capital of Judea, Jesus of Nazareth was executed by the Romans for treason. The method of the execution was crucifixion, which was a standard punishment for treason.

There is good reason to believe that the Biblical description of the Jewish authorities trumping up charges against Jesus and pressuring the Romans to execute him is false. The gospels of the Bible's New Testament, where this is described, are but four of many gospels (stories of Jesus' life). They did not come into being until decades after the events they describe and were perhaps not finalized in written form until as many as 150 years after those events. By that time, many Christians had developed some antipathy toward the Jews. This could have resulted from nothing more than recently becoming rival persecuted minorities in Rome. So it is quite possible that this demonizing of the Jews was not injected into the story until that time.

It does seem that Jesus was critical of the way the Jewish high priest was running the temple. But he was not the first prophet to come along and try to straighten up the act of wayward religious authorities.

The Romans, meanwhile, were occupiers in a foreign land where the locals despised them for being there. They were accustomed to dispensing violence in order to bring unruly native populations to heel. The Jews were particularly defiant. This Jesus fellow had a talent for drawing followers to him, and some had begun to call him the Messiah, whom Jews believed to be a future king who would redeem them from Roman overrule. That was certainly enough to place him on the Romans' watch list. They feared rebellion, and were nipping it in the bud.

Jesus was a Jew, and the community of followers who surrounded him in his life, preserved his message, and rejoiced in the continuation of his spirit was what is referred to as a *sect* of Judaism (a subset of the overall religion). As such, like all of Judaism, this sect would have held that humans are born pure and can remain so by doing good. It would have also considered God to be formless.

But then along came Saul of Tarsus, a city up the coast from Judea in Anatolia. Saul was dead set against the followers of Jesus until he had a vision and was converted to their cause. It was around this time that the leadership of the sect made the important decision to allow *gentiles* (non-Jews) to join them. This made it possible for a fully-grown Roman man to become a follower of Jesus without first having to get himself circumcised. Saul Romanized his name to Paul and went right to work on those Romans with an evangelical drive that has no

29

equal in history. He traveled far and wide in the empire, giving speeches, writing many letters, some of which are included in the New Testament of the Bible, and making convert after convert. Today he is known as *Saint* Paul for his efforts.

Saint Paul is one of the most influential humans in history, but it is not just because of his salesmanship. A very important part of what made his high conversion rate possible is that he presented the religion in a way that would make it more attractive to those of the Greek "humanist" culture, and in so doing, turned the Jewish sect into Christianity.

Paul imbued the sect with two principles that are entirely counter to the teachings of Judaism:

1. Jesus is the Son of God.
2. Adam and Eve, from whom we all are descended, committed the original sin. In doing so, they left all humanity tainted with this sin at birth. But if you accept Jesus as your savior, you will be absolved from sin and free to enter Heaven.

Number one appeals to how Greeks and Romans value the human form. God can now be pictured as the Father, in the same form as man (and one day be represented on the ceiling of the Sistine Chapel in the Vatican, reaching out his arm to create Adam). Furthermore, Jesus was his son, who walked among mortals.

Number two appeals to the Greco-Roman value of tolerance. All your sins committed on Earth will be forgiven if you but accept Jesus as savior.

Paul spread the word for nearly two decades before he, too, was executed by the Romans sometime before 68 CE.

By the middle of the 2nd century CE, small Christian communities were spread from Britain to Ethiopia. Their beliefs about the nature of Jesus and his message varied. This diversity, however, would be short-lived.

As Christian communities became more widespread in the Roman capital, they were viewed as a threat to order and began to be persecuted by the authorities, who were very creative in their punishments (think: setting lions loose in the Colosseum). In the late 2nd century, there was a bishop in the south of the Roman province of Gaul (today, that would be the south of France) who felt that the only way for Christians to survive the worsening persecution was to unify behind one set of common beliefs. His name was Irenaeus.

In 180 CE, Irenaeus, now known as Saint Irenaeus, wrote a book called *Against Heresies.* "Heresy" comes from the Greek *airesis*, which means "choice." Irenaeus was against choice. He said that Christianity needed a canon, a list of sacred scriptures accepted as the only truth. Only four gospels were chosen – those attributed to Matthew, Mark, Luke, and John (though most gospels are thought to have been written under a pseudonym).

The gospel that fits closest with the teaching of Saint Paul is the gospel of

John, which seems to have come into being in the first decade of the 2nd century, soon after one of the gospels that did *not* make the cut: the gospel of Thomas. In fact, it may have been the appearance of the gospel of Thomas that led the author of John to respond. The author of Thomas implies that Jesus taught being created in the image of God means that each person has God within them (very similar to the Upanishads' idea of the greater Self). The author of John stresses very strongly that only Jesus, himself, is God incarnate.

The gospel of John bears little resemblance to the other three gospels accepted into the canon. The earliest of those –the gospel of Mark, which the other two are thought to have used as a source—never has Jesus refer to himself as the Son of God. And only the gospel of John contains the description of Thomas as a doubter when confronted with the resurrected Jesus.

Joining Thomas on the cutting room floor were the gospel of Mary Magdalene, which echoes the Thomas viewpoint, and the gospel of Judas, among others. It seems no coincidence that these authors all play less-than-admirable roles in the eventual Christian canon: a man of no faith, a prostitute, and a turncoat.

When a religion accepts only one correct belief, it is called *orthodoxy*. As others rallied around the orthodoxy of Irenaeus over the next few decades, the several competing sects of Christianity were pretty much driven into obscurity. Meanwhile, the one *universal* church reigned supreme. The Greek for "universal" is *katholikos*. From now on, it would be called the Catholic Church.

The strategy worked. In the year 312 CE, Constantine became the first Roman emperor to become a Christian.

There was still a good deal of debate going on among Church leaders in the early 4th century. For instance, it is doubtful that the Bible was even completed, despite the 130 years that had passed since Irenaeus got started on the canon. Since debate and orthodoxy don't mix, Constantine organized a council at a place in Anatolia called Nicea, where he pressured Church leaders to get their story straight.

The Council of Nicea produced what is known as the Nicene Creed. The most important thing they worked out was the Catholic Christian conception of God, which is the Holy Trinity: There is the Father in Heaven, the Son who now sits at his right hand, and the Holy Spirit that exists everywhere in the world—the one remnant left of the formless God of the Jews.

And what of the majority of Jews who were not followers of Jesus? In the year 70 CE, the Romans had brought the hammer down on any further thoughts of Jewish independence. The Temple of Jerusalem was destroyed except for one wall that remains today: the Wailing Wall. In this rebellion, and in another that followed in the year 132, many were killed and many more fled to the corners of surrounding Eurasia in the *diaspora*, from the Greek *dia speiro* ("to sow over"), scattered like seeds in the wind.

31

◇◇◇

So let's assess the blending that created Christianity. The Greeks' infatuation with the human form comes through strongly, as does their acceptance of human foibles ("Sin on Saturday, confess on Sunday, and everything's cool" is very Greek). On the other hand, an awesome, omniscient god with a plan indecipherable to humans comes from the Middle East. So does that un-debatable sureness about the one *true* God (which now becomes the one true Holy Trinity).

In the next century, as the Roman Empire collapsed and much of the underlying Greek culture was temporarily forgotten, Catholicism would begin an unchallenged run in Europe that lasted 1,000 years. Many a heretic trying to exercise a little Greek individuality would be burned at the stake. People of science like Galileo would be forced to acquiesce to Catholic orthodoxy. But choice would return with the Reformation, and science, reason, logic all would have their day again.

In our day, Western culture can seem at times to be separating between secular humanist and evangelical Christian extremes—going back to oil and water. But there is some similarity between these seeming extremes in their sense of sureness. Devout Catholics accept the Bible as the word of God and leave no room for discoveries of the *past* about how the Bible actually came to be. But some science-informed humanists have been known to believe only what is accepted knowledge today, leaving no room for discoveries of the *future* that may prove our present understanding entirely wrong. For centuries, Europeans were sure of the Aristotelian understanding of the world. Then came the Scientific Revolution, and Newtonian physics was proclaimed to have everything solved. Then came Einstein, who shook up human understanding again. Since his time, we have learned so much more about the physical world that it has been like discovering a door, going through that door, and finding an infinity beyond it. Who knows? Perhaps the mystics have been the closest to the truth, and we are only beginning to peek beyond the veil.

CHAPTER THREE

The "Southernization" of Eurasia
(325-1205)

The far-flung borders of the Chinese and Roman empires were difficult to defend. Both made the decision to employ mercenaries from the outside in defense of those borders. It wasn't the best choice, as those mercenaries eventually turned on their employers, opening the frontiers to a wave of outsider invasions.

China's neighbors to the north were pastoralists—nomadic herders of cattle, sheep, and goats with movable encampments of tents. They were the first to domesticate the horse. Horsemen from a young age, they became excellent mounted archers. In the early 4th century, a number of smaller groups united into a confederation known as the Jin. They sacked the imperial capital of Kaifeng and brought down the Han Dynasty.

Other groups coalesced and began to migrate westward across the wide grasslands of the Asian steppe. By the 5th century, they arrived in Europe, where they would become known as the Huns. The Huns drove the Germanic Goths (the former Roman mercenaries) inward and southward to the city of Rome, which the latter sacked in the year 410.

By then, Rome was no longer the capital of the Roman Empire as, back in 330, Constantine had moved the capital east out of Italy altogether to the city of Byzantium at the entrance to the Black Sea. He renamed it Constantinople. This eastern third of the empire survived the attacks, but the west was entirely overrun.

These invasions were like a reset for the history of the world. The Silk Road, the great superhighway of trade in goods and ideas, was no more, as the connection across central Asia, from China to Persia, was broken.

But there *was* a trade route that remained. From at least as early as the 3rd century BCE, clinging closely to the Indian Ocean coast, small triangular-sailed *dhows* had been carrying goods (and ideas!) between points stretching from the east coast of Africa all the way to the Malacca Strait in Southeast Asia. Thus the center of advanced civilization now shifted south.

The invaders who destroyed the great classical empires came from the north, but until the early 6th century, India remained safe on the other side of two towering mountain ranges, the Himalayas and the Hindu Kush. From 325 on, northern India was united under the Gupta Dynasty. The Gupta were blessed with arguably the two most in-demand crops in the history of the world, cotton and sugar, and were at the very center of the Indian Ocean trade. It became India's Golden Age.

From early times, the Indians were mathematically inclined. "Geometry" and "trigonometry" are both words that come from their Sanskrit language. Before the Gupta Dynasty, they had measured both the diameter of Earth and the distance of the moon from Earth. In the former, they were off by less than 100 out of nearly 8,000 miles; in the latter, they were off by only about 300 out of about 253,000 miles.

Aside from further advancements in astronomy, the Gupta invented the 0–9 number system (so much easier to use for arithmetic than those clunky Roman numerals). They were the first to employ decimal notation. Their Hindi number system moved along with the cotton and sugar trade to the Middle East, where it was transposed into the symbols we use today (which we call "Arabic numerals" because Europeans, much later, learned about them from the Arabs).

So why do you suppose the title of this chapter is "The 'Southernization' of Eurasia"?...

In the prologue, we discussed how, since decolonization began, the Less Developed Countries have scrambled to catch up with the former imperialists. The rapid development that has occurred since the later 20th century involves one-way traffic not only in technology, but also fashion trends, worldwide branding, and the adoption of English as a *lingua franca* (a common vehicle for global communication). This cultural flooding has a name: "Westernization," the gradual spread of Western culture to and through the developing world.

In Chapter 1, we showed how geography is destiny and eliminated all the world but Eurasia and North Africa from contention for world supremacy. Now, once again as a result of geography (the protective mountains to the north and the nurturing ocean to the south), we are shrinking that area of supremacy to an even smaller percentage of Earth: the *south* of Eurasia.

It will expand again. Through the course of this chapter, we will trace how the developed world spreads north from India to China and the Middle East, each of which add their own contributions, then finally, after many long centuries, to the furthest reaches of the Eurasian hinterlands: Western Europe.

Like this:

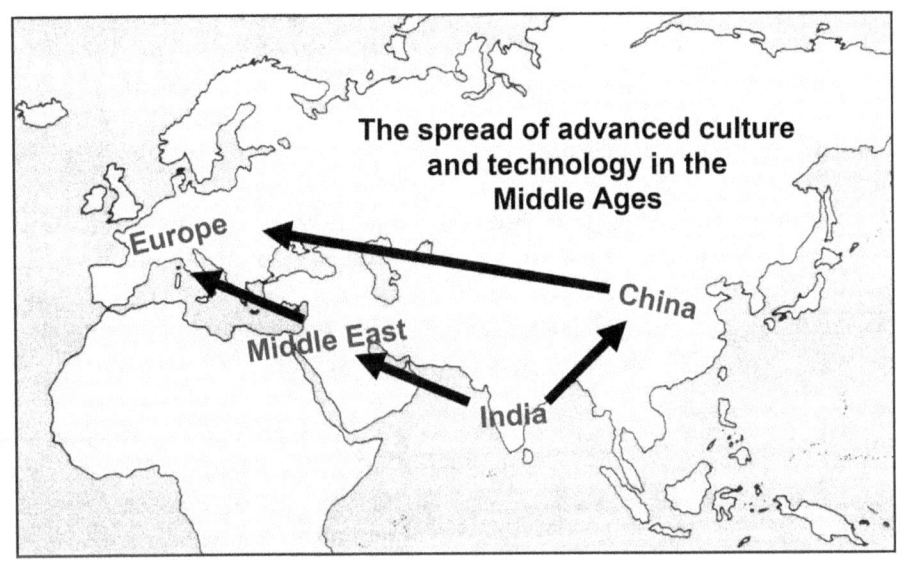

The spread of advanced culture and technology in the Middle Ages

◇◇◇

In China, during the period of fragmented rule after the fall of the Han Dynasty, life was hard on the common people. There was no rule of law. People had to deal with the destruction wrought by the armies of competing warlords and its disruption of trade. It was also a time of drought, famine, and sweeping epidemics. The time was ripe for a decline in Confucianism, with its grounds in an orderly society. The way was paved for the rise of a new philosophy, focused on the elimination of suffering. Buddhism, which lost favor in India during the Gupta Empire, was about to find a new home.

As Chinese peasants adopt the previously secular practice, they inject it with religion, adding a heavenly realm called the "Pure Land" that offers a happy reward after death. The original Buddha becomes essentially deified as *"the* Buddha." From this humble beginning, Mahayana Buddhism, the form of Buddhism with the greatest number of followers today, would eventually develop.

The history of Mahayana Buddhism mirrors that of Christianity. With the latter, the teaching of Jesus nearly died out in his homeland (Judea), but it underwent transformation into a new religion that spread widely in a neighboring region (Europe), and, centuries later, was exported to lands influenced by the Europeans. Meanwhile, the teaching of the Buddha, Siddhartha Gautama, nearly died out in his homeland (India), but was transformed into a new religion that spread widely in a neighboring region (China), and was subsequently exported to lands influenced by the Chinese.

35

Though the Jin had physically conquered the Han, the powerful Chinese culture eventually conquers the Jin. The historians' term for when invaders adopt the culture of those they conquer is *acculturation*. The concept of the Mandate of Heaven will assure that, rather than fade into history, the Chinese Empire will go on as before, becoming fully unified again by the year 581 with the establishment of the Sui Dynasty.

Throughout the short-lived Sui and for more than a century of the early Tang Dynasty, it will be a two-way cultural exchange. Daoism and Buddhism will coexist with Confucianism like yin and yang as scholars speak of how "the three teachings flow into one." The more active role of women in pastoralist communities will carry over for a time, as well. In fact, for much of the 7th century, China is ruled by one.

Wu Zetian rules as regent for her young son decades before taking over as the full-blown emperor from 690 until her death at age 80 in 705. The grueling Confucianist-centered civil service examination system has died out with the "barbarian" invasions. Now, Empress Wu resurrects it, but with one significant change. She opens the eligibility for the examination program to *all* males, no matter their status. In so doing, she breaks the strength of the noble families.

Despite her promotion of the traditional curriculum, Wu is a practicing Buddhist herself. The original secular practice, which will become known as Theravada Buddhism, will be kept alive by some members of the aristocracy and in the spread of scattered monasteries where monks isolate themselves, depending largely on the charity of others to survive.

It is written that Wu Zetian "killed her own children, butchered her elder brothers, murdered the ruler, and poisoned her mother." But even primary sources must be questioned where biases exist. Confucius once said that having a woman rule would be "as unnatural as having a hen crow at daybreak." You can imagine how purist male Confucianists felt about Wu, and *they* were the ones writing her history.

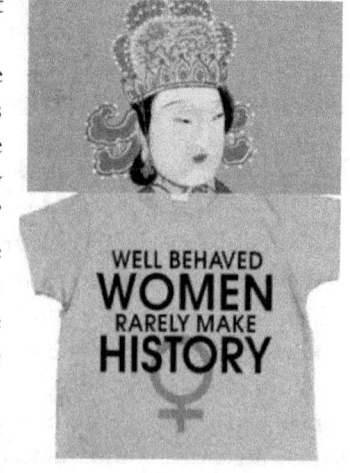

The slogan on the T-shirt pictured here (and often found on coffee mugs in classrooms belonging to female history teachers), might more accurately be transposed to say, "History rarely portrays successful women as well-behaved." (A woman need not have been ill-behaved to be portrayed as such by male historians of her time.)

From all we can tell, China thrived more under Wu's rule than under either of the male leaders that bookended her.

Granted, it does appear to be true that she slyly worked her way up the concubine ranks, passing from one emperor to the next, then finagled a way to put her dimmest son in power so she could pull his strings in the background, etc. But then, a woman's gotta do what a woman's gotta do—certainly in 7th-century China.

In the year 600, the Middle East was evenly divided between a weakened Roman Empire, centered on Constantinople (present-day Istanbul) and a reviving Persian Empire, with its capital at Ctesiphon, near present-day Baghdad. To the south of this lay Arabia, which was a patchwork of extended blood clans.

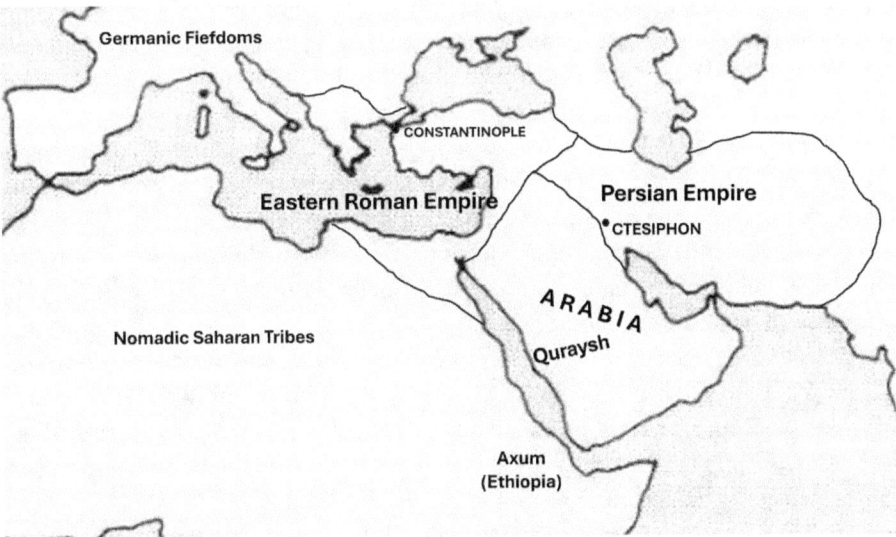

From Constantinople, the talented Justinian I ruled for nearly 40 years until his death in 565. He oversaw an overhaul of Roman law. The end product forms the basis of civil law in much of the world today, and his name is the etymon for the word "justice."

In history books, Justinian and his people are usually referred to as the Byzantines. They would not have related to that label; although their language was Greek, not Latin, they considered themselves Romans, through and through. They were also uniformly Catholic, worshipping the Holy Trinity. The Persians, meanwhile, were strictly monotheistic Zoroastrians. The Arabs were still mostly idol-worshipping polytheists.

The Arab clan of Quraysh was well-located, close to the Red Sea coast of Arabia, halfway between the Indian Ocean and the point where the two northern empires met. This made its city of Mecca a waystation for trade caravans, which was to the benefit of the local Qurasyhi merchants.

There was a particularly important religious attraction in Mecca, as well. Inside a windowless black structure at the center of a plaza, the many idols that were sacred to various clans were kept. The structure, which was (and is) called the *ka'bah*, had its own significance. It contained the "Black Stone," a stone that was believed to have been white when it came from Paradise but turned black from human sins. It was said to have been laid there in the early 2nd millennium BCE by Abraham (or *Ibrahim* in Arabic), a pastoralist leader traditionally considered the ancestor of both the Hebrews and the Arabs.

Today, Abraham/Ibrahim is considered the first prophet of the "Abrahamic" religions: Judaism, Christianity, and Islam. These three religions share many prophets (non-deities who were able to commune with God), though some are not recognized as such in all three. After Moses, Aaron, David, Solomon, Elisha, and Zacharia, Islam recognizes two more: The first is Jesus, who is not recognized as a prophet in Judaism and is deified within the Holy Trinity of Christianity; the second and last is Muhammad.

In the year 610, Muhammad was a 39-year-old Qurayshi merchant living in Mecca who, when meditating in a cave outside the city, heard a voice tell him that he was the apostle of God. He envisioned the speaker as one who identified himself as the angel Gabriel. It is questionable whether Muhammad, who could not read, would have recognized this as the angel who, in the Christian Bible, tells Mary that she will be the mother of Jesus.

Muhammad's revelations were spoken to his wife and followers, some of whom recorded them on the spot. All eventually form the holy book of Islam, the Qur'an. These revelations called on the polytheistic Arabs to forsake their idols and worship the one true God. This was very much like the Jewish prophet Amos had exhorted to the Canaanites back in the Axial Age.

But the revelations also reached out to Jews and Christians, who were respected as "People of the Book," calling on them to recognize Muhammad as God's last prophet, who was sent to sort of right the ship back on course after religious leaders took the messages of earlier prophets astray:

O People of the Book,
do not go to excess
in your religion,
and do not say of God
anything but truth.
The Messiah,
Jesus son of Mary
was only a Messenger of God....

38

So believe in God,
and do not speak of a trinity....

To forestall the tendency of the faithful to deify their prophets, Muhammad forbade his followers from ever rendering his image. Islam agrees with the formless conception of God, as in Zoroastrianism, Judaism, and the Holy Spirit. All mosques, Muslim places of worship ("Muslim" being the name for one whose religion is Islam), are free of representational images of any kind. Often, they are decorated with Arabic script taken from the Qur'an. The words above can be found on the walls of the Dome of the Rock in Jerusalem, a shrine constructed 60 years after the death of Muhammad, commemorating what is known as the Night Journey, in which Muhammad describes being taken on a magical flight to Jerusalem, where he briefly ascends to Heaven to meet with Moses and Jesus.

INSIDE A CHRISTIAN CATHEDRAL

Muhammad forbade
images of himself
(He wanted to make sure he
wasn't worshipped)

INSIDE A MUSLIM MOSQUE

The revelations come to Muhammad infrequently over the course of the remainder of his lifetime. They continually speak of God's compassion, but are demanding in their call for total submission to God, and God alone. Thus a name is given to the beliefs of Muhammad's growing number of followers: *Islam*, which is Arabic for "submission." At one point the revelations call for praying to God 50 times per day. Bowing to practicality, it is settled that five times each day will be sufficient.

As the number of Muhammad's followers increases, so too does their persecution intensify. The Qurayshi leaders are concerned about the economic impact of driving away itinerant worshippers of the various idols of the *ka'bah*. They pass laws forbidding commerce or intermarriage with the Muslims. Many are attacked, some imprisoned and tortured.

Eventually, after nearly a decade of preaching, Muhammad has rightly begun to fear for his life and decides he must lead his followers away from Mecca. By this time, his message has begun to spread beyond the limits of his clan. When doing business at one of the annual market fairs outside Mecca, he begins communication with some merchants from Yathrib, an agriculturally plentiful oasis that lies some 290 miles to the north. There are two clans that inhabit this relatively small oasis, and they suffer constant feuding. Having adopted Muhammad's message, eventually representatives of the clans invite him to come to Yathrib and mediate their conflict.

In the year 622, Muhammad spreads word among the Muslims of Mecca to begin an escape to Yathrib, telling them that he will follow close behind in secret. After this successful relocation, he is able to unite the Meccan Muslims and the clans of Yathrib into one peaceful community, over which he becomes the administrative ruler. Taking on the role of ruler distinguishes Muhammad from all of the previous Abrahamic prophets, and it sets a precedent of blending spiritual and political leadership that continues in much of the Middle East to this day.

The city is renamed Medina, "the city of the Prophet." It is the first time in the history of the Arabs that a political entity has been formed that unites multiple blood clans into a community based on something other than kinship. Knowing its significance, the Muslims create a new calendar, declaring it to be year 0. The pilgrimage to Medina will ever after be known as the *hijrah*.

But the *hijrah*, in a sense, is a wave of unemployed immigrants that the oasis cannot readily support. With all the agricultural land already spoken for, the Meccan Muslims have to take measures to ensure their survival. As leader, Muhammad, guided by his continuing revelations, decides that, since his people have been forced into this position by the Qurayshis, they will survive by raiding the Qurayshi caravans that pass nearby.

Ultimately, this leads to a great battle between the Muslims and the Qurayshis at the Wells of Badr, southwest of Medina, near the Red Sea coast. Despite being outnumbered three-to-one, the Muslims are victorious.

At the end of the battle, Arab tradition would have the victors go about killing all of the enemy wounded. But Muhammad commands otherwise; he says that enemy survivors must be encouraged to become Muslims. Tell them, he says, that "if Allah [Arabic for *God*] finds any good in your hearts, he will give you something better than what has been taken from you, and he will forgive you."

As the news of the Muslims' upset victory spreads, tales of this groundbreaking practice spread with it. Who are these people who are turning tradition upside-down, forsaking old blood ties, creating a community that blends clans and welcomes all? Who is this one god who protects them and orders them to show compassion to their enemies after battle?

Soon, pilgrims from all around the region are heading to Medina, where they find, by Arab standards of the time, an equitable community that spans not only bloodlines, but skin color and economic status, as well. Women, too, are of a higher position. Muhammad has banned the common practice of the murder of female infants. Arab men, who formerly accumulated as many wives as they pleased and treated them like personal property, are told that if they cannot treat their wives equitably then they must take only one.

Women are allowed the same education as men, and they are given inheritance rights. Except in pastoral or hunter-gatherer communities, there is no better place in the world to be a woman in the first half of the 7th century.

By the year 630, the number of converts in northern Arabia is sufficient to overwhelm the Qurayshis in their own home. Even many Meccans have begun to convert to Islam. It is time for Muhammad to make his triumphant return to Quraysh. He leads the Muslim army peacefully into the center of Mecca, where he alone rides a circle around the *ka'bah*, before entering the shrine itself and destroying all of the idols.

In two more years, Muhammad dies, and from the moment of his death there begins a schism in Islam. The majority claim that Muhammad wanted a man named Abu Bakr to succeed him, despite being outside Muhammad's direct lineage. This group will later become known as the Sunnis, or "keepers of the tradition." A sizable minority claim that the line of succession should be hereditary (though exclusively male), thus passing to Ali, who was the husband of Muhammad's eldest daughter. They become known as the Shi'ites, or "followers of Ali." The Sunnis win out, and Abu Bakr becomes the first *caliph*, the spiritual and administrative ruler over all of the Arabian Peninsula.

The division between the Sunnis and Shi'ites festers as both the second and third Sunni caliphs are murdered, after which Ali is finally chosen as the fourth caliph. But he, too, is assassinated after a turbulent five years of rule, much of which is spent at war against the governor of Syria. After a power play, accumulating allies, said governor is eventually able to wrest power from Ali's successor. He forms the Umayyad Dynasty and moves the capital north to Damascus.

Nearly 30 years after the death of Muhammad, Islam has changed in ways that would surely have disappointed him. The Prophet had always championed women's rights, but now women are being forced to sit behind a screen at the back of the mosque. They are being secluded in the home, as well, and veiled when in public.

The Prophet spoke of *jihad*, Arabic for "struggle," as a personal internal struggle to be true to the demands of Islam. He also referred to the Muslim community's *jihad* to survive as justification for making war on the Qurayshis, who had chased them from their home. But now this use of *jihad* was being abused as an excuse to make war.

41

It seems that ordinary religious leaders just can't keep their hands off the basic messages of their prophets. The ship was off course again and, Muhammad having been proclaimed to be the *last* prophet, there was no one left to right it.

◇◇◇

It would not be long before the lot of women would also severely decline in China. This begins with an attack on Buddhism...

Confucian advisers to the later Tang emperors have been regularly throwing shade on the Theravada Buddhists in their monasteries, complaining that they are neither contributing to the empire's production nor paying any taxes. As the economy begins to falter, their barbs begin to hit home with one emperor Wuzong, who, in the year 845, orders the monasteries to be shut down. Many of them are physically destroyed.

The advisers' labeling of the monasteries as unproductive is not entirely true. It is just before the time of the crackdown that an important invention comes about first in China: gunpowder. Its origin is hazy, but it is thought to have been Buddhist monks who first hit on the right combination of saltpeter, sulfur, and charcoal. The Tang will only use it in fireworks.

The destruction of the monasteries is a blow from which Chinese Buddhism will never fully recover. But the empire of the Tang has become even greater in size than the Han was at its largest extent, and Chinese ideas have spread even farther beyond those borders. Southeast Asia will become the primary center of Theravada Buddhism, and, in Japan, a variant known as Zen will take hold.

The unwieldy size of the empire will prove to be the dynasty's undoing. There are too many miles of frontier to adequately defend, and the tendency of far-flung local administrators to be tempted by corruption sours the populace.

After 900, the empire begins to crumble, and the center of power moves eastward, away from its now centuries-old pastoral roots. This, along with the suppression of Buddhism in favor of male-dominated Confucianism, gradually lessens the standing of women. It is then that the biggest blow, the consequence of which women will bear for a thousand years, begins (it is told) with a simple exclamation: "Such tiny feet she has!"

Those words are supposedly spoken by one of the last Tang emperors as he is being entertained by a traveling troupe of dancers who are putting on a show in the imperial harem. His remark is overheard by some of the higher-ranking concubines, and the word quickly spreads that if you want to impress the emperor and improve your standing in the harem, having tiny feet would be a great advantage. Thus begins the practice of foot-binding.

To fit a foot into shoes as tiny as four inches long requires that the four outer toes be bent under and pressed into the underside of the foot so that you walk on the tops of those toes. Obviously, such mutilation requires a long period of painful preparation. Beginning at age 6 or 7, a girl's feet are forced in the desired direction and tightly bound with cloth. Even though the feet swell and become feverish and the toes start to putrefy, the wrappings are made progressively tighter.

Inability to walk properly is considered a sign of status, of having the luxury to be waited upon by others. From the palace, the practice spreads to the fashionable upper-class women of the capital. It spreads down throughout society and wide across the empire until nearly every woman in China who isn't a peasant working the fields is doing it.

By this time, China is well into a new dynasty, the Song ("Soong"), and is experiencing what is often called China's Golden Age. It isn't so golden for nearly half the population.

The Islamic world, referred to as *Dār al-Islam* in Arabic, expanded rapidly from its humble beginnings in Arabia's desert oases to encompass much of Eurasia and North Africa. By 750, it extended from northwest India, across the Middle East and all of the north African coast to Morocco, then up the Iberian Peninsula through modern-day Portugal and Spain. By 1300, it would include Indonesia, reach the Philippines, and move south halfway down the interior of Africa and even further down its Indian Ocean coast.

Though the corruption of the spirit of *jihad* played a role in pockets of this expansion, the image of Arab cavalries forcing converts at the point of a sword is an almost entirely false one. Aside from the spiritual appeal of the religion, there were many worldly reasons why one might want to become a Muslim.

First, there was the intellectual attractiveness of Islamic culture...

750 was the year that the greatest Islamic dynasty began: the Abbasid. With the exception of Iberia, which remained its own caliphate, Abbasid rule would extend across all of *Dār al-Islam*, centered on a new capital at Baghdad. Because its empire bordered all of the major cultural centers of Eurasia, Islamic scholars at Baghdad could translate and further develop Chinese, Indian, Persian, Egyptian, and Greco-Roman knowledge.

All of these works were collected in a great library that came to be known as the House of Wisdom. Already a thriving center of trade, Baghdad now became a magnetic center of scholarship. It was the place where the world came together, and the native language, Arabic, would become the developed world's *lingua franca*, just as English is today's.

In the early 9th century, an astronomical observatory was added to the House of Wisdom. The century also brought a number of medical advancements. Baghdad was the location of the world's first hospitals, where, by the year 1000, elementary surgery was being performed.

There were other reasons to convert to Islam that were more concrete...

If you were a trader with business anywhere across the wide Islamic network, it was of great practical advantage to become a Muslim. In the 9th century, the Muslims were the first to develop a system of credit. And Muslims tended to give other Muslims the best terms.

If you were a lower-caste Hindu, becoming a Muslim would free you of prejudices and restrictions. If you were already living within the bounds of *Dār al-Islam*, as were many Christians and Jews, you would become free of the special tax that was demanded of non-Muslims. Plus you could marry that Muslim woman you had your eye on but was strictly off limits to those not of the faith.

So what was it like in Europe while all this was happening in Asia? Suppose you could time travel to the year 1100 and inhabit the life of three different people: one at the heart of China, one at the heart of *Dār al-Islam*, and one at the heart of Western Europe...

First, let's drop by Song Dynasty China:

You live in Hangzhou ("Hahng-joe"), the capital. It is a beautifully maintained and structured city, with all of its streets laid out in a perfect grid. The streets are quite clean, as all of the animal waste is regularly hosed off, diverted away from town via swift-flowing canals that empty into the river. There are shops selling beautiful silks or fine porcelain cups and plates, where you make your purchases using paper money.

You might go into a bookstore and peruse through books printed on real paper. Books identical to the one you hold may be found across town or even across China, as books have been being mass-printed for the last 50 years, since Bi Sheng invented movable-type printing. Since papermaking began during the Han Dynasty in the 1st century CE, the Chinese had been reproducing printed material through block printing, in which a custom block was carved for each page. Nowadays, small blocks representing each Chinese character are arranged into a page frame, making true mass production possible, boosting literacy throughout the empire.

You can see from the clock tower that it is time to join your friends at a restaurant. Eating out is a relatively new concept that began right here in Hangzhou. The clock, which is a chain-driven improvement on the old water clock, tells you not only the time, but also the day of the month and the phase of the moon.

For dessert, you enjoy a bowl of ice cream (a recent Song invention), before strolling on the promenade along West Lake, where someone is setting off fireworks. You know that the powder that causes their explosion has been put to another use by the emperor: launching bunches of arrows at the barbarians who occasionally trouble the northern border.

Before you end your day, you head to the public bathhouse. Once home, still smelling like liquid soap made from peas and herbs, you strike a match, light an oil lamp, and crack open that book. Later, as you put out the lamp, you reflect on how lucky you are to live in the "Middle Kingdom," the place that (from your perspective) the rest of the world revolves around. (Assuming you're a man, so you don't have to deal with the feet thing.)

Now let's apparate westward to Baghdad into the body of an Abbasid Muslim:

The city is much dirtier than Hangzhou: dusty, with lots of camel dung to keep dodging. But what an exciting place! You explore the warren of the bazaar. Easy to get lost in these narrow passageways with merchant stalls full of every type of good: glass, ceramics, spices, trinkets from exotic places. There is a jumble of languages being spoken, as well, primarily your own Arabic, but quite a smattering of Chinese, too.

After your exciting but hot and dirty outing, you come home to clean up. Your home has a marble bath you can fill with water that runs through metal pipes, and you clean your skin with a bar of pulverized ash.

In the cool of the evening, you decide to visit the House of Wisdom, where you climb to the astronomical observatory. The stars are bright, and a man is using an astrolabe to study them.

Then, poof!—Suddenly you're even farther west, living the same day, but in Paris:

You walk along rutted, unpaved streets, where blood from the butchers runs in the gutters. At one point, you see a scrawny pig rooting in some garbage. You drop into a tavern filled with rowdy men. They are playing a game of dice. One is munching on a chicken hindquarter. He tosses the bones on the floor, where they

45

disappear into the rushes. You assume that the owner will be sweeping those out soon and replacing them, as they are starting to smell.

Back outside, you hear a commotion coming from a couple streets over. On your way to it, you pass a house with a door open to a back bedroom, where you can see someone is sick. The doctor is there, and he is letting the patient's contaminated blood out into a bowl.

You are in luck. The sounds you heard came from a crowd beginning to gather for a performance by a traveling company. You know they will be acting out a scene from the Bible. There is a good chance it will be a familiar one, perhaps one of your favorites. But it would be good to learn something new, too; you don't have many chances, as you are illiterate. You did once see a big book that had been inked by hand on pages made from animal skin. You admired the pretty pictures.

To get home, you decide to take the shortcut along the River Seine, but you immediately regret it. The stench of rotting animal carcasses is especially strong today.

It is getting dark, so you retire early. Taking off your outer garments, you rub the dirt off your skin as best you can. It's been a month since your last bath. You should probably chance one again soon, but you worry it might make you sick.

Maybe we had better back up and trace how Western Europe has gotten to this point...

While *Dār al-Islam* and Tang and Song China were advancing civilization to new heights, Western Europe remained a collection of warlords' fiefdoms and petty kingdoms. Political leaders were uniformly as illiterate as their people.

But there was one centralized organization that survived, although in a fragmented form: the Catholic Church. By the 8th century, the Bishop of Rome had acquired the title of pope. He answered to no political authority, and he maintained communication with a network of distantly dispersed monasteries and nunneries. Communication between and within these Catholic centers was in Latin, the language of the Romans, while various vernacular tongues were spoken in the lands around them, some derived from Latin, some from the mostly-Germanic invaders.

Catholic environs were the only areas where much *written* language could be found. Here, a monk labors over a hand reproduction of a massive illustrated

Bible, inked on parchment (the dried animal skin referred to in the last section). He may be drawing and coloring this very illustration, immortalizing himself inside a letter "N" that begins a new book.

Eventually relics—bones of those who would later become saints, along with such items as purported fragments of the cross used to crucify Jesus—were collected, stored in golden reliquaries, and housed in monastery treasuries. One of the most remote of these, at Lindisfarne in northern England, was raided by Vikings in 793. Undefended Catholic treasures were easy pickings for these Scandinavian raiders, who would continue to make trouble far and wide throughout Western Europe for the next two centuries.

In the feudal system, the warlord apportioned most of his fiefdom to knights, whom he could then call up to raise an army to engage raiders. Don't imagine chivalric knights fit out with lances on horseback; these were the earliest knights, much rougher sorts. While the Abbasid and Tang dynasties were expanding in Asia, Western Europe was engaged in constant warfare, which prevented the region from making any significant progress.

By the year 1000, the Vikings had either been repelled or permanently acquired land, such as the Normandy coast of present-day France, where they settled and became farmers.

Farther east, the Vikings established the first political order of any kind north of Constantinople, centered on their capital at Kiev, in present-day Ukraine. Through their close trading ties with the Eastern Romans, they acquired Christianity.

But this did not immediately create peace. Wherever weapons and armies abound, war will find a way. Now, many of the warlords who had engaged the Vikings turn on each other in a quest to expand their landholdings.

By this time, the Eastern Roman Empire is not much larger than present-day Turkey and Greece. The head of the Church in Constantinople is called the patriarch and is appointed by the emperor. As the pope in Western Europe becomes more powerful, tension develops between the two Church leaders. The pope, who answers only to God, feels he should have the last word on Church practices and observations. The patriarch feels that, as the representative of the empire, he should be the ultimate authority, not some guy from the hinterlands.

When the goal is orthodoxy, there can be no variation. Thus the only possible outcome is a schism—in this case what comes to be known as the Great Schism of 1054. Sure that their interpretation is the correct one, the eastern sect calls itself the Orthodox Church, while the western sect continues to be known as the Catholic Church, even though it is no longer katholikos (the one universal Church).

Nevertheless, the pope continues to gain power. Only two decades later, he has a chance to demonstrate just how powerful he is. Kingdoms have been growing in some areas of Western Europe. In Saxony, one King Heinrich IV decides his has grown large enough that he ought to have the power to appoint his own bishops (regional Church leaders), rather than have them imposed on him by the pope, who is so far away down in Rome.

In response, Pope Gregory VII threatens Heinrich with excommunication. When one is excommunicated by the pope, they are cast out from the Church. Under Catholic doctrine, no one who is outside the Church can have salvation; they will remain stained with original sin and roast in Hell forever after death.

Whether Heinrich truly believes in Gregory's power or not, he is pretty sure that most of his subjects do. Once they receive word of his excommunication, they would no longer feel bound to submit to his rule.

Gregory comes north to Germany, lodges himself in some suitable quarters there, and waits for Heinrich to come to him. When he does, Heinrich has to wait outside in the snow, begging Gregory to reinstate him (barefoot, as the story, perhaps exaggerated, is often told).

The next power move by a pope comes in 1095, when Urban II launches the First Crusade. Urban urges the more powerful kings to unite their forces and march to the Middle East to take back Jerusalem and its sites that are sacred to Christians. Though his ultimate motivation may be solidifying his place atop Western Europe's feudal hierarchy, it truly benefits the people at the bottom of that power pyramid, who no longer have to worry so much about the armies of neighboring kings and warlords sweeping periodically through their farms and villages.

A Crusade... Fight Muslims, not each other!

1) Sends all the fighters away to the Middle East, restoring peace

2) Solidifies the power of the Church

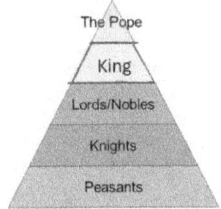

Altogether, the series of Crusades that occur over the next 100-plus years will be a military failure. Jerusalem will be held only briefly by the Christians. Yet the side benefit of the Crusades is the best thing to happen to Europe since before the Fall of Rome: It deepens the contact between the Europeans and the much more advanced Arabs.

Just prior to the First Crusade, a Spanish army in Iberia had entered Toledo, the capital of that lesser caliphate. They were awed by what they found: "homes with marble balconies and courts with lovely waterfalls" and public lamps that "lighted roads for as long as ten miles." They also found those Arabic numerals in use. The Muslims withdrew south to Granada, but the Spanish frontier continued to be a source of one-way knowledge transfer. Now an even greater fount of knowledge opens up at the other end of the Mediterranean, with an ongoing stream of returning armies carrying it back through Italian ports.

In 1204, armies of the Fourth Crusade, failing once again to take back Jerusalem, turn on Constantinople and plunder it instead. The Eastern Roman Empire recovers, but in an even weaker state. Yet, as the empire weakens, the surrounding Mediterranean world begins to awaken. Through the years of Constantinople's decline, many of the writings of the ancient Greeks were lost. But this knowledge was preserved in Baghdad's House of Wisdom. Now, because of the Crusaders' contact with the Arabs, it is beginning to make its way home.

Though the Muslims are chased south by Christian armies in Iberia and overrun by Turkish pastoralists migrating west across Persia, the culture of *Dār al-Islam* remains strong. The Turks become converted and acculturated, only changing the title of the theocratic ruler from caliph to sultan. Under their leadership, Muslim armies push deep into the Eastern Roman Empire (Turkifying what will become present-day Turkey).

But before the empire disappears altogether, a new and even more fruitful frontier will open up to the northeast. The Southernization of Europe, only just begun, is soon to get kicked into high gear.

CHAPTER FOUR

The Mongol Conquest: Three Hugely Different Fates
(1206-1368)

This chapter begins in 1206 because it is the year that the opposite fates of Europe and *Dār al-Islam* are sealed.

It happens far away from either, north of China's Great Wall, north of the great Asian steppe, among a ragtag bunch of pastoralists known as the Mongols. Like pastoralists of the steppe whom we have encountered before, the men are fabulous horsemen and expert mounted archers. The women herd cattle and manage the packing and unpacking of seasonal migration. They have begun to gain exposure to neighboring Chinese goods and ideas.

So why "ragtag"? Two reasons:

1. Like the Arabs before the coming of Muhammad, they are fragmented into blood clans.
2. These clans are constantly feuding with each other, if not in outright warfare, then in regular raiding of each other's livestock and women.

Given these two things, you wouldn't think that anyone in Hangzhou or Baghdad or Constantinople would have any reason to be concerned about these guys, and they weren't. But then some Mongol raiding the clan next door decides to swipe the wrong woman, and the rest is history.

That woman is the wife of one Temujin (Mongols don't have family names; they are only called, for example, Temujin of the Borjigin clan). After her kidnapping, Temujin makes a name for himself by taking the unusual action of going after the perpetrator and bringing his wife back.

It is right about this time that the Borjigin clan is uniting with a couple of other clans, with an eye toward further expansion. They need a leader, and Temujin seems like the perfect guy.

It is a wise choice. Temujin knows how to win people over. Even though pastoralists are more egalitarian than "civilized" societies, the Mongols are not without some basic social leveling. Temujin exploits this each time his coalition is victorious in battle. He invites the lower class into his ranks while executing the

51

rich and equitably redistributing their possessions. This makes the newcomers happy and the old-timers grateful for the newcomers.

By the year 1206, Temujin has become the sole ruler of all the Mongol clans. In a ceremony, he is named "Universal Ruler." In the Mongolian language, that translates to "Genghis Khan." Look out, civilizations of Eurasia! He'll be coming for you next.

One of the first actions of the newly titled Genghis Khan is overseeing the codification of a single set of Mongol laws. He makes thievery of women punishable by death. In the violent and disorderly milieu of male Mongol society, this is an incredible accomplishment. As is imposing discipline and unity within the ranks of his fighting forces. Less than five years later, he has them marching south to invade the world's most advanced empire.

Subduing China's Song Dynasty would be a multi-decade process, during which time the Mongols also sweep west across central Asia all the way to the Caspian Sea. They are able to advance with limited resistance because they make examples of cities that fight back, sometimes executing entire populations. One story spread of how Genghis Khan, himself, made an example of a city leader who had unwisely resisted, pouring hot liquid silver in the leader's ear until it started to run out his eyes. In this way, the Mongols' reputation having preceded them, the next city up the road would open the gates and roll out the welcome mat.

After Genghis Khan's death in 1227, his four grandsons split up his empire into four khanates and expand it further. It takes 60 years to subdue the Song Dynasty, the Mandate of Heaven finally passing to Kublai Khan, who declares himself emperor. By this time, Kublai and the Mongols have learned much of Chinese culture. As with the pastoral conquerors of the past, they become acculturated. Thus, in keeping with Chinese tradition, a new dynasty is declared: the Yuan.

There would be a few differences. The capital is moved to a new site, halfway between Hangzhou and Mongolia, just below the Great Wall: Beijing. To the disdain of the native Chinese, who refer to themselves as Han Chinese, yurts and grazing animals appear in the palace compound. Worse yet, Mongol women do not bind their feet, and even upper-class women go hunting on horseback with the men.

But the palace where Kublai Khan receives merchants from Europe is just as opulent and Chinese in style as the one left behind in Hangzhou (we have one of those merchants, by the name of Marco Polo, to thank for his detailed descriptions). Though the Han Chinese might mutter to themselves about the improper habits of their leaders, they get on quite well. Unlike after the fall of the Han Dynasty centuries before, the great Chinese Empire hardly skips a beat. And in 1368, after less than a century of Mongol rule, the second Yuan emperor is deposed and a native Chinese dynasty, the Ming, is returned to the throne.

But wait! (you say). What are *European* merchants doing in Beijing? There hasn't been a Silk Road for more than 1,000 years.

It's time to back up and relate those opposite fates mentioned above...

In 1258, a Mongol horde led by Hulagu, another grandson of Genghis Khan, arrives at the gates of Baghdad. Hulagu sends word to the caliph, al-Musta'sim, demanding that he surrender the city. But al-Musta'sim must have not gotten the memo on what the Mongols were capable of. The summary translation of his reply is: "Take a hike." He, his fellow citizens, and indeed all of *Dār al-Islam* will pay for this impudence.

The great capital is destroyed, and 100,000 of its citizens are slaughtered. Al-Musta'sim, himself, is executed by being rolled in a carpet and trampled by horses.

The House of Wisdom is looted and its books tossed into the Tigris River. Stories are told of its waters turning black with ink.

Some scholars, who are able to get out ahead of the attack, make their way to India. It is like the knowledge that came from India and was increased by the Arabs is going back where it came from. Meanwhile, the center of a much-reduced and less learned and influential *Dār al-Islam* is shifted in the opposite direction, to the safety of Cairo, Egypt.

With Baghdad in ruins, the Mongols move the khanate's capital to Persia. Though much of the culture is eviscerated, the religion of Islam remains. It is adopted by the invaders.

While Arab fortunes are crashing, those of the Europeans are poised to rise...

After the Mongols sweep across the south Russian steppe, subjugating the Viking principality of Kiev, they do truly call for peace. Their empire, the largest the world has ever known, now spans over 11 million contiguous square miles.

Except for a little raiding in Poland and Hungary, the rest of Europe is spared. The Kipchak Khanate (later called the Khanate of the Golden Horde by Europeans) is ruled from its capital near present-day Volgograd, though in a very decentralized fashion—something feudal Europe could relate to.

The Mongols have been fast learners, applying what they learned from the Chinese in their later conquests. First is the art of siege warfare. Then is the use of gunpowder. These now make their way to Europe.

Though divided into multiple khanates, the Mongols work together to reopen the Silk Road, all the way from Yuan China to Eastern Europe. They establish guard stations at regular intervals all along the several thousand-mile route, keeping trade caravans safe from attack by thieves. Over the next century and a half, in what comes to be known as the Mongol Peace, the spigot will open and the advanced learning of the Chinese will gush Europe's way.

Having already been exposed by the Arabs to the Indian number system and the compass, Europeans now acquire firearms, papermaking, movable-type printing, and many everyday Chinese conveniences from renewed Silk Road trade. Constantinople becomes the gateway through which all of this passes. From there, these ideas tag along with the trade goods by sea to Venice and Genoa. Northern Italy, already a crossroads en route to the Crusades, will become a center of even more wealth—and learning.

But before we can call this a Renaissance and declare the Southernization of Europe to be complete, one other thing will tag along the above route with those trade goods: rats. Which is nothing unusual in the holds of ships, but these rats carry fleas that are infected with the bubonic plague.

Over a five-year period from 1347 to 1351, Europe loses 40% of its population to the Black Death, around 25 million souls. On the bright side, once it's over, there is a great need for workers, and the economy rapidly recovers. Plus, you know, what doesn't kill you...

CHAPTER FIVE

In a Flash,
The Course of Human History is Altered
(1369-1488)

For the first several decades of the Ming Dynasty, Chinese leaders continued to have the Mongols on their minds. The Great Wall was shored up and expanded, and repetitive military expeditions were sent deep into Mongolia.

By 1400, the Ming ruled over 2.5 million square miles of territory, small by Mongol standards yet more than ten times the size of Europe's largest kingdom. Despite active trade along the Silk Road, the "Middle Kingdom" showed signs of becoming even more insular, becoming reasonably cautious about what foreigners were beginning to do with its inventions.

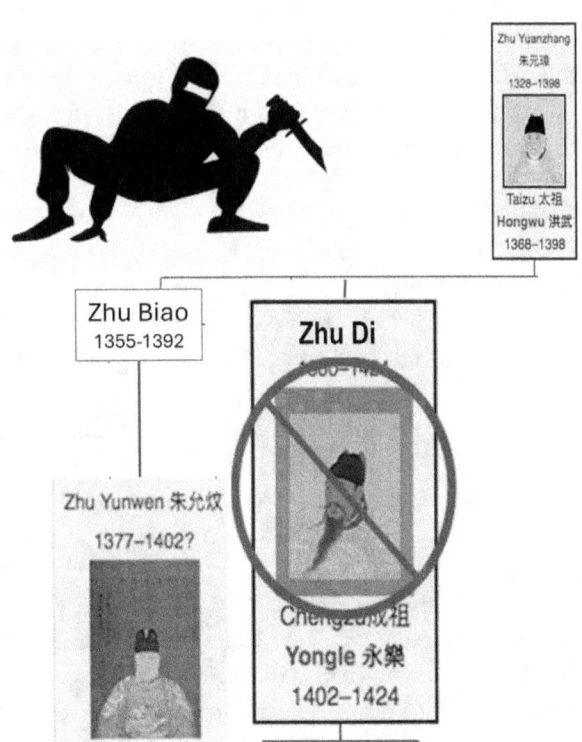

All that would change when a certain emperor came along, who was in many ways unlike any emperor China had before...

Zhu Di ("Jew Dee") only came to the throne through a bit of palace intrigue. This occurred because the first Ming emperor outlived his eldest son. In this case, the rules of succession made the eldest son's son the next in line. Thus, immediately upon the first Ming emperor's death, his grandson, Zhu Yunwen, became the new emperor.

Zhu Di was the deceased emperor's eldest surviving son, and, to head off any possible dispute about the succession, Zhu Yunwen's advisers persuaded him to arrange to have his uncle murdered...

Before we continue this story, we need to recap a prior episode in the history of China. Recall the importance of the Civil Service Examination System: that really tough, competitive series of Confucian-inspired tests that one needed to perform extraordinarily well on to land a position in the government, where failure meant reducing one's entire family status and often resulted in suicide. The ultimate success—passing the very highest level—would make you a scholar-adviser, an integral part of the emperor's court. (Today, the West knows these figures as "mandarins," a term which—although much more associated with China—originated in India, and was an adaptation of the Sanskrit word for *adviser*.)

Also before continuing, we need to introduce an equally important figure in the Chinese imperial court: the eunuch. A eunuch, of course, is a castrated male. Their most well-known purpose was to serve as guards of the imperial harem. Chinese emperors were known to have hundreds of concubines, and their harems had rigid hierarchies, from "Number One Concubine" on down. Aside from the imperial family and the concubines, the eunuchs were the only ones allowed to stay overnight in the inner sanctum of the palace. Because they could not match the eunuchs' physical proximity to the emperor, the mandarins developed a natural dislike of them. One historical account, written by a mandarin, describes the "effeminate, cringing eunuchs, slavishly dependent upon the emperor for their very lives."

In fact, eunuchs were not always effeminate. Many of them served in the army. In Nanjing, where the Ming moved their capital, eunuchs guarded not only the harem, but the palace itself. Which brings us back to the current action...

Zhu Di is tipped off to the assassination attempt. Learning that the mandarins proposed the idea, he decides to take advantage of the long-simmering eunuch–mandarin rivalry. He raises an army to march on the palace and secretively contacts his nephew's eunuch palace guard. They open the gates and let his army in.

At some point in the resulting melee, the inner sanctum is set on fire. Zhu Yunwen is declared to have died in this fire, but his body is not identified, and it is rumored that he escapes China altogether. At any rate, he is never heard from again, and Zhu Di becomes the third Ming emperor.

And so begins the most extravagant reign of all the Chinese emperors. From the moment he takes control, Zhu Di has *big* plans. To begin with, he wants to aggressively expand China's ocean trade. The mandarins advise against this. If we have sea trade, they say, then we must build a naval fleet to protect it, when

56

instead we should arm and supply our land army and send them north again to keep the Mongols at bay.

We *will* build a fleet, answers the emperor, the greatest fleet that the world has ever seen. *Big* ships capable of crossing the open ocean, not just clinging to the coastline. Exploring ever outward, our ships will awe those who inhabit the shores beyond the Middle Kingdom.

The mandarins are shocked by the sweep of their master's ambition. They also are disturbed by his motive. Confucius taught that merchants are only parasites, making money for themselves from the work of others.

But Zhu Di, it seems, is only obsessed with recognition of China's power. Trade is secondary. The goods the ships carry will be gifts to the rulers of the lesser lands, in exchange for paying a nominal tribute and pledging allegiance.

As he ignores the mandarins' counsel and initiates construction, Zhu Di begins to turn to his most trusted eunuchs for advice instead. He chooses a eunuch named Zheng He ("Jung Huh") to be the admiral of his fleet.

By 1405, three years into his reign, Zhu Di's vision has become real. Zheng He takes a fleet of 62 ships down through the South China Sea, up through the Straits of Malacca, and west across the Indian Ocean to Ceylon. It will be more than ten years before Portuguese sailors begin to inch their way down the Atlantic coast of Africa in their caravels. By that time, Zheng will have made three more voyages. Soon after, on his fifth voyage, he will reach the east coast of Africa.

To get a better idea of the massive size of Zheng He's ships, here is one shown alongside Columbus' flagship, the *Santa Maria*. The Santa Maria is about the same length as the *rudder* of one of Zheng He's ships.

The Chinese ships are also far more technically advanced. Each one of the nine masts

can be swiveled to allow the sails to adjust to the wind. With their massive holds laden with Chinese goods and inventions, many unfamiliar to the recipients, they become known as the Treasure Ships.

Ships this big need a *big* man at the helm, and Zheng He is that. He is said to be seven feet tall and have a five-foot girth. He was captured by the Chinese in a war when he was an adolescent and made a eunuch, then a common practice. As his fame increases, he becomes known as the Grand Eunuch.

Soon, to be a eunuch adviser in Zhu Di's court becomes such a sought-after position that it necessitates passing a new law:

It shall hereon be a capital crime for any man to engage in or arrange for self-castration.

Pause for a moment and imagine being one of Zhu Di's mandarins at this point in time. Perhaps you come from modest means. You engage in the exam process, knowing how your family depends on you, the weight of Confucian obligation toward them heavy upon you. You study hard and begin to advance through the multi-tiered system of tests. It is likely you know at least one other who failed and whose shame was so great that they took their own life. Keeping your head down, remaining humble, you persevere, until finally you complete the highest level and you pass! You have brought great honor to your family, and you head to Nanjing to become a member of the emperor's court. But now the throne has passed to this man, who ignores the wise counsel of the elder mandarins whom you respect, who spends recklessly on such an extravagance. And now he begins to shun you and your fellow mandarins altogether, in favor of his eunuchs! With public praise for this "Grand Eunuch" ringing in your ears, your hatred for Zhu Di and his "Treasure Ships" grows...

If the mandarins think that things can't be worse, this thought is premature, for in 1406, the year after Zheng He's initial voyage, Zhu Di announces his next *big* project. He launches plans for moving the capital back to Beijing, where the Mongols ruled, but not until completing construction of what will become, by far, the *biggest* palace complex in the world. It will take the next 15 years to complete the Forbidden City (which remains the largest palace complex in the world today). Six-tenths of a mile long by nearly half a mile wide, the complex will contain 1,000 buildings with nearly 10,000 rooms.

In the meantime, Zhu Di contents himself with the many gifts of tribute from the leaders of the growing list of tributary states. He creates what is probably the world's first zoo to house the exotic creatures his admiral brings back to him.   (1)

Finally, in 1421, to inaugurate the completed palace complex, Zhu Di announces that he will entertain 28 heads of state in a month-long orgy of feasting and drinking. To set the proper submissive tone, Zheng He will sail the fleet from place to place, collecting heads of state and bringing them to Zhu Di so they can kowtow before him (prostrate themselves, tapping the forehead three times on the floor). At the end of the month, a second voyage will carry them home.

Now, by this time the mandarins are beginning to think that, if they only bide their time, an end to their misery may be near. The treasury is being strained. Taxes have already been increased and there is little benefit to the people for all the added expense. After all, every Chinese, no matter how lowly, has been brought up in a Confucian society where humility is prized. Zhu Di is no tyrant, but his actions, which seem designed to bring glory to himself, can hardly be considered ruling with virtue. How much longer can this man be entrusted by Heaven to do the best thing for China? The mandarins begin to court Zhu Di's eldest son, Zhu Gaochi, in anticipation of a kinder future.

The first indication of that future comes in the middle of the night, shortly after the month of private revelry comes to an end, when a lightning storm sweeps through Beijing. One lightning bolt strikes a direct hit on the inner sanctum of the Forbidden City, igniting a fire. Large sections of the newly-finished complex are destroyed and the emperor's Number One Concubine is killed. To the common people, if ever there was a clearer sign from Heaven, this is it...

Badly shaken, Zhu Di retreats into seclusion. No doubt the synchronicity of this fire and the one caused by his army so long ago, which led to the fall of Zhu Yunwen, gives him pause.

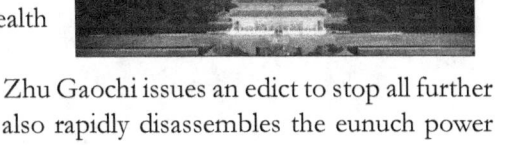

With Zhu Di's powerful personality neutralized, the mandarins become emboldened, continuing to meet with Zhu Gaochi. And soon, Zhu Di's health begins to fail.

On the day of his father's death, Zhu Gaochi issues an edict to stop all further voyages of the Treasure Ships. He also rapidly disassembles the eunuch power structure and returns the mandarins to their rightful positions.

Hate is a strong emotion, and the mandarins' hatred for Zhu Di long outlasts his death. When a later emperor decides to take the fleet out of mothballs and calls up Zheng He for one more ocean voyage, all that emotion comes rushing out again. This time, the mandarins' desire to stop exploration will not be denied. They warn the emperor that Zhu Di's hubris, built up by the gifts of his tributaries, ultimately led to his downfall and question whether the dynasty can survive a repeat occurrence.

Later, after the death of Zheng He, the mandarins convince the emperor to allow them to seek out and destroy all records of the Treasure Ship voyages. Which is why we knew nothing about China's period of ocean exploration until 1962, when divers in the South China Sea made the first of many discoveries: one rudder the size of the Santa Maria.

Since that time, other sunken ships have been reclaimed from the ocean depths. A fully-working model has been assembled. After combing the shores of the Indian Ocean, tales of the voyages have been found. Records of Zhu Di's reign have been studied and reinterpreted. Together, the pieces of a forgotten history have been assembled like the shards of an ancient urn.

There is a story told, perhaps only legend, of salt being plowed into farmland along a part of the coast of China. It was thought that if the land could not be farmed, then the population would have to live inland, turned inward, preventing any thoughts of what might lie beyond the ocean's open horizon.

Meanwhile, the Portuguese, in their small ships, were moving farther south along the Atlantic coast of Africa. Just nine years after the records of the great Chinese voyages were destroyed, the first Portuguese caravel would round the Cape of Good Hope... into a newly empty Indian Ocean.

How different our history might have been had that lightning storm swept a mile north or south! For little do the mandarins know, ocean exploration, now to become the exclusive domain of Europe, not China, is what provides the power to become master of the world.

CHAPTER SIX

Conquering the New World Enriches Europe and Destroys Africa, But Neither Happens in the Way Most People Think
(1489-1833)

While it took all of Chapter 5 to explain why China did *not* continue to engage in ocean exploration, Europe's reason *for* ocean exploration can be mostly explained in one word: Greed.

But, although religion played a much lesser part in motivating exploration, developments in Christianity at this time do impact our present, so before we get to the part about greed, it requires a rather long digression...

As already mentioned, Italy was at the forefront of Europe's Southernization. Politically, it was a collection of small city-states. As the port cities of Venice and Genoa got richer (and smarter) from their role as entrepôts of Silk Road trade, inland cities like Florence and Milan got richer (and smarter) as banking centers. Wealth also flowed to the Catholic Church in Rome, where it seems to have had a corruptive effect on certain popes.

By the turn of the 16th century, the old basilica of St. Peter, the principal church in Christendom, was falling into disrepair and, as is common during economic upswings, thoughts turned to remodeling. In 1513, under a new pope, Leo X, those thoughts became rather grandiose.

Leo wanted a big, brand-new basilica, and he turned to one of the leading Renaissance artists of the day to design it: Michelangelo. Here is what they came up with:

Even though the Church was doing well, this was going to cost more than it had. So Leo designed a scheme to raise the needed funds.

Catholics believed in this thing called *purgatory,* a place your soul must go after death to suffer for all its worldly sins before finally getting into Heaven. The Church would sometimes issue a free pass out of purgatory called an *indulgence.* You had to have done something especially pious to receive one.

Leo's idea was to start *selling* indulgences to all comers.

This did not go over well with a particular monk-turned-professor at a backwoods university in Saxony. His name was Martin Luther.

In 1517, Luther posted a list of "95 Theses" on the church door in the town of Wittenburg, stating his displeasure with paid indulgences and 94 other ways he felt the Church bureaucracy was misleading the people. The church door was quite like the equivalent of a social media post in those times, and oh, brother, did it ever go viral!

Little by little, going back to the time of the plague, some minds had begun to wonder about the power of the pope. Luther seemed to be bringing out those deeply-suppressed suspicions, and it just so happened that movable-type printing had recently arrived in Europe (Buddhist monks in Korea had improved Bi Sheng's invention by creating type out of metal, and a German named Johannes Gutenberg employed this in something he called the printing press). So before long, all Germany was abuzz with Luther's ideas.

Leo's eventual excommunication of Luther had none of the effect that Gregory VII's excommunication of poor King Heinrich had on his subjects centuries before. Instead, hordes of the populace showed up to support Luther at his trial for heresy. Some even kneeled before him as if he were a saint, which Luther didn't like at all because the worship of saints and relics and so forth, which he considered a distraction from Jesus Christ alone, was part of what he had attacked in his Theses.

Though he would not repent, Luther escaped being burned at the stake for heresy because his sly patron, the prince of Saxony, Frederick the Wise, had him kidnapped after the trial and secreted away to one of his minor castles. In his isolation, Luther worked on translating the Bible from Latin (the only language allowed by the Church) to German, so that ordinary people could read it themselves for the first time.

While Luther was in hiding, the People (with a capital "P") came under the influence of other rabble-rousers who wanted to turn this grass-roots groundswell into a social revolution. Generally, all hell broke loose in Germany, and tens of thousands were killed. But finally, in 1555, a peace was declared whereby each prince had the power to determine whether their domain would remain Catholic or become what was now being called Lutheran.

This peace, however, was only the harbinger of greater Europe's Wars of Religion. As anti-Catholicism spilled out of Germany into other areas and acquired variations in addition to Lutheranism, the term "Protestant" began to be applied collectively to those who *protested* the stipulations of the Church in Rome and advocated *reformation*. These on-and-off wars will tear the subcontinent apart for the next 93 years, with Catholics shedding the blood of Protestants and vice versa.

Relevant to ocean exploration, all of this is only a lead-up to one thing: the Counter-Reformation...

In addition to fighting back physically in the Wars of Religion, the Catholic Church fights back politically, campaigning for the hearts and minds of the people, just like a modern presidential candidate. They have lost worshippers to the new Protestant sects, and they need to stop the bleeding. In order to maintain their numbers—their numerical advantage over the Protestants—they know they need to straighten up their act, so they get rid of paid indulgences and try to stamp out all other forms of corruption.

They do, however, maintain those practices that distinguish them from the Protestant sects: They keep doing masses in Latin (which ordinary people don't understand). They keep insisting that only the Church knows best when it comes to interpreting the Bible and that excommunication is still very bad because there is no salvation outside of the Church. To put a positive spin on all of this, they create the Society of Jesus, better known as the Jesuits, to form a system of Catholic schools with a curricula that emphasizes the *good* points of Catholicism.

Finally, to *really* boost their numbers, they start going after *new* worshippers where none have existed before: in the *New* World. They call on the Jesuits to launch this campaign by sending missionaries out on the waves. And *that* is the major way that religion influences European oceangoing exploration.

The Jesuits are quite successful, as today Catholicism is the dominant religion in all of Latin America. Much of this is attributable to Portugal and Spain being the early leaders in European ocean exploration, two countries that had remained 100% Catholic.

Those who grew up in the USA may be less familiar with those who came to the New World to evangelize than they are with those who came for their own religious freedom, like these guys:

That search for religious freedom also resulted from the Reformation. It had to do with a Protestant sect created especially for this guy of wife head-chopping fame:

King Henry VIII took advantage of the anti-pope sentiment running through northern Europe by forming the Church of England so he could divorce his wife. This "Anglican" Church was very much like the Catholic Church, except that Henry replaced the pope as head of the Church and divorce was okay. He also had all the English people swear an oath of loyalty to his new denomination and said that, if they didn't, it would be illegal to own property. This immediately created two sets of religious refugees:

1. Puritans (i.e. Protestant purists) who said, "You can't fool me; this isn't Protestantism—it's too *Catholic!*"
2. Catholics who said, "You can't fool me; this isn't the true Church unless it's the pope making the rules."

The Puritans wound up in New England. The Catholics eventually ended up in the colony of Maryland, named for Queen Mary, a.k.a. "Bloody Mary," Henry's daughter with his first wife, who inherited the throne since he never produced a son who lived to be an adult (all the time blaming his wives, whom he alternatively divorced or executed). Mary, like her mother, was a devout Catholic. Like her father, she was partial to having folks executed, though in her case the target was Protestants and, rather than head-chopping, her method was burning at the stake.

In sum, there were only a tiny few brave souls who came to the New World seeking religious freedom; most of the Christians who got out on the waves were Catholics with evangelical zeal in their eyes. But if, standing next to that Jesuit missionary, you picture a sailor with *another* kind of sparkle in his eye—one that anticipates fabulous wealth—nine times out of ten, your visualization would be accurate.

If the color of that sparkle is gold or silver, however, although you may be reading the mind of an uninitiated sailor correctly, you (and he) will soon learn that those are not the colors of the fabulous wealth that is about to come Europe's way. No, the color that will ultimately provide them the power to become master of the world is...

White.

But we're not there yet. Let's begin instead with black. As in black pepper.

After years of parsley, sage, rosemary, and thyme, newly Southernized epicurean Europeans were loving the spice trade that flowed their way along the safe,

Mongol-patrolled caravan routes running west from China (ginger) and north from Ormuz at the entrance to the Arabian Sea (cinnamon from Ceylon, black pepper from the Spice Islands of the Indies). *Until* the Ming mandarins shut down the China trade. From that point on, Europe had to rely on trade with Muslims going through Alexandria, Egypt. Said Muslims, knowing they had Europeans over a barrel, jacked up the prices. To make matters worse, the Egyptians weren't keen on what Europeans had to offer; they mostly wanted gold.

It so happened that Africa contained one of the places in the world where gold was plentiful. That was nearly 4,000 miles west of Egypt, in the Malian Empire, centered on Timbuktu. In the 14th century, the Portuguese would get there by camel caravans, heading straight south across the Sahara Desert, but now they were able to sail down the west coast of Africa. The part of the west African coast that turned to the east, which became known as the Gold Coast, was where Portuguese merchants traded European cloth goods and other items for Malian gold. They then paid Venetian or Genoese merchants gold in exchange for spices that had been paid for (in gold) in Alexandria. Start with high demand and reduced supply, then add the double mark-up, and you have the understandable reference to pepper as "black gold."

You also have a very strong impetus for the Portuguese to figure a way to crack this trade. They do it by sending a spy to India. In 1489, a year after Bartolomeu Dias gets around the Cape (and then returns home), a man named Pero de Covilha hitches a ride on an Arab *dhow* from Jedda (near Mecca), down the Red Sea and due east to Calicut, India. From there, he works his way back up the coast to Ormuz, scouting out nautical details like winds and currents, as well as the trickier points of culture and politics.

Back in Lisbon, the Portuguese king rejects a harebrained proposal from a Genoese adventurer named Christopher Columbus and instead doubles down on the Indian Ocean project. He orders a fort to be constructed at the entrance to the Red Sea in order to cut off trade with Alexandria (also cutting out the Genoese and Venetians). At the same time, preparations are made for a maiden voyage beyond the Cape and up the east coast of Africa, then following de Covilha's route over to India.

Plans are put temporarily on hold when news gets to Lisbon that Columbus actually *did* find land by sailing west, which he claims to be the Indies. But after the king's consultation with his experts, the consensus is, "Nah—Can't be." So they send Vasco da Gama 'round Africa, and he seals the deal. The Portuguese own the Indian Ocean now.

Though the Portuguese experts were right, Columbus—and Spain—would have the last laugh.

After his rejection by the Portuguese, Columbus pitched the same proposal to their Iberian rivals, the Spanish king and queen, who took him up on the deal. In October 1492, he landed three ships on an island in the Bahamas. Going south from there and back along the north coast of Cuba, he winds up on Hispaniola (the large island that in the present day is split between Haiti and the Dominican Republic). Here is what he had to say in his journal about the native Taino people who greeted him: "They are... far from being ignorant. They are the most ingenious men, and navigate these seas in a wonderful way and describe everything well."

He returned home to great fanfare (he had dealt himself a smart contract, which said that, if successful, he could call himself "*Lord* Christopher Columbus" and that his "sons and successors... may call themselves Lords, Admirals, Vice-Roys..." etc.). This made him feel emboldened, so, striking while the iron was hot, he told the king and queen, "Their Highnesses may see that I shall give them all the gold they require, if they will give me but a little assistance...." So he was given the funding for another voyage.

This time, he makes a fateful stop-off at the Canary Islands, a Spanish possession northwest of Africa where they have been growing sugar. Sugar, you will recall, was traded in the Middle Ages from the Indians to the Arabs (it is indigenous to New Guinea and passed from there to India at least as long ago as the Axial Age). It is too cold to grow it in Europe, even in the Mediterranean. But as soon as the Portuguese and Spanish start sailing southwest down the African coast, they start to grow it in the islands they pass there. Now, Columbus thinks to load some cane starts on one of his ships to see how the crop will fare on the other side of the Atlantic.

The sugar is mostly an afterthought. He knows this is a race for gold against the Portuguese, which is why he dangles the prospect of gold to the Spanish monarchs in order to secure their continued backing. Shortly after he returns to Hispaniola, he makes another entry about the indigenous population in his journal: "[They are] such cowards.... With fifty men you could subject everyone and make them do what you wished."

Something has changed in the relationship. Columbus met these people the first time with thoughts of new discovery and adventure paramount in his mind. This time, he is thinking about gold...

The Taino had previously given the Spanish gifts of gold jewelry, which led Columbus to make his guarantee to the Spanish monarchs. He now looks at the indigenous population as under his command, and he demands that they bring him more.

But in fact there is not much gold to be found on Hispaniola. When the indigenous people return with little in hand, the Spanish become more aggressively demanding. Before long, they are setting their dogs loose on these gentle people, whom they had earlier admired.

Though the search for gold has gone badly, the sugar cane has taken well to the soil and climate of the island. Sugar, like spices, can be turned into gold. With little acreage to date under Spanish control and intense demand from all over Europe, most sugar has to be supplied through trade with the Muslims. The opportunity for revenue abounds.

The cut into profits occurs on the expense side. Growing, harvesting and processing sugar is extremely labor-intensive. You have to hack it down with a machete, then carry the heavy bundles back to the plantation house, then peel and press it to get out the juice. The juice is clarified and boiled until it crystallizes. The vat then has to be spun by hand to separate the crystals from the syrup, and these have to be dried in the sun.

But if the cost of labor is free...?

The solution is that the Taino will be worked—many to death—as plantation slaves. Thus the change in Columbus' journal entries. From here on, the only way for the Spanish to reconcile their inhumane actions with their own humanity is, in their eyes, to strip the humanity from the Taino.

In this roundabout way, Columbus would indeed supply the Spanish monarchs "with all the gold they require." And then some.

With Columbus stubbornly insisting until his death in 1506 that he had made it all the way to the Indies, his name for the islands forever sticks, which necessitates labeling them as the *West* Indies and the Spice Islands as the *East* Indies.

The West Indies were a bust as far as spices went, but of course Columbus had discovered far more: an entire hemisphere that was replete with edibles that no one in Eurasia or Africa had ever been exposed to. No Italian had ever eaten tomato sauce, nor had any Irish person ever had a potato:

THE "COLUMBIAN EXCHANGE"			
Previously only in Western Hemisphere		Previously only in Eastern Hemisphere	
turkeys	tobacco	horses	coffee
corn	chocolate	livestock of all types	sugar
beans	vanilla	wheat	grapes
potatoes	pineapples	rice	citrus fruit
tomatoes	avocados	onions & garlic	apples
peppers	pumpkins & squash	olives	bananas

Those in the Americas acquired many new things, as well. Some—like wheat, rice, and the horse—were quite useful. Sugar turned out to be a less welcome exposure.

Another unwelcome exposure unpictured in the above chart and invisible to the naked eye was disease germs. Smallpox, typhus, influenza, even measles; all were deadly to those who had no immunity.

We don't know the exact population of the Americas prior to 1492. Estimates vary widely. We do have a good idea of the *remaining* indigenous population. It is possible that as many as 90% of indigenous people in the Americas died in the great wave of disease that spread over the hemisphere in the decades after the arrival of the Europeans.

Europeans, of course, had immunity to the germs they were spreading; they might become ill, but they rarely died. But why weren't they struck down with some strange *American* diseases for which *they* had no immunity?

The answer, once again is: Geography is destiny. It is the livestock that existed in the Eastern Hemisphere that carried all of the disease germs. Eurasians long ago had caught and spread these diseases from their pigs, sheep, and goats, which they kept in close quarters in pens or sometimes even at the back of their houses. They had drunk the milk of their cows, horses, sheep, and goats. The result was great plagues that had killed many in centuries past. Now they were immune.

Indigenous Americans had no livestock. They did not milk their llamas and alpacas. They had never experienced sweeping plagues—until now.

Overall, the great dying was advantageous for the Europeans, delivering to them a rich land, swept clean of most of its inhabitants. But for the early Spanish plantation owners –and the Portuguese, too, who had accidentally discovered Brazil as they swung out a little wide en route to the African Cape and found it an excellent climate for sugar—the deaths were a puzzling disaster. They had just set up shop and begun to collect the fruits of their slaves' labor, and now those laborers were dying out from under them. What were they going to do?

The Atlantic Slave Trade would enrich Europe and destroy Africa, but if, when thinking back on that time, you imagine pitiable, weak Africa being immediately subjugated as it is overrun by the Europeans, then your post-colonial mindset has misled you. In fact:

1. Africa was not weak.
2. The whole of Africa was not overrun.
3. The worst of the destruction did not occur until the slave trade *ended.*

Since the 14th century, Timbuktu, the capital of the Malian Empire, had been a center of learning; its famous Sankore University library housed more than one million manuscripts. In 1324, Mansa Musa, a Malian king and a convert to Islam, had made a very famous pilgrimage from Timbuktu to Cairo. Mali, you will remember, was a center for gold, and along his way, Mansa Musa made lavish gifts of it. When he got to Cairo, he gave away so much of it that its value dropped by 25% for the period of time that he and his entourage were in town.

To the south of Egypt, Ethiopia had been a center of Christianity since the early days of the religion. While stories of great wealth spread north across the wide Sahara from Mali, stories of a spiritual nature spread across the desert (and the swath of *Dār al-Islam*) from Ethiopia. Pero da Covilha, the Portuguese scout, died there while searching for the legendary Christian king known as Prester John.

At the time of Columbus, the little that Europeans knew of sub-Saharan Africa came from stories of places like Mali and Ethiopia, which rightly engendered their respect. These kingdoms were at least as advanced as the city-states of Renaissance Italy and the Iberian kingdoms of Portugal and Spain.

But when the enormous wealth of sugar production began to suddenly slip through their fingers, it was to Africa that the Portuguese and Spaniards turned to replace their slaves. This only made sense because they were already using African slaves on their sugar plantations in the Canary and Madeira Islands. Slavery of all peoples had been going on since the generation of food surpluses had kickstarted "civilization." Africans, like most people, only used prisoners-of-war and criminals as slaves, and this was the background of those people they sold to the island plantations.

As Columbus' about-face in his assessment of the Taino shows, racism did not lead to slavery; it was the other way around. Just as Columbus showed no racism toward the Taino in his first voyage, no racism was shown toward the Black Africans of sub-Saharan Africa until Black slaves were put to work in American cane fields. Once the inhumane treatment began in the name of greed—and the objects of that treatment happened to look different—racism became a convenient psychological adaptation that allowed the dispensers of that treatment to live with themselves.

It is another common maxim of world history that if you want to find the cause of evil, you need only follow the money. Slave-enabled sugar production made untold numbers of Europeans filthy rich. Whole economies came to depend on it, as indicated by this argument against abolition, made in England in 1790:

> If... abolition shall take place,... the revenue will suffer an annual [decline] of three millions at least; the price of sugar, which is now become a necessary article of life, must be immediately [increased]; discontentment and dissatisfaction may dismember the empire!

While the Spanish produced sugar in Hispaniola and Cuba and the Portuguese in Brazil, the British got into the act in Jamaica and Barbados. In the more northerly English colonies of the North American mainland, two other plantation crops became lucrative, as well. One, a New World novelty, was tobacco; the other, a mainstay of trade for over a millennium that happened to have varietals in both the Old World and New, was cotton. Like sugar, both crops were labor-intensive.

The addition of tobacco and cotton contributed to England overtaking the Iberian kingdoms in the slave trade. In 1619, the first African slaves arrived in Virginia. By 1672, the Royal African Company was established for the purpose of procuring a regular supply.

The upshot of all this was that there soon was as intense a demand for human beings as there was for sugar, tobacco, and cotton. Africans, themselves, were not immune to greed. Just as Europeans' eyes had sparkled with the thought of fabulous wealth coming their way from selling sugar, some Africans' eyes now sparkled with the thought of fabulous wealth coming *their* way from selling human beings.

Europeans—familiar only with the Arab lands of the Mediterranean, a few camel routes to the southern edges of the Sahara, and the Gold Coast—had never penetrated the interior of sub-Saharan Africa, and they weren't about to now. Africa's rivers were full of dangerous rapids and its jungles rife with malaria-infected mosquitoes. Native African adventurers, out to strike it rich, were better-equipped to venture inland, where they bargained for slaves. They marched the slaves to the seacoast, where they dealt them at a precipitous mark-up to Europeans awaiting them on the shore. The Gold Coast came to be called the Slave Coast, as Black slaves were now key to producing those *white* commodities, sugar and cotton, that yielded so much more profit in the long run than simply trading for Malian gold.

The further you go down this rabbit-hole of profits, the more evil you find lurking in the shadows. As some African kingdoms run out of their own slaves to sell (POWs and criminals), they begin raiding their neighbors, enslaving ordinary citizens.

In 1526, a Congolese king writes to the King of Portugal about the growing problem:

> Very often it happens that they kidnap even noblemen and the sons of noblemen, and our relatives, and take them to be sold to the white men who are in our Kingdoms.... We beg of Your Highness to help and assist us in this matter, commanding your [people] that they should not send here either merchants or wares, because it is our will that in these Kingdoms there should not be any trade of slaves nor outlet for them.

We know of no response.

This is the first step toward the disintegration of Africa. Wars begin to erupt between neighbors. Some have the attitude that if you can't beat them, you need to join them, and they start getting into this expanded slave market themselves. Others refuse to be aggressors but now must constantly worry about defending their own people. And this creates yet another hot market...

Europeans have long since put to work the firearms and gunpowder they received in the Asian trade. As with printing, they have made incremental improvements. They are now the principal makers of the world's most advanced guns. Whether using them offensively or defensively, no one needs guns more desperately now than the kingdoms of Africa.

At this time, there is an economic theory in vogue among the European rulers. Called *mercantilism*, the theory says that a kingdom must sell more to others than it imports in order to increase its supply of gold and silver. It is the opposite of free trade. To achieve this goal, European rulers impose legal restrictions on their colonies, forbidding them to:

- manufacture goods from the produce of their plantations
- sell that produce to anyone but the home country
- buy those manufactured goods from anyone but the home country

This results in something like this:

- England buys cotton from a plantation owner in the colony of Georgia at a low price
- England manufactures cotton cloth that it exports to other kingdoms in Europe and Africa; because of the low cost of the raw material, they make a large profit
- In order to make a large profit on the raw cotton despite the low price, the plantation owner uses African slaves to keep overhead even lower
- Because there are so many plantation owners in the Americas who depend on having African slaves to keep their overhead low, slaves demand a high price
- Because slaves demand such a high price (and are in continual demand because it is cheaper to work a slave to death than it is to properly maintain them), Africans start raiding their neighbors to have more slaves to sell
- In order to defend their kingdom (or have the upper hand as slave raiders), African rulers have a need for guns
- Because of the high demand for guns, England and other European gunmakers can sell them at high prices to Africans, literally making a killing

71

If you're keeping score:
- England is rolling in the dough from cotton goods because of the low cost of cotton (to them)
- England is rolling in the dough from guns because high African demand enables high mark-up
- Georgia plantation owners are doing just fine, despite their home country's restrictions, due to their low overhead resulting from African slavery
- The most successful (and least principled) African kingdoms are doing just fine selling slaves

But Africa as a whole is suffering. It isn't just that it is torn by war and losing a large percentage of its population (mostly male). As the continent's economy begins to depend more and more on the slave trade, other exports fall by the wayside. Even the domestic market begins to run out of those products, so that what once was exported is now imported instead. Where once there was a vibrant, diversified economy, a card castle is being built in its place. In the game of mercantilism that England and the other European colonial powers are winning, Africa is losing big-time.

There is one other participant in this dirty business who is doing quite well, and that is the owners of the ships that now circumnavigate the Atlantic in what becomes known as the Triangle Trade. They carry sugar, tobacco, and cotton from the Americas to Europe on the inbound leg of their voyage; textiles, rum (made from the molasses that is a by-product of sugar production), and guns to Africa on the outbound leg; and slaves to the Americas on the "Middle Passage," thus assuring that they are fully laden with cargo on every leg.

The human "cargo" of the Middle Passage is treated no differently than sacks of sugar, packed tight. One in five do not make it alive to the Americas, if not dying from disease, then from being thrown overboard for disciplinary reasons or becoming sick (the shippers having first cut off their ears as proof of purchase).

Women are kept above decks, where they are often the victims of rape by the crew. Men are kept below in horrid, cramped conditions, as described by one Olaudah Equiano, who survived to tell his tale:

> The stench of the hold while we were on the coast was... intolerably loathsome... but now that the whole ship's cargo were confined together, it became absolutely pestilential. The closeness of the place, and the heat of the climate, added to the number in the ship—which was so crowded that each had scarcely room to turn himself—almost suffocated us. This produced copious perspirations, so that the air soon became unfit for respiration, from a variety of loathsome smells, and brought on a sickness among the slaves, of which many died.... This wretched situation was again aggravated by the galling of the chains, now become insupportable; and the filth of the necessary tubs, into which the children often fell, and were

72

almost suffocated. The shrieks of the women, and the groans of the dying, rendered the whole a scene of horror almost inconceivable.

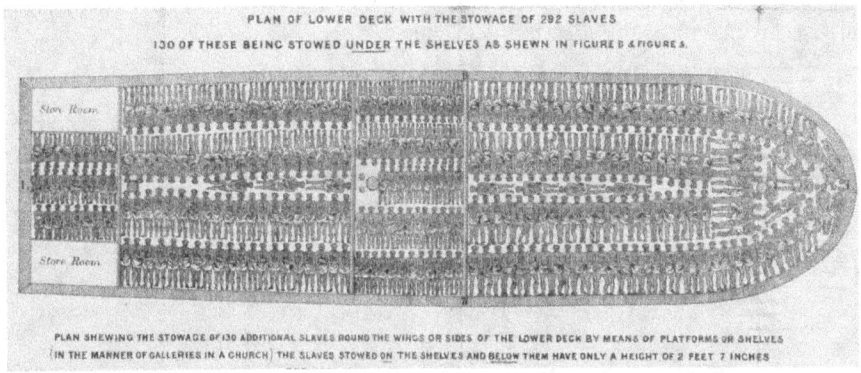

A ship's crewman, sickened by his experience, later writes of the horrors,

> The sick and dying were chained together. I saw pregnant women give birth to babes, whilst chained to corpses, which our drunken overseers had not removed. The blacks were literally jammed between decks, as if in a coffin; and a coffin that dreadful hold became, to nearly one-half of our cargo.

Throughout the more than two centuries when slavery was the driver of the British economy, it was outlawed within the country itself. What happened on the slave ships and plantations was out of sight, out of mind, until at last, in 1833, a growing abolition movement succeeded in making slavery illegal in the colonies. It continued in the United States until 1865 and in Brazil until 1888.

Abolition may have freed individual African slaves from their torment, but it was the last big blow to Africa's collective standing in the world. The card-castle economy came tumbling down. With nothing left to replace the slave trade, on which the continent's finances had become completely dependent, Africans were plunged into poverty. On top of this, deep hatreds had been established between formerly peaceable kingdoms, and now they were awash with guns.

Meanwhile, two centuries of the slave economy were enough to move the West (Europe and eventually the United States) to the top in contention for world supremacy. One by one, their competition had fallen away: The Mongols took out the Abbasids, China handicapped itself through the mandarins' reaction to the excesses of Zhu Di, and now the Atlantic Slave Trade had destroyed Africa.

China remains the richest economy in the world throughout those two centuries, with much of the wealth extracted from the Americas flowing its way in trade, but the British investment in oceangoing exploration will finally pay off, and they will overtake them. Sugar had gotten the British into the game, and by 1833, cotton had secured its victory. Both goods will play a role in their becoming the world's first industrial power.

But before we go there, we need to back up to understand how the same chapter of history that contains the cruel inhumanity of the Atlantic Slave Trade can also give birth to the idea that "all men are created equal"...

CHAPTER SEVEN

A Movement for Rights and an Expansion of Slavery Both Contribute to the Birth of the USA
(1651-1789)

Paraphrasing, the words are: All men are born with the inalienable rights of life, liberty and property. The purpose of government is to protect these rights. Whenever a government tries to take away or destroy the property of the People, or to reduce them to slavery, the People are absolved of any further obedience to that government.

The action that accompanied these words was removal of a king from power by the People.

The year was 1688. The place was England. The man whose words are paraphrased is John Locke. The action has been called the Glorious Revolution.

Locke's words were inspired by the Social Contract, a concept first defined by Thomas Hobbes in 1651, at the end of the English Civil War.

Prior to that time, Europeans generally believed that their monarchs ruled with *divine right*. This wasn't just a mandate, like the Chinese assumed their emperors had; it was in most cases believed that monarchs had an absolute God-given right to rule as they pleased, granted to them hereditarily.

The English were the most liberal of the bunch. By this time, their land-holding class already had a long history of possessively guarding their property against those above them in the feudal hierarchy. In 1215, the Magna Carta, signed under duress by the king of that time, decreed that a ruler must at least make their laws known before enforcing them. It went on to say that they cannot seize property arbitrarily, but only after securing a lawful conviction.

The English went from liberal to radical in 1649, when they chopped off the head of King Charles I. An alliance of Puritans under the leadership of one Oliver Cromwell had taken exception to his marrying a Catholic.

Hobbes evidently was shaken by the experience, as you can imagine many of the common people were. After two years of chaos, he deduced that "The condition of Man... is a condition of war of everyone against everyone" and that the People therefore needed a strong king who could keep order.

"Just how is this going to inspire a Glorious Revolution in which the People dump their king?" you ask.

Because of the "Social *Contract*." The word "contract" implies an agreement that is freely entered into by two parties, the People being one of them. It says that the People do in fact *have* individual freedom; it is just that, in order to receive protection, they bargain some of it (well, in 1651, quite a lot of it) away.

And that's the deal that they struck with Charles II (son of the guy whose head they previously chopped off) when they asked him back to the throne...

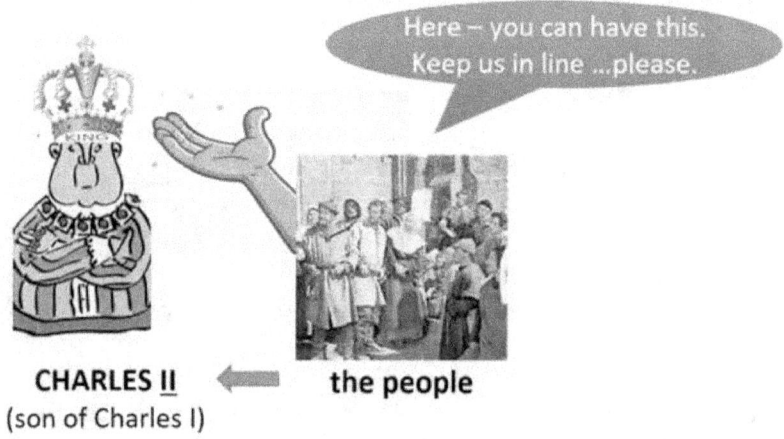

Here – you can have this. Keep us in line ...please.

CHARLES II ⟵ **the people**
(son of Charles I)

Charles Junior is careful not to upset the People too much, but he is succeeded by his younger brother, and you know those younger brothers! James II was but a teenager when his father got the axe, and he continues to act like one, recklessly ignoring the provisions of the Magna Carta, then thumbing his nose at his lords by suspending Parliament.

The People decide they have had enough. They contact James' daughter Mary, who is the wife of the Stadtholder of the Dutch Republic, to tell her they would fully support her husband, William, if he were to bring an army across the North Sea and lead a coup. With 20,000 Dutch troops marching on London and his defenders standing down, James flees for France without a drop of blood being shed. William III and Mary II become dual monarchs.

Inspired by the revolution, John Locke—after the fact—writes his seminal *Two Treatises on Government,* in which he expands on Hobbes' Social Contract to make its terms more specific and to address any breach of those terms. He says that the job a king (or any government) is hired to do is: to protect the People's natural rights of life, liberty, and property. In case of a breach of terms: Revolution is justified.

◇◇◇

Fourteen ninety-two was a busy year in European history. While Columbus was making contact with the Americas, the Turks were laying siege to Constantinople, finally putting the Eastern Roman Empire out of its misery. At the same time, the Spanish drove the Muslims out of Grenada and out of Iberia altogether, completing a flip-flop between religions in two corners of Europe, Iberia becoming fully Christian and Anatolia going to Islam.

Soon after, the Turks were knocking on the gates of Vienna. Their military was never able to conquer the city, but a certain beverage did. In 1669, we find Venetian emissaries introducing coffee to the court of the "Sun King," Louis XIV, at his palace at Versailles, just outside Paris. By the start of the next century, the coffee house had become a thing in France. Its popularity grew hand-in-hand with the popularity of what historians would call Enlightenment philosophy.

Under King Louis' highly autocratic rule, the coffee house was a perfect place for a surreptitious conversation about how government should best be structured or what rights people should expect *in addition to* life, liberty, and property. The Baron de Montesquieu is famous today because he proposed a structure of government that would actually be realized, though not until 30 years after his death. Francois-Marie Arouet, who would write under the pen name Voltaire, championed rights that would one day be enumerated in the constitution of that same government, also posthumously by a little over ten years.

Montesquieu, like many others, proposed a republic where laws are made by a legislative assembly of representatives voted in by the People. He went further to say that this legislature should be separated from the head of state and that both of these should be separate from a judiciary where violations of those laws are prosecuted. No one branch of government would be more powerful than the others.

Voltaire didn't have as long to hang out in French coffee houses, as his early writings got him exiled. He spent most of his time in England, whose constitutional monarchy (with its strong parliament to hold the king in check) he very much admired. Especially when compared to his home country, where he saw an ignorant common class duped by a corrupt Catholic Church and nobility while lacking any kind of rights at all. He believed strongly in freedom of choice in one's religion, and, given his experience with the censorship of his works, in freedom of speech, as well.

Voltaire wasn't the only one to sing the praises of the British government.

Those inside the British Empire, even those in the American colonies who were subject to the Crown's monopolies, were also more than happy with it. Let's have a visit with a Viginia tobacco farmer in 1750 to see what he thinks...

1750: Good times in the colonies

I'm a Virginian!

We have a colonial assembly, and we pretty much govern ourselves

- If you have enough property, you can vote for your representative
- And there's more property to go around here than back in England, so quite a few of us qualify
- The King is on the other side of the ocean, and doesn't pay much attention

So, first of all, this guy is very proud to be an Englishman. He knows that since the English defeated the Spanish Armada way back in 1588, they have been the top dog in the ocean trade. He knows he comes from the same stock as Francis Bacon, who launched a revolution in science by teaching that truth is not found at the beginning of inquiry (as that Greek, Aristotle, asserted), but at the *end*, and from Isaac Newton, who used this experimental method to unlock all the secrets of nature. He knows how the English property-owning class has always stood up for its rights, how they formed the world's most powerful parliament, which must approve the king's acts of war and taxation, and how they made King James pay for trying to ignore it. He believes in the monarchy and would rally behind the present king (George III), if need be, but like a manager in a highly decentralized company, he feels empowered to make his own day-to-day decisions.

Like all property-holding Englishmen, he gets to vote for someone like himself to be his political representative. But instead of being part of the English Parliament, they are part of a local colonial assembly, which is like a mini-Parliament just for Virginia. Being an ocean away from the king has its advantages, like being a manager in a *remote office* of a highly decentralized company.

But then comes the Seven Years' War. It is another routine conflict between Britain and France, but it spills over into North America, of which each country has claimed a good chunk.

There are by this time 13 separate British colonies. These colonies are in no way unified. In fact, when, in response to the threat of war, one Benjamin

Franklin tries to get them to form a loose confederation for defense purposes, all 13 reject the idea. This goes to show that our tobacco farmer, who thinks of himself as a Virginian first and foremost and is also proud to call himself an Englishman, doesn't think of himself as an American at all.

The British have been really into clearing land and putting up fences, establishing their property. They have been working their way inland from the coast, banishing the wilderness. The French, meanwhile, have been thriving in the interior wilderness, trapping for furs, establishing only a scattered network of forts. Their lighter footprint has kept them, for the most part, in the good graces of the indigenous Americans, so most of them take the French side, which is why Americans today call the conflict the French and Indian War.

Most of the war is fought back in Europe, where each country has several powerful allies, and the British side ends up winning. But the biggest *effect* of the war—by far, if you count the ensuing chain of effects—is on America. First, all of the land claimed by the French –what today is eastern Canada, plus everything west of the Appalachian Mountains, down to the Gulf of Mexico –is ceded to Britain. Second, there is nothing more costly to a government than a war, and when governments need to cover a cost, they often get creative with taxation...

Another advantage that our Virginia tobacco farmer has had versus his equals back in England is that he hasn't been paying as many taxes. Now, that is going to change. The Stamp Act of 1765 says most everything printed in the colonies—legal documents, news sheets, even playing cards—must hereon be on paper supplied by the Crown and embossed with a "revenue stamp." This sneakiness doesn't fool anyone about it being a tax, and it likely leads our tobacco farmer to grumble a bit. But up in Boston, where they have shorter fuses, a bunch of hotheads start a big protest. They harass the poor revenue collectors who supply the special paper, even going so far as to tar and feather one of them!

The rabble wins round one and King George backs off on the plan, but this is only the start of a back-and-forth where the latter keeps coming up with alternative ways of raising revenue and the former only harden in their resistance.

It is not the idea of taxation, the amount of tax, or even the sometimes-devious methods of collecting tax that is at issue here. After all, the colonies would still have a lower overall tax burden than those living back in Great Britain. The issue is that *those* property owners have an elected representative who voted on whether to approve their tax increases. Colonial property owners' only representative is in their own colonial assembly—and they didn't have a say in the vote; only the big Parliament back on the mother ship did.

Thus, when Massachusetts patriots (as they are beginning to call those in the radical resistance) start rallying behind the slogan "No taxation without representation!" our tobacco farmer down in Virginia can relate. It is an affront to his English pride.

Things come to a head eight years on, when Parliament passes the Tea Act of 1773. The British East India Company—the world's largest company, with a charter from the British government that allows it to dominate Indian Ocean trade—has been going through a rough patch. They haven't been able to sell any tea to the colonies because colonists can do better through foreign sources. That means the government hasn't been able to collect taxes on it, either. Parliament figures it can get two birds with one stone by passing this act, which allows "the Company" to sell its tea directly to retailers and individuals in the colonies, skipping the wholesalers, thus lowering the price below that of other sources.

Once again, those Boston patriots see past the sneakiness. One evening, a bunch of them, loosely disguised as indigenous Americans, board one of the Company's ships and chuck most of its tea into the harbor.

Incensed by this action, the king's government passes a series of punitive laws they entitle the Coercive Acts, but which are referred to up and down the colonies as the Intolerable Acts. The king has crossed a line here. For nearly a decade, the source of his ongoing headache has been pretty much confined to those Northern patriots. But now he has done something to rouse the ire of proud property owners of English stock clear down to Georgia:

He shut down the Massachusetts colonial assembly!!!

Our guy in Virginia never thought the amount of new taxes was unreasonable (he knew he was getting a pretty sweet deal before). But he *was* put on edge when his elected representative didn't get to approve them. Still, he never liked the radical tactics of the patriots. But now!... The king has taken away those property owners' rights as English citizens. What next?!

It has been 20 years since Ben Franklin's proposal for unity got the thumbs down, but now things are changing. The colonies call the First Continental Congress, with 12 of the 13 sending representatives to Philadelphia to discuss the crisis. Their unanimous decision is (wait for it)... Write the king a letter of protest. So nothing much happens for the next six months.

Six months later is April 1775, when in Boston they light lamps and Paul Revere goes for a late night ride. Since the Coercive Acts were passed, there have been more and more soldiers arriving in Boston. On this evening, a column of them head out under cover of darkness to confiscate arms the patriots have in what was supposed to be a secret store out in the western exurbs. The first shots of an armed rebellion are exchanged at Lexington and at Concord, and the king's troops are harassed with musket fire all the way back to the city.

This leads to a Second Continental Congress in Philadelphia the next month. Though the rebellion hasn't made its way south, the Congress does authorize a Continental Army and appoint George Washington as its commander. The delegates are split between those who wish to seek reconciliation with the king and those who think all-out war is inevitable. The former send the Olive Branch Petition to the king, while the latter begin a period of watching and waiting.

The Congress does not disband while it awaits word from the king, and it keeps an eye on how the new army is doing. In August, the king responds to the petition by issuing a Proclamation for Suppressing Rebellion and Sedition. So much for the olive branch approach. The following March, the rebels are able to drive all of the soldiers out of Boston, though the British still hold New York, effectively dividing New England from the other colonies.

It does not appear that there is any way a rebellion can be successful without some outside help, and Britain's ongoing rival, France, is obviously the place to go for that. But the French aren't going to want to get in on this unless they know it is going to be a success. The only way to convince them success is possible is to get all of the colonies on the same page. So Franklin and John Adams, a talented Boston lawyer who, oddly enough, made his name defending the occupying British troops in the so-called Boston Massacre, go to work at convincing the others to get behind a Declaration of Independence. They farm out the job of writing it to Thomas Jefferson of Virginia...

In CONGRESS. July 4, 1776.

The unanimous Declaration of the thirteen united States of America.

Note above that the date Americans celebrate as their Independence Day is not yet the birth of the United States of America; it is the birth of the united States of America. "United," like "unanimous," is an adjective, not part of the name of a new nation. They are important adjectives, thus the redundancy for emphasis. It is important to show the world (code word for France) that all 13 of these sovereign nation-states are united in their conviction to turn this rebellion into a revolution.

In 1776, to be a "state" means to be a nation-state, just as it is defined today in the Oxford dictionary:

> A nation or territory considered as an organized political community under one government --for example "Germany, Italy, and other European *states*...

Not until the advent of federalism, which we will get to before this chapter completes, will there be states under one government that at the same time are part of a larger state.

That is why this document was produced by a *Continental* Congress in an effort to support a *Continental* Army. If they were part of a nation-state called the United States of America, they would call it a *National* Congress. But there are no thoughts of such a deeper union at this time. Just getting delegates to agree to sign a document with the adjectives "unanimous" and "united" is a major accomplishment.

Thomas Jefferson is a true product of the Enlightenment, but also, it seems, of the Age of Romanticism. The first several lines of the Declaration—the familiar part—are almost all lifted straight from John Locke, with a bit of Thomas Hobbes. Jefferson refers to Locke's concept of natural rights as "inalienable" rights (in either case, it means the rights you are born with). He iterates Locke's job description for governments: "To secure these rights, governments are instituted among men..." and ends that sentence with a nod to Hobbes' Social Contract: "... deriving their just powers from the consent of the governed." He wraps up the intro with more Locke: "... whenever any Form of Government becomes destructive of these ends, it is the Right of the People to alter or to abolish it."

But in the few instances where we get original Jefferson, the romanticist comes across strongly. The bland (but all-important) natural right of property is replaced by the "pursuit of happiness." And before stating those rights, he says it is self-evident that all men are created equal, as in not just the property-holders who will sign their names to this document, several of whom, including Jefferson, hold numbers of men and women among what they consider their property.

In the long list of grievances against King George that takes up the majority of the document, there are many uses of melodramatic phrasing ("... sent hither swarms of officers to harass our people & eat out their substance"; and "... plundered our seas, ravaged our coasts, burnt our towns & destroyed the lives of our people"). But only the very last item comprises several lines. It starts by seeming to blame the king for the slave trade:

> He has waged cruel war against human nature itself, violating its most sacred rights of life & liberty in the persons of a distant people who never offended him, captivating & carrying them into slavery in another hemisphere, or to incur miserable death in their transportation thither.

This is but a lead-in to the real gripe:

> He is now exciting those very people to rise in arms among us, and to purchase that liberty of which he has deprived them... thus paying off former crimes committed against the liberties of one people, with crimes which he urges them to commit against the lives of another.

This is a reference to Dunmore's Proclamation. The year before, just shortly after the battles of Lexington and Concord, the Earl of Dunmore, who was also the royalist governor of Virginia, issued a proclamation that offered freedom to any slave who joined a special "Ethiopian Regiment" of the British army. It was also rumored around this time that Parliament was working on a bill that would legally emancipate *all* the slaves in the colonies.

The passage above appears only in Jefferson's draft. It is kept out of the signed version, probably at the behest of editors Franklin and Adams, who are keen not to dissuade the representatives of the southern states from their moment of accord. In fact, it is Dunmore's Proclamation that does more than anything else to drive the Southern representatives to the cause of Frankin, Adams, and the Northern patriots. Many in Virginia are one day loyalists and, upon hearing news of the proclamation, become born-again patriots the next.

With a sigh of relief, and only some trepidation about having officially signed on to treason, the Declaration is made public. Come December, while Washington and his army spend Christmas crossing the Delaware to ambush Hessian mercenaries in New Jersey, Franklin is off to revel in the delights of the court of Louis XVI and Marie Antoinette in Paris so he can put in a good word. After a year and a half of his charming the courtiers and finally some battlefield successes worth bragging about, France decides to become the American states' ally.

In the fall of 1781, surrounded by the land forces of Washington and the Marquis de Lafayette and the sea blockade of the Comte de Grasse, the British forces of General Cornwallis are trapped on a Virginia peninsula near the village of Yorktown. For all practical purposes the war is over, yet an official peace agreement is not signed until two years later.

Since late 1777, the Continental Congress has been operating under a document called the Articles of Confederation. For the sovereign states, this is a step above signing a declaration that they are all individually independent; from this point on, they will be a bona fide confederation. Furthermore, this confederation will be called the United States of America (big "U"). The Continental Congress will become the Congress of the Confederation (but everybody keeps calling it the Continental Congress because they are stuck in their ways and you can say it a lot faster).

A confederation is not highly binding. Getting in and out of a confederation is much easier than, say, becoming independent of an empire. (Present-day example: Although it took several months of discussion, getting the UK out of the confederation known as the European Union was no harder than amicably dissolving the marriage of a financially-entangled couple.)

Article 3 of the Confederation of the United States of America says it is a "firm league of friendship" right after stating the new name, but then it says, Don't worry, everybody will retain sovereignty (the authority to govern yourself) over anything that isn't specified herein.

That's just the way confederations work: The members retain nearly all of their sovereignty, but, being united for some common purpose, they give up some autonomy where it is necessary in order to achieve that purpose.

In November 1777, the purpose of the Confederation of the United States of America is to win the dang war. In the fall of 1783, it becomes, more generally, to secure the liberty and general welfare of the confederation's members and to provide for their common defense. Its simple stipulations can be summed up as follows:

- Citizens of each state enjoy free ingress to any other state and are treated fairly compared to the residents of that state. Fugitives from one state are not harbored by another. Free trade is maintained; states cannot charge each other tariffs or embargo goods outright.

- Any alliances or treaties that states wish to make with each other or with other sovereign nations must first be approved by Congress.

- Every state is responsible for keeping its own militia at the ready. The size of its forces and numbers of warships, however, must be approved by Congress, and a state cannot go to war with some other sovereign nation without approval of Congress unless the state is invaded.

- The cost of providing for this general welfare and common defense is apportioned between the states according to the total land value of the state. It is up to the state legislature to get the money from its citizens.

84

- Just as in the Continental Congress, each state (no matter how big or small) has one vote on any future changes.

So how exactly is life in the Confederation different from life before the revolution? Depends on who you talk to…

For slaveholding Southern plantation owners, life is a notch better than before. There is no law saying you can only sell your produce to the home country. Now you can sell on the open market to the highest bidder. You can even sell to the northern states, who can manufacture textiles or cigars without interference from a mercantilist king. You can be sure there will be no king's soldiers coming for your stockpile of rifles. Jefferson made it sound like you may need them when –betraying his conflicted state with regard to slave ownership—he recently wrote,

> I tremble for my country when I reflect that God is just: that his justice cannot sleep forever; that considering numbers,… a revolution of the wheel of fortune, an exchange of situation is among possible events.

Having gotten back several of your slaves who had escaped in the revolution (and exacted harsh justice), you are armed up and ready to prevent any such "exchange of situation" from occurring on *your* plantation.

Eighteen percent of Americans remain enslaved. A few escaped to British Canada, but none of the rest will see any relief from a miserable existence, despite those inspiring words with which Jefferson began his Declaration.

For the 20% of Americans who remain loyalist to the end, the choice is to either grumble in private or emigrate to the old home country or to Canada.

Massachusetts, of course, has its elected legislature back. The patriots are free of the king's creative taxation and can thumb their nose at him, but soon state legislatures will have their own taxes to collect and will have to deal with resistance among their own unruly citizens. At least they can buy tea from whomever they please.

But are Americans any more democratic? Hardly. Remember, they had it pretty good before; the colonies had their independent assemblies. Some states begin to allow non-property owners who pay taxes to vote. Only Massachusetts, New York, New Jersey, Pennsylvania, and Maryland allow free Black people to vote. A few women who live in New Jersey are given the vote—only those who are single and own property (New Jersey does not allow married women to own property or non-property owners to vote.) No state allows Native Americans to vote.

In summary, let's try to put a fork in several commonly held myths about the American Revolution:

MYTH	REALITY
Americans were first in declaring that the People had a right to overthrow a tyrannical leader.	British philosopher John Locke first wrote about this, and the People in England actually *did* it more than 80 years before the American Declaration of Independence.
Prior to the Revolutionary War, Americans had no say in their government.	Prior to the troubles with the king that began with British victory in the Seven Years' War, Americans pretty much governed themselves.
Oppressively high taxation is what led to the American Revolution.	The taxes on Americans meant to recoup costs of the Seven Years' War were not that high, nor did they lead directly to the revolution. The fact that the colonial governments were *not consulted* about the new taxes caused protests that led to shutting down one of these governments, and that was the last straw.
The patriotic citizens of all 13 colonies were quick to unite in opposition to the British.	The patriots were considered radical by most colonial citizens, who were happy to remain part of Britain. But when the king shut down the Massachusetts government, many came around to supporting the revolution. Many *Southern* holdouts only came around when it was rumored that the British were going to emancipate the slaves.
With the defeat of the British, a strong United States of America was established.	From the time the British were defeated, and for several years after, the states were only loosely united as a confederacy, with very little central government and no president.
Having become free of the king, the USA was now a democracy.	After the revolution, less than 25% of Americans could vote. This was almost the same as before the revolution.

Rebellion in the state of Massachusetts is what led to the American Revolution. A second rebellion in Massachusetts is what caused the American confederation to morph into the American nation.

In the summer of 1786, a mob of disgruntled farmers upset with taxes far higher than any they had owed during British rule marched on a debtor's court in western Massachusetts and disrupted the proceedings. Their rebellion would continue deep into the winter. In a February correspondence, George Washington wrote,

> The moment is, indeed, important!—If government shrinks, or is unable to enforce its laws, fresh maneuvers will be displayed by the insurgents—anarchy & confusion must prevail—and everything will be turned topsy turvey in that State, where it is not probable the mischiefs will terminate.

The Articles of Confederation were failing on multiple counts. That "firm league of friendship" was being strained. New York and New Jersey were about to come to blows over charges on shipping levied by the Port of New York. Congress was supposed to arbitrate these sorts of disputes, but without any written law above the state laws (other than those few restrictions and requirements of Congressional approval mentioned above), there was nothing for them to base any resolution upon.

Now the troubles in Massachusetts magnified concerns to a point where a convention was called to see about shifting a bit more power away from the states. Washington was skeptical about its chances of achieving any meaningful reform.

Before May was out, delegates from the states were meeting in Philadelphia (Washington had, under pressure from friends James Madison and Henry Knox, reluctantly given in to attending). Fairly soon into the process, it became apparent that something greater than a few patches to the Articles was brewing. Some, like Madison and Knox, were determined to produce an entirely new type of government with centralized power, and they knew they were going to have to structure it in a way that somehow kept the many delegates who favored individual state sovereignty on board.

Their solution was called *federalism*. Its basic definition is "an organization within which smaller divisions have some degree of internal autonomy." The result is something much more binding than a confederacy but—unlike a centralized, hierarchical form of government—also quite empowering of those smaller divisions:

 **NOT like this →**

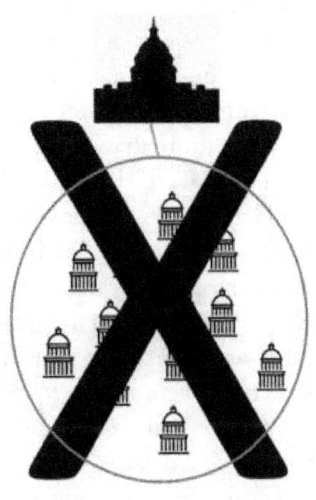

87

LIKE THIS:

FEDERALISM

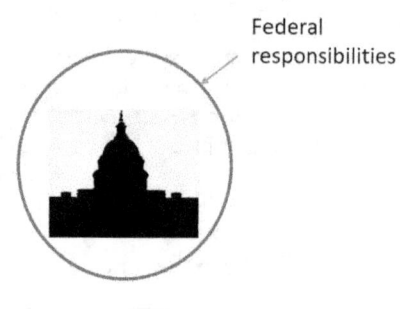

Federal responsibilities

Power is <u>distributed</u> <u>between</u> the national government and the states

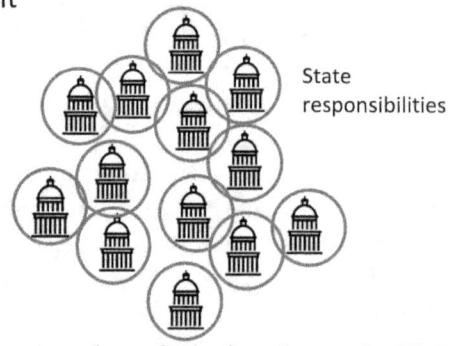

State responsibilities

The idea was that the national government (hereafter referred to as the "federal" government to distinguish from the hierarchical government in the first picture) would wrest back some of what the states had been managing themselves but remain hands-off on the rest.

Under Madison's influence, an outline was created for a federal government with limited power. It would retain the power to tax, raise a military, regulate interstate commerce, and override only those state laws that infringed on its own sphere of power or were deemed unjust.

For the structure of the government, the "framers," as the delegates to the Convention would later be called, turned to the writings of Montesquieu. There would be more than just a national Congress; there would be an executive branch and a federal court system. Not only would each branch have its specific role; they would also have the means to cross-check each other. Congress, as the legislative branch, would author all bills and vote on whether they became law, but the head of the executive branch, who would be called the president, would have to then sign them into law. The president would have veto power. It would require two-thirds of Congress to override the veto.

There were issues to be worked out. First, there were items of particular interest for only a certain subset of the delegations —for example, Northern bankers or Southern slave owners. Second, there was the question of whether states with greater populations should have a greater say in the federal government. These issues would become intertwined in the dealing that occurred.

Sometimes deals were made as a direct trade-off. For example, bankers wanted federal control of the money supply because some states were printing wads of their own money, which led to inflation, which reduced the value of the banks' loans. Meanwhile, slaveholders wanted to prevent the harboring of fugitive slaves in northern states. So each delegation might vote for the other's item in order to assure passage of their own.

At other times, deals could have been made *indirectly*. For example, the most populous states, like Massachusetts and Virginia, were tired of only getting one vote in Congress, which made them feel that their electorate was underrepresented. But if each state was given a number of votes relative to its population—with the smallest like Rhode Island and Delaware only receiving one vote, those with twice that population receiving two votes, etc.—then states losing voting power would outnumber those gaining voting power 7 to 6. Obviously, without some dealing, such a proposal was bound to fail.

Slaveholding states pushed to include their slave population in determining any apportionment of votes. All northern states probably would have initially opposed this. But once they got into the details of the math, it would have become apparent to a highly populated state like Massachusetts that, if North and South Carolina, both of whose slave population was significant, were to receive just enough compensation for their slaves, the numbers would flip; both states would move from losing power to gaining power, thus providing an 8 to 5 majority in favor of basing Congressional representation on population.

Eventually, a compromise was worked out breaking Congress into two houses: One, the Senate, retained the all-states-equal tradition; the other, the House of Representatives, would be based on population. And, yes, slaves would be counted among that population as precisely three-fifths of a person each. Both houses could write bills, which, if passed, must be approved by the other house before they could be forwarded to the president to be signed into law.

A draft of the Constitution for the United States of America was readied and signed in September, and the Convention disbanded. Tension remained between those who thought that federalism was the perfect solution and those who didn't want to give up so much of their state's sovereignty or feared that a president would become another kind of king. So during the months that followed, as the debate over ratification played out, Madison, Alexander Hamilton, and John Jay wrote a series of persuasive entreaties. These became known as the Federalist Papers. Hamilton, who was the strongest advocate of centralized government, was the most prolific of the three, but it was Madison who shepherded the document through by working with the Anti-Federalists to draft ten amendments that reiterated the sphere of power maintained by the states and specifically stated rights of the People that could never be infringed.

89

Once again, the framers were standing on the shoulders of the Enlightenment thinkers who had gone before them. The ten amendments, collectively, were called the Bill of Rights after England's Bill of Rights, which was based on the writings of John Locke and enacted after the Glorious Revolution. A response to the impunity of James II, England's Bill of Rights had enlarged the powers of Parliament and specifically prohibited cruel and unusual punishment. The American Bill of Rights also had this prohibition, in addition to those rights of free speech and freedom of religion so cherished by Voltaire.

The American Constitution was ratified the following June. The states had come a long way, from unity of purpose to union in confederation to "a more perfect union." If gaining independence from the British Empire had not been particularly revolutionary, when the last vote for ratification was cast in 1788 and Washington was sworn in as president in 1789, it was indeed a milestone in world history. The federalist model would be copied many times over the decades, as more and more areas of the globe won their sovereignty.

The significant role of slavery in the formation of the United States of America cannot be overstated. Without Dunmore's threat of emancipation, would initial unity behind the drive for independence have even been achieved? Though they would remain enslaved for another six-and-a-half decades and be denied rights as citizens for far longer, it was slaves who tipped the balance toward greater democracy, with the Three-Fifths Clause making a House of Representatives based on population possible. Finally, slaveholders' ongoing fear of a slave rebellion, particularly in those areas where the slave population outnumbered the White, as in South Carolina, gave impetus to the prominent inclusion of a specific right to bear arms in the Bill of Rights.

Slavery, though ingrained in the country's formation, would nearly become its destruction, as the South would temporarily loosen the binds of federalism and return to confederacy seven decades ahead. After its defeat in the American Civil War, the South would be brought to heel during the Reconstruction period, but would soon again resist federal control. The road toward justice for Black Americans would be long, indeed, and, as of the moment that just passed, still has not reached its end. But Jefferson's idealistic opening words, so incongruous with him and his times, continue to guide its arc.

CHAPTER EIGHT

The Industrial Revolution Occurs in the English Midlands, But it Begins in America
(~1760-1789)

The next time you buy something from Amazon, or go out of town on vacation, or attend (or send your kids to) a free public school, or go to a movie, or go to your job as a mid-level technician... thank a slave. All these things were the biproducts of the Industrial Revolution, and the Industrial Revolution began with cheaply-grown and -harvested cotton in the plantations of what today is the American South.

Eventual freedom for the slaves of Jamaica and Barbados was another biproduct of the beginnings of industry. Remember this? "If... abolition shall take place,... the revenue will suffer an annual [decline] of three millions at least;... discontentment and dissatisfaction may dismember the empire!"

It didn't happen. Abolition did not dismember the empire any more than losing the American colonies did, because six years after the treaty for the American Revolution was signed, England gained something that would more than make up for the loss of those colonies and slaves: A textile factory in the English Midlands became the first to be outfitted with a steam engine, heralding the beginning of our industrial era.

Before that history-altering moment, England already had a thriving "cottage industry" in textiles...

In the early 18th century, the English Midlands, like all of England aside from the capital, London, was highly rural. Picture an idyllic village with one square Norman church tower at one end, a thatched-roof pub at the other, and cottages in between. And in the gently rolling fields radiating in all directions from the village, loads of sheep grazing.

This was most peoples' world. Few got out to other villages. After all, the roads looked like this:

There were a lot of rivers, but they were too narrow and fast flowing to be easily navigable.

Because there were so many sheep, there was also a plethora of skilled weavers. So when cheap plantation cotton started to arrive from overseas, to these weavers it came. Fortunately, Great Britain is an island, and a narrow one at that, especially up in the Midlands. With commercial interests driving the investment, a network of canals was created to connect key villages to the seaports.

In a typical cottage setup, the man of the house might run a shop downstairs where he makes useful things on order—perhaps some kind of farming tools. Meanwhile, upstairs, his wife spins while grandmother uses a hand loom to weave. They used to only make things for individual orders, as well, but now that the canal is up and running, there's a man from "the company" who comes by every other Tuesday to pick up the work they've finished and drop off a new load of cotton.

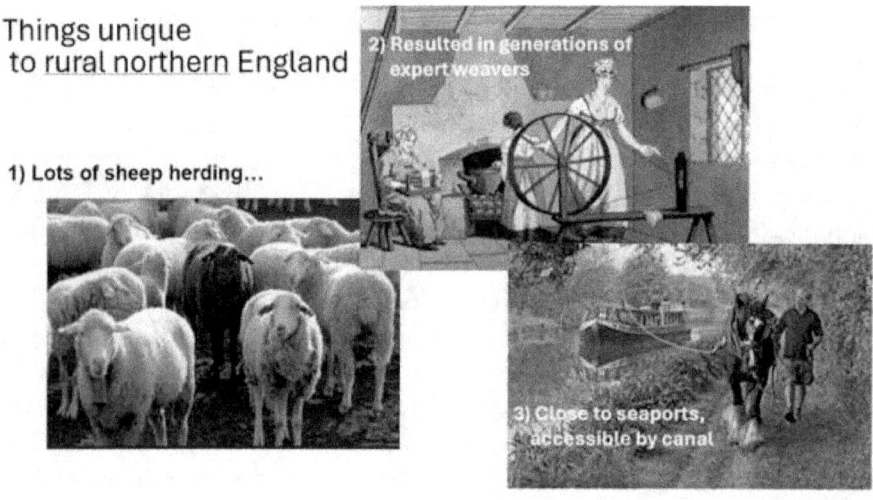

Things unique to rural northern England

2) Resulted in generations of expert weavers

1) Lots of sheep herding...

3) Close to seaports, accessible by canal

(2)

This man from the company is, of course, a buyer of slave-produced cotton arriving in Liverpool on an inbound ship and brought inland by a horse-drawn barge like the one pictured above. He's a seller of considerably marked-up cotton textiles going outbound. It is a proto-industrial process, because the goods are being produced *before* they have been ordered, in hopes that they will sell hundreds or even thousands of miles away from the village to buyers in France or some African kingdom.

The production rate increases considerably once Edmund Cartwright invents the mechanical loom, a device that both spins and weaves as you sit at it like a piano and pump its pedals. Watch one of these in action and you can't help but think: So repetitive. If we only had a continuous nonhuman power source...

And if you've been paying attention, you know that we do have one. Those fast-flowing rivers that were a headache to navigate are just what we need to drive a waterwheel that can drive an axle that can drive our loom.

It isn't just cotton that makes this revolution happen; sugar will play a big part, as well. For as the abolition movement becomes stronger, Jamaican plantation owners begin to see the writing on the wall. Most had begun their lives in temperate England and only came to the New World to strike it rich. Never having been made for the weather of the semi-tropical Caribbean to begin with, they now are ready to return home.

Most plantation owners likely did not come from titled families. Now, with their success and wealth, they feel they are deserving of a landed estate equal to the one they have become accustomed to in the New World. This would normally present a problem as, in the Old World, all the land was already taken. But there is great change afoot in the land situation of England...

So many agricultural improvements were happening that the period was later dubbed by proud Englanders as the Second Agricultural Revolution. There was the discovery of nitrate-based fertilizer. There were new inventions like the seed drill that did all the planting for you, with perfect spacing. But perhaps the most important discovery wasn't a technological one, but simply a better understanding of what crop rotation meant for fertility.

FOUR-YEAR CROP ROTATION SYSTEM

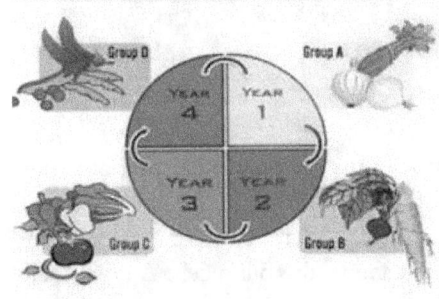

Since the First Agricultural Revolution millennia before, farmers had been leaving fields fallow every third year to allow the soil to refurbish itself. A third of the agricultural land left empty: What a waste! But now, English farmers had experimented enough with crops to know the nutritional requirements of each one. Crops differ greatly in what they pull from the soil, and if you plant a complimentary crop the next year that uses entirely different nutrients than the first crop, it allows the soil to recover just as well as if you had left the field fallow.

With this greater attention to the country's farm production, there was an interest in putting more land under the plow. This coincided nicely with the expatriate sugar plantation owners' desire to return home as landowners.

Most of the land around an English village would have been owned by the lord, who lived in a big fancy manor house a mile or two up the road. But most villagers maintained kitchen gardens, and some even had a head or two of livestock. Having nowhere in their little plot to graze the animals, they instead walked them up the lane every morning to the Commons, a large area the lord left open for communal grazing.

You know what came next: Desire to expand agriculture + Influx of "new money" landowners from America = Goodbye, Commons.

There were two ways in which this contributed to the Industrial Revolution...

First, by putting all the small livestock farmers out of business, it created a ready labor force for the first factories. The agricultural improvements and the import of brand-new high calorie crops like the potato led, as bountiful harvests always do, to an increase in the population. Now, at the same time, a chunk of that population was looking for jobs.

Enclosure movement *The Co**mm**ns*

When rich plantation owners from the colonies start coming home,
they buy up the commons and start fencing out the "commoners."

COW FOR SALE
–Goin' cheap!

Second, it provided a business opportunity. Because the emigrant, newly ex-plantation owners are new money and fully look upon themselves as equals of the old, they are into conspicuous consumption. As with conspicuous consumers today, expensive imports displayed in the home fit the bill nicely. A costly set of "china" laid out for tea was the 1780 equivalent of a Maserati in the driveway. Better yet if the lady of the house showed up for that tea in a floral cotton dress woven in India. Imagine what it cost to ship that garment to England. If only there were a way to manufacture it as cheaply...

94

So we had

» cheap, slave-grown cotton
» a ready-made ship-in/ship-out distribution system already up and running in the Midlands
» plenty of available labor
» an influx of moneyed customers looking to spend

What were we missing to make this an Industrial Revolution?

Oh right, *industrial* machinery—something that would scale these stationary water mills up about a thousand notches to give us a true economy of scale.

Conveniently, not only did the English Midlands have expert weavers, nearness to seaports, fast-flowing rivers, an expanding and partially out-of-work labor force, and an influx of new money; they also were sitting on extensive veins of coal. In 1781, James Watt adapted the steam engine to produce rotary motion. It used coal to turn water into steam that was injected into a single piston. The movement of the piston up and down drove a lever that, through a system of belts and gears, could drive a loom.

By 1789, the factory system had begun. It was no longer necessary to situate by a fast-flowing river. Wherever you could transport coal and set up a steam engine, you could drive a long axle with multiple belts used to drive multiple looms.

But wait! We have the staff you see in the picture at left, but who is going to be the *owners* of these new factories?

This is not a question you answer with "Duh!" European nobility have always been interested in only one thing: land. New money is after the same thing. To all of these landholders, owning a line of factories is considered scarcely above owning a corner shop. Get into *trade*!? They wouldn't be seen dirtying their hands with it.

But fortunately for England, and for those of us whose lives have been defined by the Industrial Revolution, just as there is a ready-made group of available laborers, there is a ready-made group of available entrepreneurs.

Remember those Puritans who refused to join the Anglican Church—not the ones who emigrated to Massachusetts, but the ones who stayed behind and followed Oliver Cromwell for a bit? Despite some of them being well-educated, they still aren't allowed to own land. But as for owning a business...

(4)

◇◇◇

The Industrial Revolution gave us more stuff, faster. But that was not nearly as revolutionary as all of its secondary effects...

Before industry, consumers initiated contact with a craftsman in their own village and told them what they needed, then waited for it to be made. Now, companies produced products that they expected to be able to sell. Advertising began for the first time. And salespeople.

Factories were magnets for employment. They brought *strangers* to your town (which previously had been extremely uncommon). As factories grew larger, foremen and middle managers were required. Technicians to keep the machines in working order. Accountants to handle the growing complexity of finances. The world was no longer split between an idle landed gentry, a slew of peons, and a few shopkeepers and craftsmen. A true middle class was born.

The middle class had other needs that did not exist before. They wanted the same comforts for their children as the wealthy and, lacking the tutors that were hired by the landed classes, demanded public schools. Unlike the peons and shopkeepers and craftsmen, they had leisure time. On the "week-end." To the landed gentry, one day was like any other, but to this new class, two days of the week were special. Leisure businesses arose. Newspapers. Theaters. Steam power led to the creation of railways that took middle-class workers on holiday. Hotels sprung up to house out-of-towners.

The railways transported coal and raw materials to the factories and distributed manufactured goods across the country. For the first time, it mattered whether Liverpool and London set their station clocks to the same time. Standard time was born.

It was a period of rapid urbanization. Before industrialization, London was the only city in England of any size. By 1800, across the formerly rural Midlands, Leeds, Manchester, Sheffield, and Birmingham all had more than 50,000 inhabitants, as did Liverpool, Bristol, and Plymouth, where the ships of the Triangle Trade came and went.

Great Britain got off to a two-decade head start in this new world. It solidified its position atop the heap of rising European nations and prepared it to overtake China in the next century. When it lost the American colonies and its monopoly on American cotton and tobacco, it hardly skipped a beat. In ten years, it would be starting up a "land tenure system" in India, enforcing the same cotton monopoly there.

The British got themselves to this place because of their decision to pursue oceangoing exploration. Most importantly, this supplied them with cheap, slave-grown cotton. But it also caused a repatriation of new-money types, ready to spend, and exposed them to imports of Indian textiles and fine Chinese porcelain at exorbitant prices that manufacturers could undercut. The influx of new landowners caused a wave of unemployment in a labor force whose numbers were increasing from a diet supplemented by New World foods.

Of course, British ingenuity must be credited for part of that population increase, as the Second Agricultural Revolution was a significant step up for the world's food production. Britain was also a supportive environment for entrepreneurial investment because of its longstanding history of protecting merchants' rights and private property, beginning with the Magna Carta and continuing through the Glorious Revolution and the writings of John Locke.

But luck, too, had much to do with the British being the first to industrialize. Once again, geography is destiny. Why else would one of the two greatest revolutions of human history begin in the cramped upstairs rooms of quaint cottages, miles of washed-out road from the nearest city? From expert weavers to fast-flowing waters to rich coal deposits, the steps were laid for British inventors to follow.

And a supportive environment for entrepreneurship meant nothing without available entrepreneurs. Perhaps the greatest luck of all was how religious persecution wound up creating a class of educated owners—ones who may have been reading Adam Smith's recently-published *The Wealth of Nations*. Mercantilism was out, said the "father of capitalism"; a 100% free market was the way to go. The top rungs of European feudalism (kings, lords, etc.) weren't about to jump on board. But their days were numbered. England's Puritans were the first wave of a new political order.

CHAPTER NINE

Thoughts of Social Equality Lead to a Bloody Revolution in France, and Seep Across Europe and Latin America
(1789-1829)

Before the new politics could take shape, industry would have to spread in tandem with notions of social equality. The latter will be formed by the French Revolution and spread by the subsequent Napoleonic Wars.

In Latin America during the same period, there will also be revolutions, but notions of social equality will be stillborn and there will be no industrialization, resulting in an entirely different political order.

In the same year that George Washington began his presidency under the new constitution and Great Britain opened the first truly industrialized factory, the citizens of Paris stormed the Bastille and started on the crazy rollercoaster ride that was the French Revolution.

How could they not revolt? After seeing decades of impassioned coffee house conversations come true as the new nation across the Atlantic put a French design for government into practice—a nation of people that their own dashing military hero, Lafayette, had helped to set free?

It was French involvement in the American cause that started it all, not just by inspiring the French, but by causing them to become stone-cold broke. Just as the Seven Years' War drained the treasury of King George III and led to dissension about its replenishment, helping the Americans win their revolution drains the treasury of King Louis XVI and leads to dissension about *its* replenishment.

King Louis, seeing that the direct approach didn't work out well for King George, takes a more indirect path by calling a meeting of the Estates-General, the nearest thing France has to a parliament—and a rather poor approximation of one. It hasn't convened at all for the past 150 years.

The Estates-General has representatives divided into three "estates." Here is how they compare:

	Composed of	Privileges	Amt. of population represented	# of votes *entire Estate* gets in E-G
First Estate	clergy	pay zero taxes	~100,000	1
Second Estate	nobles	-pay very few taxes -only people allowed to hold jobs in the government -miscellaneous others, e.g. hunting ground access	~400,000	1
Third Estate	everyone else	none (pay nearly all of the taxes)	~24 million	1

Despite paying no taxes, the Church owned about 10% of the land in France. The country was 100% Catholic. Protestants and Jews were persecuted.

At any given time, a few of the most favored nobles were invited to hang out at the extravagant Palace of Versailles as courtiers. Otherwise, when not hunting in their private hunting grounds, they inhabited their own castles or manor houses throughout France.

Although the Third Estate was mostly peasants, poor farmers, laborers, and small shopkeepers, it also included doctors and lawyers. The latter were a minute percentage of the Third Estate overall, but made up nearly its entire representation in the Estates-General because what peasant, small farmer, laborer, or shopkeeper has the time to go to meetings? Or the means to travel 25 kilometers to Versailles, where the meetings were held?

This physical distance between the monarch and the people of Paris was metaphorical of the chasm between palace life and life in the fields and streets. It also didn't help that Louis XVI had very little charisma. Much has been made (and exaggerated) of the People's disdain for his queen, Marie Antoinette. In fact, it was she who had all the charisma and who, before things turned for the worse, was responsible for whatever love the People showed to their monarchs. But being Austrian made it easy to turn on her once revolutionary fervor began to build—that and her propensity for overdressing while people were starving (though she never did utter the phrase "Let them eat cake," which is a reference to the crumbs left behind in the oven once all the bread has been spoken for).

When the doctors and lawyers head to Versailles to represent the People in May 1789, there is indeed a bread shortage, as well as runaway inflation. Louis knows that he can't press the People any further. He has called the Estates-General together to see if he can somehow entice the First and Second Estates into ponying up the cash needed to bail his government out.

As you can see from the chart, without some prior back room dealing, any proposal to shift the Third Estate's tax burden onto the other two is sure to be defeated by a vote of 2 to 1. And when Louis, perhaps with the best intentions for the Third Estate, calls a meeting with the first two Estates alone, the Third Estate, rather than standing by like good third-class citizens, takes matters into their own hands.

They search the nearby streets for a place large enough to hold their own meeting, settling on an indoor tennis court (probably more along the lines of a racquetball court today). There, they proclaim themselves to be the new National Assembly. (Louis soon will learn that this is not his great-great-great-grandfather's meek Third Estate of 150 years ago; these representatives are modern, Enlightenment-inspired intellectuals whose generation has been waiting for this very moment for years.) One and all, they make a pledge to not disband until a new constitution has been written.

Though there is no industry yet in France to swell their numbers, the men who take this so-called Tennis Court Oath are the vanguard of what will become the upper crust of a new middle class. They are of the same social level as the leaders of the American Revolution –Franklin, Adams, Madison et al. It is the French that give them a name: the *bourgeoisie*.

Despite the character of its leadership and other similarities, the French Revolution will differ hugely from the American Revolution. It will require more than cutting ties with a geographically separate master; all will be fighting for the same physical country here, and there will be vastly different ideas about how that country will be run and how to get there. It is going to be a true social revolution. The commoners will not be content to be led.

When the news of the Tennis Court Oath reaches Paris and rumors spread that King Louis is planning to crush any response from the People and they react by storming the old Bastille prison, raiding its armory and killing the captain of the guard, it is clearly evident that...

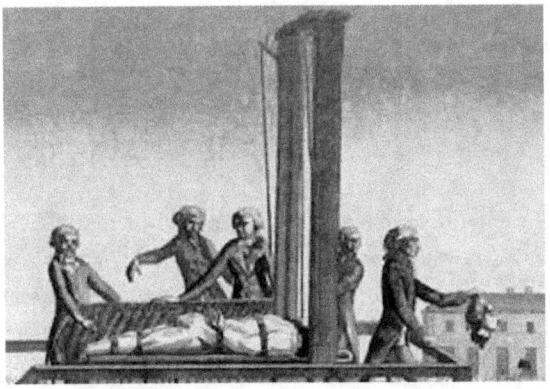

...heads will roll!

◇◇◇

The first hero of the French Revolution is the same Marquis de Lafayette who was a hero in the American Revolution. He is the leader of the National Guard, which, when called to disperse the mob at the Bastille, sides with the revolutionaries instead. He is also the author of the Declaration of the Rights of Man and of the Citizen (let's just call it the DOROMAC hereon), a sort of outline of principles to enshrine in the new constitution.

Progress on the constitution has been slow. The Tennis Court Oath had been taken in late June and the Bastille breached in mid-July. Now, with the calendar turning to August, the city government of Paris, known as the Paris Commune, takes it upon itself to represent the People, and they are running out of patience.

But one of the reasons the constitution isn't coming together is that there are now more people to debate its contents, and that's a good thing: A number of members of the Second Estate have joined, and they agree to step up to pay their fair share of taxes. The scales having tipped, King Louis officially recognizes the National Assembly.

It soon becomes clear that this progress is the result of some political maneuvering in which the First Estate is the big loser. Louis decides to bring the church under his control (sorry, pope!), and his first action as its new boss is to start selling off its excess landholdings. He uses the proceeds to pay down the debt.

Though things are looking up for the government financially, the common folk are not going to sit on their hands waiting for the trickle-down effect. Spontaneously, a group of poor women, finding little to buy at the market one day, decide to band together and *walk* those 25 kilometers from Paris to Versailles to show their displeasure to the king.

The group of women quickly becomes a mob, led by women with pitchforks, with their men, some with rifles, mixed in. Concerned about keeping order, Lafayette decides to follow along with a detachment of the National Guard.

By the time the procession gets to the gates of the palace the next morning, the objective has morphed from a protest into a kidnapping. The angry mob demands to see the king step out on his balcony. Inside, Lafayette advises Louis to comply.

Someone begins chanting for the queen to step out. Aware of the explosiveness of the situation, she not only complies, but also curtsies to the crowd.

There seems to be no alternative that can keep the peace other than to hastily hitch up a procession of carriages in order to transport the royal family back to the city, led by the mob, with the bourgeoisie general and his troops trailing behind.

The principles in the DOROMAC go beyond even those in the American Declaration of Independence or Constitution of that time, drawing from a later Enlightenment philosopher named Jean-Jacques Rousseau. Rousseau thought all citizens had a responsibility to support the *general good*, ignoring personal advantage and focusing only on what is in the public's best interest. He also was a bit of a socialist, once stating that private property is the source of all inequality.

Lafayette draws upon all but the socialism. With nods to citizenship, inequality, and the general good, he writes, "All citizens are equal in the eyes of the law," and, "Social distinctions may be founded only upon the general good." But he also retains *property* in the DOROMAC's version of *natural rights*: "liberty, property, security, and resistance to oppression."

Thus the boundaries of the revolution that he draws are that no one will identify as being from this or that estate; all will be simply citizens. There will be no privilege, no *social* leveling. But neither will there be economic *un*-leveling; property rights will be protected.

This emphasis on social equality becomes the rallying cry of this first phase of the revolution, with its motto, "Liberty, Equality, Fraternity."

After the constitution is finally written and presented for ratification, there is a big celebration on the anniversary of the storming of the Bastille, led by Lafayette in the huge park known as the Champs de Mars ("Shahm duh Mar"), with the royal family showing off pasted-on smiles and the king saying a few words. Among the diverse attendees, you might see and hear a lot of this:

The person on the left, of noble birth, has agreed to give up his traditional privileges and greets his fellow citizen of lower birth as he would any other.

They are both happy because the royal family is now permanently ensconced in the Tuileries Palace, right on the Seine, in the center of town. The king has been stripped of most of his power. From now on, he will function like the American president. Every male property owner will be able to vote for his representative in the National Assembly, which will be the lawmaking body. France is about to become a *constitutional* monarchy, rather than an absolute one. It seems the revolution has been won in just one year, with hardly any blood spilled.

But somewhere in the crowd that happy July 14, 1790, lurks a man named Maximilien Robespierre. He is a thoughtful, quiet type and a very smart lawyer. He isn't smiling and cheering like most everyone else because he is a skeptic.

The king and queen are not exactly all smiles, either, when the focus is not on them. In the following months, Louis corresponds with Marie Antoinette's brother in Vienna. Austria at this time owns the Austrian Netherlands, on France's northern border, today known as Belgium. Plans are made. Come one late evening the next spring, Louis packs his family secretly into a simple carriage without a royal seal... and heads out of Dodge.

Well past midnight, several kilometers north of Paris but still well short of Belgium, the carriage is stopped at a checkpoint. Louis is identified from his likeness on a coin, and the family is apprehended.

Despite this blatant show of displeasure with his new role, both the National Guard and the National Assembly decide to go easy on the king and give him another chance.

The bourgeoisie seem to keep forgetting that, although they are the leaders, they aren't ever totally in charge. An angry crowd forms a protest on the Champs de Mars to call for the king's removal. Lafayette leads a detachment of soldiers to disperse them. The crowd starts throwing rocks at the soldiers. The soldiers fire on the crowd and at least a dozen are killed. This "Massacre at the Champs de Mars" erases the good feeling from the celebration almost a year earlier.

Meanwhile, some nobles get the same idea as Louis, and they are more successful. Longing for the a*ncien régime*, they become émigrés to Austria, Prussia, and other surrounding kingdoms where nobility will still get you a hunting ground or two and keep you secure from the riffraff. Hearing stories from inside France, leaders of these other kingdoms become concerned; they certainly don't want their *own* people to get ideas.

In February 1792, Austria and Prussia form an alliance and issue a declaration to the French National Assembly announcing that they will send troops to crush France if the royal family is harmed. The assembly, perhaps somewhat overconfidently, votes to strike first. Troops are sent marching north to attack the Austrian Netherlands.

The war goes badly for France. By summer, the Prussian army is drawing close to Paris.

A social revolution often progresses like the stages of a serious flu. It bursts out suddenly and then it seems to come under control, but lurking below the surface of an optimistic recovery, signs of the illness remain.

Not all of the discontented nobles have emigrated. Now, with the national forces weakened by the threat from without, some provinces have begun to counter-rebel, trying to undo the revolution in hopes of reinstating the king to full power.

On the other extreme, food shortages continue off and on, threatening to destabilize the masses, who are already on edge because of the news of the Prussian advance.

Inside the National Assembly, the initial optimistic unity has splintered into various factions. All support the revolution, but whereas some are staunch defenders of the constitution, others, disillusioned by the lack of commitment from the king and the Massacre at the Champs de Mars, want to take it in a new direction.

On the evening of August 9, the radicals act. They begin by walking into a meeting of the Paris Commune, dismissing it, and convening in its place.

Their leader is Georges Danton. His confidant and adviser is Maximilien Robespierre. They are an odd match. They know each other through Camille Desmoulins, a revolutionary pamphleteer whose speech had inspired the storming of the Bastille. Though politically aligned, Danton and Robespierre have little in common. Danton is charismatic, a boisterous leader and womanizer. Robespierre is a bit of a prude. Although he is the godfather of Desmoulins' child, he is a childless, unsocial bachelor himself. But he is slyly influential. He uses Danton and his popularity to enact his own vision for the revolution.

Danton recruits troops from the south of France to the cause. In the early morning hours of August 10, the army wakes and marches to the Tuileries Palace. Members of the National Guard defect and join them, rotating the palace cannons to point inward. Only the king's small detachment of Swiss Guards remains loyal, and they go down in a futile exchange of fire.

The royal family is taken to different quarters and placed under arrest. Complaining of their ignominious treatment, the queen's closest consort is hauled away to an actual prison.

Danton is appointed minister of justice. As such, he begins rounding up "traitors to the revolution," tossing them in the prisons as a backlog of trial dates is set.

The calendar turns to September. The Prussians draw ever closer to Paris. A panicky group of citizens forms an ad hoc meeting in response. One of them steps to the front and shouts that when the Prussians enter the city, they will go to the prisons, now full of traitors, and release them all. A cry goes up: "To the prisons! Kill the traitors now!"

From this moment, and for the next four days, mobs armed with clubs and tools and farm implements control Paris. They storm the city's prisons, killing any guards who attempt to stop them. Once inside, they break into every cell and butcher every prisoner they can find. There is of course no distinction between accused traitors (many of whom may be innocent) and petty criminals or common debtors. When Marie Antoinette's consort is found among them, she is tortured and decapitated. Her head is placed on a pike. Later that evening, a torch-bearing group parades it by the window where the queen is imprisoned.

Danton is wise enough to know that this is the wrong time to try to impose control. He reasons that, as the news spreads to the rebellious provinces, the counter-revolutionaries will back down in fear.

Somewhere in the field of battle, the news reaches Lafayette. Incredulous that he is now considered an enemy of the true revolution by Danton and his faction and sickened by the turn that it has taken, he says farewell to his troops and decamps for the northern border.

Less than three weeks after the massacres in the prisons, French troops turn back the Prussians with a decisive victory at Valmy. On the very next day, a new National *Convention* is called into session to replace the National Assembly. A suggestion of Robespierre's, it is cleaned out of any of the king's supporters.

A new constitution has been drafted that will abolish the monarchy altogether. Danton is cheered as he presents it for ratification, and in a mood of giddy jubilation, a representative proposes that the calendar be changed to make this the first day of a new Year 1.

One day in the fall, as the Convention is in session, the inevitable occurs. A representative named Louis Antoine de Saint-Just steps to the lectern and calls for the execution of the king. As long as the king lives, he reasons, those who secretly harbor loyalty in their hearts will continue to hope or even plot for his restoration. A king is born to rule, he says. A king must either rule... or die.

And so charges are made formal. A trial begins. Louis—now addressed as "Citizen Capet"—appears before the Convention to defend himself. The vote is taken and he is sentenced to be executed by guillotine.

At this point, the guillotine is considered a positive symbol of the revolution. It is an equitable means of execution. In England, they still remove heads the old-fashioned way. The rich are able to hire the best swordsmen. Bargain axe wielders often do a sloppy job, sometimes requiring multiple chops.

On January 21, 1793, Louis Capet's life ends like that of any other convicted citizen, in one swift, clean slice and a plop into the bucket —with the exception that they fire off a 21-cannon salute and a large crowd roars their approval. The cannon fire alerts the former queen, back in her quarters, that the act has been completed. To her and all the remaining royalists, her seven-year-old son is now King Louis XVII.

Those scattered royalists are still a worry for Robespierre, who becomes more insistent in his private advice to Danton. In their quiet conversations, the revolution's third phase is about to begin.

When a patient has the flu and is well past the optimism of false early recovery, as the illness really takes hold, the body's immune system steps up its response. This is when the fever builds higher and higher, and the misery that the patient feels comes from their own system of defense.

Certain words are commonly spoken at this point in social revolutions. Danton would have heard them from Robespierre:

Our opposition is back—like an incurable illness.

Our **people** don't want to **go backward**. They know we must win this war **at any cost**.

Exceptional times call for exceptional measures.

Note how confidently the bourgeoisie claim to know what the People want.

These "exceptional measures" are always an infringement on liberty—even if liberty is the very thing that inspired the revolution in the first place.

What happens to a social revolution when it feels threatened?

It suspends liberty in the name of the revolution

In March, at the urging of Robespierre, a Revolutionary Tribunal is established. It is no more than a kangaroo court set up to rapidly try, and in almost all cases execute, those accused of **crimes against the revolution**. A Committee for

Public Safety is formed, with Danton at its head, that has power above and beyond that given to the Convention by the constitution. Special Watch Committees are set up within neighborhoods so that people might report their own neighbors as potential **counter-revolutionaries**.

This is the beginning of "the Terror." Over the next 16 months, more than 40,000 people will lose their head to the cause. Most of those executions occur in Paris, where they have to keep moving the guillotine from square to square as nearby residents complain that the smell of blood is driving their housing prices down. Prisoners are loaded onto a tumbril that pulls up to the side of the raised platform where the guillotine stands. Bodies and their severed heads are tossed back into the tumbril. Once the executioners finish with one group, the tumbril is wheeled away to make way for another.

It is all very efficient—very industrial, you might say. It has to be. Two-thirds of the 40,000 executions are carried out in June and July alone. Do the math: It comes to over 430 heads a day.

Danton can see that the revolution is eating itself. He quarrels with Robespierre, steps down from the Committee, and leaves Paris for his country house, where he spends his time fishing.

Since the formation of the Committee, Robespierre has stepped out of the background and become more and more vocal. Now he steps to the fore-front. Under his leadership the Committee begins to obliterate all things that smack of monarchy. Playing cards and chess are outlawed because both have kings and queens. Next, they turn against the Church and begin a program of "de-Christianization." Across the country, church icons are destroyed. To replace Catholicism as the state religion, Robespierre invents his own, which he calls *The Cult of Reason*.

In October, Marie Antoinette finally has a date with the guillotine. By now, Desmoulins can see that Robespierre has lost it. He journeys to Danton's country home and pleads for him to return.

Danton comes back and gives a speech to the National Convention, directly opposing the desires of Robespierre for the first time in his life. He tries to steer the Committee toward some sense.

For the next four months, a power struggle ensues. In the end, Robespierre is able to engineer trumped-up charges against Danton. He expresses regret that the web in which he snares him also sweeps up his friend, Desmoulins. But this doesn't stop him. Danton, Desmoulins, and Desmoulins' wife are all sent to the guillotine, leaving Robespierre's own godson an orphan.

As his public speeches become more and more bizarre, Robespierre loses the support of the people. The National Convention turns against him, as well, and on July 28, 1794, he becomes one of the last to lose his head to the Terror.

◇◇◇

After stumbling through a complicated new oligarchic governing structure that ends the Terror but cannot seem to accomplish much else, France decides to go full tilt the other direction and hand power to one man. His name is Napoleon Bonaparte.

Dashing general, hero of the revolution's battlefield (perhaps not as much from his success as from the positive press he is so good at generating), confident and seemingly magnanimous, Napoleon is just what the country needs at this point in time. To carry on the flu analogy, when a body has been through the worst fever imaginable and barely survived, all it craves is some chicken noodle soup and "Dr. Mom" to tell it what to do. The French Revolution is entering its convalescence phase.

Napoleon is responsible for two significant compromises that help to heal France. The first is the Concordant of 1801. After all of Robespierre's cult craziness, it reinstates Catholicism as the "preferred faith" of France; yet, at the same time, it guarantees protection from persecution for Protestants and Jews.

The second, the establishment of a new law code, takes much longer to finalize. While that is being worked out, Napoleon's predilection for riding at the head of an army takes control of him and he sets out to expand France into an empire. By the time the law code is ready for prime time in the spring of 1804, he has acquired lands from the Austrians in northern Italy and expanded French territory northeastward to the Rhine River.

The Napoleonic Civil Code contains something for each of the former divisions of French society...

For the nobility, it restores property to returning émigrés as long as they swear an oath of loyalty to the new government.

For peasants, it protects rights to property that they have *legally* acquired, even if it was bought at a fire sale from a fleeing noble.

For the bourgeoisie, it assures that all government jobs are open to every class and filled based on merit alone. Social equality will be maintained, with every man equal before the law.

Every *man*. But there will be no gender equality, as was anticipated in the heady early days of the revolution, when Olympe de Gouges penned her *Declaration of the Rights of Woman*. She was yet another casualty of the Terror.

Napoleon has been holding plebiscites (votes after the fact) to confirm his actions. All of them won the People's approval (anything you say, Dr. Mom). Now, with plans to launch another wave of expansion, he crowns himself emperor. The People approve of that, too.

By 1808, the French Empire includes Piedmont and Genoa in western Italy, Catalan Spain, and all of the Netherlands. The remaining Italian states and the Duchy of Warsaw also give their allegiance to the emperor.

As they marched across the continent, French forces, feeling superior due to their having won social equality, exposed the rest of Europe to nationalism. In response to French arrogance, Germans may have thought, Hey, we're not just Saxons or Bavarians or Schwabians; we're *Germans!* And the same was true in Italy. As the century wore on, both would ultimately unify into new nations.

At the same time, drives for social equality put princes and monarchs on edge, wary of their subjects getting too many ideas. Though most of these drives were contained, they would cause widespread instability in the decades ahead.

When French armies marched into Madrid, the Spanish capital, Napoleon installed his brother Joseph on the throne. This meant that Joseph ruled over all of Spain's vast holdings in the Western Hemisphere, comprising the two vice-royalties of New Spain, which stretched from Florida to Panama, administered from its capital at Mexico City, and New Castille, which stretched from Colombia to Argentina and had its capital at Lima.

New Spain had evolved from Spain's conquest of Mesoamerica's Aztecs in 1521, New Castille from the Spanish conquest of South America's Incas 11 years later. In both cases, it required only a small number of Spaniards to subjugate rich empires that were mighty by New World standards but lacking in Eurasian technology (due to the several geographical factors related in Chapter 1). Of course, as described in Chapter 6, the real conquerors were the disease germs the Spaniards were carrying without even knowing it.

The culture that had developed in Spanish America was quite different from that which the British had established in their North American colonies. Whereas the British had been into clearing land for settlement, the Spanish who came to the New World, like their *conquistador* ancestors, were into exploiting resources that could make them rich. And both the Aztec Empire, with its great capital of Tenochtitlan (which became Mexico City), and the huge Inca Empire, with its rich Andean silver deposits, had the riches to exploit.

Also, whereas immigrants to the North American colonies usually came with wives, Spanish immigrants were more often single men. They sought out native wives, leading to many multiracial descendants, a rarity in the north.

An unfortunate result of this mixing in the south was a prevalence of both class and race prejudice. Those who only came to make their fortune, never intending to stay, were known as *peninsulares* (their true home being the Iberian Peninsula). This upper crust made up 100% of the positions in colonial government. Those of the White race who were born in the Americas were known as the *criollos* (also referred to as *creoles,* not to be confused with French creoles). Though educated, the *criollos* were looked down upon by the *peninsulares.* They, in turn, looked down upon those who were multiracial—mostly *mestizos,* who had a mix of both Spanish and indigenous ancestry and made up the largest percent of the population.

The first revolution against this social hierarchy occurs in Mexico. It begins with the insistent clanging of a church bell, as a provincial priest calls poor *mestizos* to arms. The *criollos* at first support them, but before long they are switching sides. They join the *peninsulares* in running the insurgents to ground. The revolution will only simmer in the background for the next several years.

In South America, there are *peninsulare*-led efforts to break from Bonaparte-controlled Spain. Venezuela declares itself a republic, but not really, as at the same time it pledges loyalty to the deposed Spanish king.

Colombia (then known as New Granada) also breaks away, after relying heavily upon the help of a young Venezuelan calvary commander who has begun to envision something much more grandiose than his countrymen's pseudo-republic. His name is Simón Bolívar.

Bolívar is a *criollo.* The vision he has begun to form is that of an America for the *Americanos*: *criollos, mestizos,* and indigenous people united together across South America in one uprising to oust the *peninsulares.* He will soon get his chance to enact the first step of his plan, as the situation in Europe is about to change again.

That is because Napoleon is about to bite off more than he can chew. In the summer of 1812, he leads his army into Russia. Russia is a huge land, and by September he has only made it to Borodino, which is still 130 kilometers short of Moscow. There, a great battle ensues. Although the French suffer significant

111

losses, they eventually begin to gain ground.

The Russians go into full retreat, all of the way east of Moscow, abandoning the city. But it is a planned retreat, luring the French army ever deeper into their homeland, knowing that the early Russian winter is just around the corner.

Napoleon waits in Moscow, believing he has won, but no message of surrender comes. By the time he moves out to track down the Russian army again, it has begun to snow...

In total, more than 300,000 French troops perish in the failed Russia campaign. On December 5, 1812, the emperor ignominiously flees by sled for Paris, leaving the remnants of his starving troops behind. By the time he makes it back to his capital, news of the debacle having preceded him, the last of Dr. Mom's mojo is gone. Napoleon is exiled to the Mediterranean island of Elba, 200 miles northeast of Corsica.

The so-called Four Great Powers—Prussia, Austria, Russia, and Great Britain—come together at the Congress of Vienna to determine what penalties should be imposed upon France. It goes without saying that all of the conquered land must be returned. Equally important to the peacemakers, as each of these powers is ruled by a monarchy: There must be a king!

So after all the twists and turns from "Liberté, Égalité, Fraternité!" to "A king must rule... or die!" to "Exceptional times call for exceptional measures" to "Anything you say, Dr. Mom," France ends up bringing back a king. By this time, young Louis the XVII had died in prison, so they brought in Louis XVI's brother (an émigré who had wisely not returned) and made him Louis XVIII.

This isn't quite going all the way back to where they started. They are to follow the British model, a constitutional monarchy, much like in the first constitution created by the original National Assembly. It is also time to state another repetitious maxim of human history, which is: You can never put a genie back in the bottle. Not all the way. Social movements nearly always proceed four steps forward and three steps back. From 30,000 feet, this setback will hardly be noticed. There is no stopping the forward arc of history.

As Napoleon stews in exile on Elba, on the other side of the world, Simón Bolívar's star is rising. In 1813, Bolívar returns to his homeland at the head of a force, liberates it from the royalist *peninsulares*, and establishes the Second Venezuelan Republic. He then works tirelessly to shepherd the creation of a new constitution.

Unfortunately, the other Venezuelan *criollos* turn out to be more akin to cats than sheep. They cannot settle on one president but instead set up *three*, and they give very little power to the central government. This is much like the early American states when they were only loosely grouped under the Articles of Confederation, whereas Bolívar wanted to emulate the finished product after those states had become the USA.

What Bolívar *really* has in mind is an entire United States of South America, comprising all the pieces of a fully liberated New Castille. How was he ever going to achieve that vision if Venezuela by itself couldn't pull its pieces together?

Ultimately, Spain, now free from the Bonapartes, takes advantage of the dissension to invade and, once again, reclaim the colony. Bolívar, once again, heads for the hills of New Grenada.

But France, it turns out, is *not* free from the Bonapartes. Napoleon, who still has a reduced but loyal fan base, receives assistance in making an escape from his island prison. He sails to the French mainland, where he is greeted by others in that fan base, puts together a small force, and begins marching north.

The king sends an army to intercept him, but, so legend has it, Napolean walks unarmed into firing range and cries out, "Here I am! Kill your emperor if you wish."

And the army embraces him. Merging the armies together, he continues his march all the way to Paris, where he finds rousing support and an empty throne, King Louis having fled.

So begins what is known as Napoleon's 100 Days, a last burst of glory before he "meets his Waterloo." It is a typical example of how a popular autocrat can be fooled by the admiration of a sizable but highly vocal minority into thinking that they are invincible. He tries to replay the Napoleonic Wars from the beginning by leading his forces north into Belgium, where, near the town of Waterloo, they are thoroughly defeated by the British and Prussians.

As Louis XVIII returns to the throne, Napoleon is exiled, *much* further away this time, to a tiny island called St. Helena, miles from anywhere, in the vast South Atlantic Ocean.

Bolívar's return to his homeland goes quite a bit better. After expanding his army with some foreign support, he mounts a second invasion. The Spanish withdraw from Venezuela for good, and the *Third* Venezuelan Republic is declared.

Soon after, Bolívar leads his army southward as far as the country that now bears his name: Bolivia. South of there, another *criollo* general, Jose de San Martín, liberates Chile and Argentina.

In Mexico, the rebellion instigated by the lower ranks of Mexican society is contained but not extinguished. Then, in 1820, ten years since that lone church bell rang out for freedom, a revolution in Spain changes everything.

Inspired by France's revolution and temporary occupation of their country, liberal Spaniards overthrow their king and begin setting up a new government. Worried that the new Spanish constitution will create social equality, Mexico's *criollos* swap sides again to support the *mestizos*.

With *criollo* support, the revolution is finally successful in kicking out the Spanish and establishing a Republic of Mexico. But for the *mestizos* (and indigenous and multiracial people), it only means that their subjugation by a higher-ranking class (the *criollos*) will continue... whereas if Mexico had remained part of Spain, it may have ended.

In South America, liberated multiracial people fare no better. Bolívar's vision of uniting the social classes into one group of *Americanos* is unrealized. The *criollos* who led the revolutions never give up control. They only become the new *peninsulares*. In Europe, the seeds of social equality had found fertile ground, but in Latin America the old class/race-based structure has proved to be too ingrained to overcome.

By this time in Europe, it is a different world. Ground-shifting change had occurred during Napoleon's first exile. His defeat at Waterloo had been big news, but it was really just a last gasp of *old* news. In hindsight, it was far from the most important thing going on in Belgium at that time. For while he was away on Elba, two Belgian brothers got hold of plans showing how to use the Watt steam engine to drive textile machinery. Industrialization is no longer a British secret. The spread of industrial technology will soon combine with the spread of ideas about social reform, and the result will be the politics we were still arguing about in the moment that just passed.

CHAPTER TEN

Industrialization Completes the Formation of the Modern Political Spectrum
(1830-1884)

In 1842 in the English Midlands, the average lifespan of a farmer was 38 years. The average lifespan of a laborer in the industrial city of Manchester was only 17 years.

In Leeds and Birmingham, the other cities that had boomed with the advent of industry, it was the same. Workers and their families existed in cramped, unsanitary, light-deprived slum housing. Outside, the air was thick with coal smoke. Inside the factories, workers labored for upwards of 12 hours six days a week in 80-degree heat, enveloped by the constant clanging din of the machinery. Respiratory infections from the polluted air were common, as were lost limbs resulting from malfunctioning equipment or a moment of carelessness brought on by exhaustion.

Women were particularly susceptible to harm, as their long skirts and hair were more likely to become entangled in the machines. They also were more often employed in the textile mills, where the air, filled with cloth dust, was the most destructive to the lungs.

Children were particularly useful for crawling into hard-to-reach spaces to fix the machines. Even more so in the coal mines, where, affixed to a coal cart by a chain running between their legs, they would crawl steeply uphill through passageways as low as 18 inches in height, often covering upwards of 10 miles per day in this way.

The mines were damp and full of coal dust. Fatalities were not uncommon, sometimes from drowning when the mines would flood, sometimes as the result of a gas leak, which might either silently poison the miners or, set off by candle-flame, cause a sudden explosion.

As displaced farmers migrated en masse to the new cities, factory owners rushed to throw together blocks of worker housing, long rows of connected units where 20 families would share a single toilet and water pump. According to an 1843 Edinburgh magazine article, reprinted in *The Times of London*,

> These streets are often so narrow that a person can step from the window
> of one house into that of its opposite neighbour, while the houses are piled
> so high, storey upon storey, that the light can scarcely penetrate into the
> court or alley that lies between.... All refuse, garbage, and excrements of
> at least 50,000 persons are thrown into the gutters every night, so that,
> in spite of all the street sweeping, a mass of dried filth and foul vapors
> are created.

Diseases like typhoid and cholera were rampant.

Aside from the miserable living conditions and the dangers and physical toll of the work, there is a terrible impact on mental health, as well. To this first generation of industrial labor, it was a shocking transition. Imagine having grown up poor in a rural hamlet, working a small plot of land, walking your cow back and forth to the Commons each day. Your diet is sparse and your life is hard and you rarely meet anyone new, but you are your own boss and your day is comprised of multiple tasks that vary with the seasons. Or perhaps you are a craftsperson—a weaver creating handmade clothing in a proto-industrial setting. Or a blacksmith or farrier who takes custom orders from other villagers. Now, suddenly your world has changed. In the factory, every day is the same. Nearly every minute or two is a repetition of the one or two before. You are taught to perform one generally simple task over and over. You have no input to the planning of your work and no cognizance of its fruition.

In the first few decades of the Industrial Revolution, as automated machinery was first becoming widespread, there was some resistance to this new world. A group called the Luddites, active in England during the 1810's, wrote threatening letters to early adopters, which they sometimes followed up with nighttime raids to vandalize the machines.

But as new businesses boomed, there was, of course, no stopping the onslaught of profiteers. The new class of bourgeoisie factory owners elbowed its way into the social ranks, bending the labor class to their own needs and, as their wealth

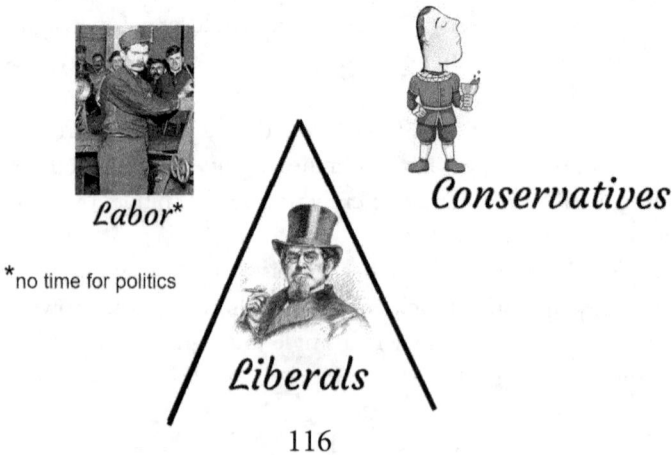

Labor*

*no time for politics

Conservatives

Liberals

expanded, challenging the status of the conservative landholding class, as well.

The new factory owners became a new political bloc. They were known as "Liberals." If you transported one of them into our own time, they would be shocked to find that the label they so proudly represented designates an entirely different ideology in the 21st century. The ideologies represented by the "conservative" and "liberal" labels keep changing over time. That is because, in a greater sense, they have two very general (and time period-immune) definitions: A liberal is someone who embraces change; a conservative is someone who either doesn't at all or is much more careful about implementing it.

Relating this to the specifics of the early 19th century, Conservatives were the "Second Estate" types, lords who favored the king, believed in mercantilism, and lived in their manor houses some ways out of town, devoting most of their time to fox hunting and other forms of leisure, while managing at a distance their vast landholdings, looking down on those Liberal losers who dirtied their hands with business.

The Liberals believed in republican forms of government, with representation in assemblies or parliaments filled with people like themselves. Economically, they were devotees of Adam Smith, whose seminal work, *An Inquiry into the Nature and Causes of the Wealth of Nations*, published just as the first factories began, was still all the rage.

Smith, who is known as "the father of capitalism," paved the way for the independence of these new Liberals when he wrote, "It is the highest impertinence and presumption...in kings and ministers to pretend to watch over the economy of private people." He was not only telling kings to back off from mercantilism and allow free trade; he was telling *ministers*, i.e. all government, to back off from *business owners*, as well.

This was capitalism in its purest sense, without the wider spectrum it would encompass even before the 19th century concluded. As a subset of that spectrum, it will acquire the label *laissez-faire* capitalism (French translation: *hands-off*).

Smith had a very realistic (some would say highly negative) view of human nature: basically that we're all out for ourselves, and ourselves alone. And, from his dispassionate high-level perspective, he said, That's absolutely okay. It's all going to work out in the end because our competing interests will keep each other in check. He used the now-famous analogy of the Invisible Hand: "Man is led by an invisible hand to promote an end which was no part of his intention. By pursuing his own interest he frequently promotes that of the society." This example from the entertaining and informative *The Cartoon Introduction to Economics* by Grady Klein and Yoram Bauman, PhD, shows the intersection of interests between two merchants and one consumer:

117

(5)

"Selfish jerk!" indeed. Smith wrote,

> It is not from the benevolence of the butcher, the brewer or the baker
> that we expect our dinner, but from their regard to their own self-
> interest. We address ourselves not to their humanity but to their
> self-love.

Thus, with the widely-sanctioned belief that being greedy was doing your part for the good of all, the bourgeoisie Liberals ran their factories and managed their worker housing with profit only in mind.

It wasn't until the decade of the 1840's that more sympathetic attention began to be paid to the laboring class. Friedrich Engels grew up in Germany, the son of a wealthy family that happened to own a textile mill in England. While still in his early twenties, his parents sent him to Manchester to learn the business, hoping it would draw him away from some radical views he held. It had the opposite effect: In *The Conditions of the Working Class in England*, he communicated directly to that class from his position implanted among the bourgeoisie, writing,

> Be their words what they please, the middle-classes intend in reality
> nothing else but to enrich themselves by your labour while they can
> sell its produce, and to abandon you to starvation as soon as they
> cannot make a profit by this indirect trade in human flesh.

118

Soon after, he would befriend expatriate German philosopher Karl Marx, who, more realistically, expected that the laboring class, which he termed the "proletariat," was not ready to properly digest any such awareness of the politics that bound them.

Marx, who is known as "the father of communism," conjectured that a natural progression would occur in the various countries of the world, whereby the bourgeoisie would cause republican governments to form in support of industrialized capitalism; industrialization would give birth to the proletariat; over time, the proletariat would learn what he termed "class-consciousness," and only then rise up to overthrow the capitalist system, creating an entirely classless society. It was important, he emphasized, that this revolution be led by the laboring class *themselves*, not by those of his own and Engels' class.

In hindsight, we know that this idealized world has not materialized (as of the moment that just passed). There were two significant developments that Marx did not anticipate, which had everything to do with this.

The first was the rise of *reformers*. Take a look at the political spectrum of 1840, compared to the modern equivalent. What's missing?

Radicals   Liberals   Conservatives

Pictured: Karl Marx   factory owner   lord

Believe in: communism   republican govt   monarchy
                                   w/limited suffrage
                                   laissez faire capitalism

Modern
equivalent: Socialists   Republicans (USA)   don't exist

(6)

To be accurate: The Liberals of the 19th century were a bit more right-wing than modern-day American Republicans, few of whom embrace totally laissez-faire capitalism, while the Radicals of the 19th century were quite a bit more left-wing than modern-day socialists, few of whom would label themselves as communist. Despite both groups' move toward the center in recent times, there is still a very big gap between them that today, in the USA, is filled by the Democrats.

The reformers are their 19th-century equivalent:

Radicals   Reformers   Liberals   Conservatives

	Radicals	Reformers	Liberals	Conservatives
Pictured:	Karl Marx	a member of the new middle class	factory owner	lord
Believe in:	communism	reform laws & universal suffrage	republican govt w/limited suffrage laissez faire capitalism	monarchy
Modern equivalent:	Socialists	Democrats (USA)	Republicans (USA)	don't exist

Marx failed to differentiate between bourgeoisie factory owners and the brand-new rising middle class, represented by all those accountants, lawyers, advertising folks, and salesmen who worked for that fat cat, stogie-smoking Liberal to their right. Perhaps the father of communism was too much of a utopian visionary, whereas the reformers were more practical. Their plan was to work within the present system instead of blowing it up—to reform government in order to gradually bring about a kinder world for the laboring class.

Middle-class women would eventually be particularly active in reform movements. Professional jobs in factory offices were limited to men. Their wives, eager, in their new station, to fulfill the proper role of the lady of the house, busied themselves by joining societies, many of which were focused on helping those who were less fortunate. Their drive to expand suffrage (the right to vote) to factory workers would eventually fire a drive for women to get votes for themselves.

An early group of reformers in England were called the Chartists. The name stuck after their publication of the People's Charter, which demanded

- a vote for every man, rich or poor
- payment for political office (so you could serve without being rich)
- constituencies of equal population (so lords in the countryside with few neighbors to represent didn't get all the power)
- term limits of one year

Eventually, they also championed public education, with women taught the same knowledge as men.

There are a number of revolutions across Europe in 1848, but most are just trying to get to Marx's step one: members of the bourgeoisie establishing republican government. The largest is in France, where they hit the barricades, arming themselves with rifles and stacking furniture and construction material in the streets to stand behind and fire, *Les Miserables*-style. The king has to flee, and the Second Republic is declared. (7)

While putting together a new constitution, a group of reformers push through measures to help the laborers, such as shortening the allowable workday and imposing a minimum wage.

It is just what Marx would have hated, knowing it would push back the world's progression toward his communist ideal, which required enough dissatisfaction to trigger an explosion. "Religion is the opiate of the masses," he is famous for saying, i.e. faith in a beautiful afterlife pacifies those who are struggling in this one. He would have considered the reformers to be "pushers" of the same opiate as the clergy.

By the latter part of the century, reform laws will begin to be passed into law across the industrialized nations. This will help to keep the radical vision of Marx and Engels at bay.

Meanwhile, France's Second Republic ends up going the way of its First Republic. Napoleon's nephew Louis-Napoleon is elected president, but four years later, he mimics his uncle and declares himself emperor. (You can't make this stuff up.)

This particular Emperor Napoleon keeps any thirst for empire mostly in check. But when the Prussians win a war over the Austrians in 1866, he begins to feel the need to flex his muscles a bit to keep the ascendant big boy on the block in his place.

Prussia's president is the wily Otto von Bismarck, who allows Napoleon to feel threatened enough to declare war. Von Bismarck uses the provocation to stir up German nationalism, which had boiled up in a brief 1848 uprising and had been simmering on a back burner since.

The little Franco-Prussian War of 1870-71, won by the Prussians, has several important outcomes:

- France has to cede the province of Alsace-Lorraine to the Germans, for which it will stew in a funk for the next 40-plus years, craving revenge.
- Germany unites as one nation under a system of federalism (similar to the American states) with an emperor called the *kaiser* at its head. The new German capital is Berlin, which was Prussia's capital; the new

kaiser is the former king of Prussia; the new chancellor, charged with the day-to-day running of government, is Bismarck.
- Louis-Napoleon is booted off his throne, and France declares the Third Republic.

A dozen years later, just as Germany's factory laborers are beginning to edge their way toward class-consciousness, Otto von Bismark announces a raft of reforms. Among these, first of its kind in the world, is mandatory universal healthcare. The German workers' infatuation with communism fades.

And what was the second significant development that Marx failed to anticipate, which would keep a worldwide communist revolution from coming about?

In *The Communist Manifesto*, Marx and Engels write about a serious flaw in Adam Smith's capitalism that was severely exacerbated by industrialization. Too much of a good thing, produced too fast, and the inability to predict consumer behavior will regularly throw the system into chaos:

> In these crises, there breaks out an epidemic that, in all earlier epochs, would have seemed an absurdity—the epidemic of over-production.... Industry and commerce seem to be destroyed; and why? Because there is too much industry, too much commerce.

With laissez-faire capitalism, overproduction, typically on the crest of a boom, leads to a bust. The result is painful. And pain always falls to the bottom. Due to the fickleness of the consumer or simple oversaturation of the market, suddenly sales plunge. Yet there is so much invested in the pipeline of industrial production that it is impossible to just throw the off-switch and stop the bleeding. The bleeding continues in the cost of parts that cannot be repurposed and inventory that cannot be sold. Immediately, financial managers look for the biggest expenses to cut, and the biggest expense is invariably labor. When cuts in wages and benefits alone cannot make up the difference, jobs fall by the wayside.

Marx and Engels expect these epidemics of overproduction to occur with more and more frequency as industry spreads and more competitors clash for the same consumers. Class-consciousness cannot be far behind.

Capitalism, now as then, is like a deadly, wild beast that we have tamed and dare to ride upon. We use its power for our benefit, but it must be fed with constant growth. Since the first days of Keynesian economics in the 1930's, governments have regularly inserted themselves into the machinations of markets, interfering with the Invisible Hand in order to smooth out the natural market's rollercoaster high–low cycles, kind of like administering a sedative to the beast. In the 19th century, there are no sedatives, and the industrialized nations are concerned.

But they have an out. In 1884, the various European powers come to Berlin, the capital of the new Germany, for a critical discussion. As they sit at the table, a map before them, they take out their knives and begin to carve. Africa is about to be fed to the beast.

Chapter Eleven

Feeding the Beast:
Industrial Capitalism is Unleashed
Upon the World
(1793-1912)

By way of review: Oceangoing exploration by Europeans gave them lucrative trade in slave-grown cotton and sugar that, along with the coalfields of England, enabled an industrial revolution that allowed the first few who adopted it to master the whole remaining world.

We have arrived at the so-called Age of New Imperialism. Though it is the traditional name given to the era, it is an inaccurate and highly misleading term. Its resemblance to original imperialism—the forming of great empires like those of the Chinese, the Romans, or the Mongols—is superficial at best. "Imperial" indicates empire, vast landholdings ruled by an emperor. In those cases, *government* was the driver of conquest. Nineteenth-century "imperialists" were really industrialists. Though they were eventually sponsored by governments, conquests were driven by the interests of *business*. And if conquest could be avoided, as long as business was satisfied, it was all that mattered.

The industrialists have a problem, and they think they know how to solve it. The boom of production and consumption that has spread through much of Europe has reached its peak; market saturation is about to take it on that rollercoaster dive. But there's a world out there! Every industrialist country has already established itself as a global trader. Markets abound.

In some cases, as in Asia, those markets are already established; the problem is getting them to accept the merchandise that needs to be moved. The interior of Africa, on the other hand, is a dark mystery where only the obstacles to entry are known, but now there are advancements that can tame these.

To get the fuller picture, we are going to leave those carving knives poised above the African map and back up to the building of the framework for this new "imperialism": global trade. Before industrialization turbocharged trade, those same countries who would become leaders in industry—particularly Great Britain, but also France and the Dutch Republic—had already established global trading centers and routes that industrially-manufactured goods would eventually traverse.

By the early 1600's, the Portuguese had been booted from their dominant position in the Indian Ocean trade, first by the Dutch, then also by the British. The Dutch had come up with the idea of forming a joint stock company to sponsor expensive and risky ocean voyages. The English copied them, and their British East India Company took it to the extreme, militarizing their operations, even waging small wars.

As the name implies, India was initially the Company's focus. At that time, most of India was an empire for only the third time in its history. Islam had established a firm foothold in the northwest ever since scholars and others fled there after the Mongols destroyed Baghdad. Then, in 1526, the conqueror Babur, a descendant of the Islamized Mongols of the Central Asian khanate, swept down from Samarkand and established the Mughal Empire. By the mid-1600's, nearly all of the subcontinent had been united.

Throughout the 1600's, the French and British vied for footholds in Mughal India. (The Dutch were content to dominate the Spice Islands from their capital at Batavia, today's Jakarta, and would become the only Western trade partner allowed into Tokugawa Japan.) By the end of the century, Britain had outmaneuvered France and built well-established trading posts at Bombay, Madras and Calcutta.

In the early 1700's, the Mughal Empire collapsed, leaving the country once again a collection of disconnected local administrations, more vulnerable to foreign dominance. Thus, over the rest of the century, the Company's clutches deepened, expanding beyond trading posts to the acquisition of land. Once the textile mills were up and running in the English Midlands and the monopoly on American cotton was ended by the American Revolution, the British established a land tenure system that gave monetary encouragement to Indian aristocrats to convert farmland into cotton plantations.

In the mid 1700's...

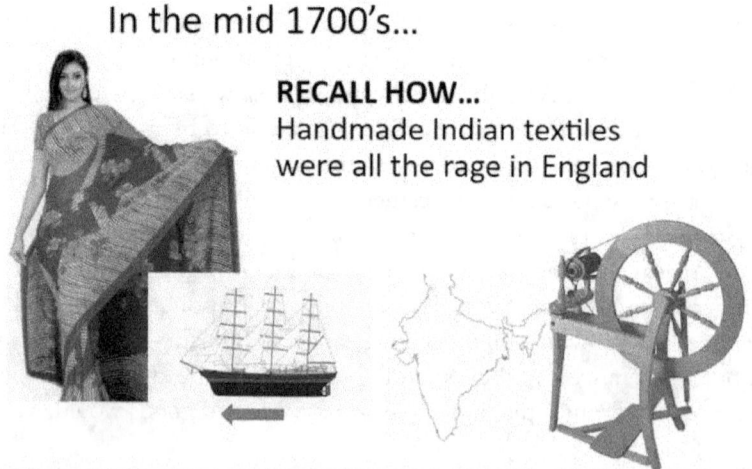

RECALL HOW...
Handmade Indian textiles were all the rage in England

126

Rapidly, what used to be a lucrative trade of handmade Indian textiles to England flip-flopped. India began furnishing cheap cotton to industrialists in Birmingham, Manchester, and Leeds, who would engage in a lucrative trade back to India, undercutting Indian weavers and putting them out of business.

Britain starts shipping machine-made textiles to India

...which completely destroys the Indian weavers

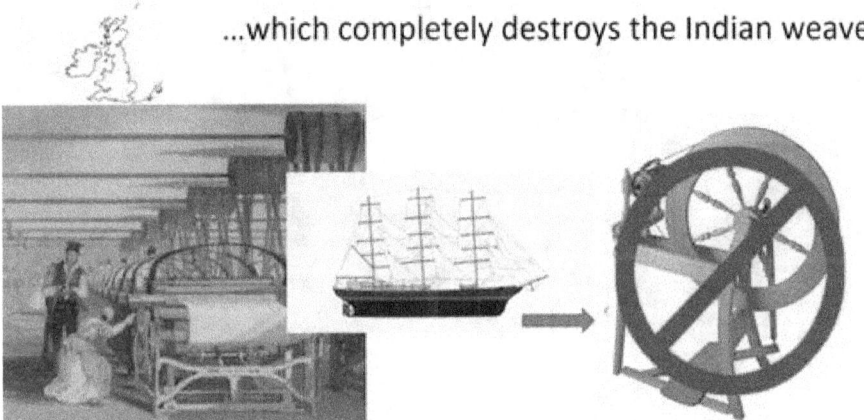

China will be a tougher market to crack, but a similar reversal is about to happen there, as well.

In 1793, nearly three centuries on from the time when European traders began to take over the Indian Ocean and the South China Sea, Emperor Qianlong of the Qing Dynasty sends a letter to England's King George III. It is the king who had initiated contact. He is desperate to establish trade relations with China, as his subjects have acquired an insatiable taste for Chinese tea. The reply he receives is,

> Our Celestial Empire possesses all things in abundance and lacks no product within its own borders. There is no need to import the manufactures of outside barbarians in exchange for our own produce. But as tea, silk and porcelain are absolute necessities to yourselves, we have permitted, as a favor, that your wants might be supplied.

What can the British do now that the emperor has made it clear they have no bargaining power? Some enterprising early British industrialists are beginning to experiment with knocking off Chinese porcelain, but those fine cups will sit empty without continuing to cough up silver for high-priced Chinese tea. As late as the early 1830's, China still has an annual trade surplus with the British of over five million ounces of silver.

In the early 1830's the Chinese have a trade surplus of over 5 million ounces of silver

It is British expansion into agricultural land in India that will bail them out. In the far northwest, poppies thrive. Opium poppies. The drug, in small doses, is common in England and other parts of the West as the basis of *laudanum*, taken for any number of small ills without the need of a prescription. In Southeast Asia, it is mixed with tobacco and smoked in pipes. This habit spreads to the south of China.

Opium processed in India under British supervision is soon being shipped from Calcutta and sold to Chinese smugglers who begin to operate in the many inlets off the Pearl River Delta, just east of the old Portuguese trading center of Macao. As the supply of the drug increases, smokers begin to forego the tobacco and fill their pipes with it. Soon there are a significant number of addicts... and a thriving black market. Not only the British, but also the Americans and others begin to set up permanent trading centers at the port in Guangdong (Canton).

And in only a few years, the British–Chinese trade imbalance completely reverses itself (much as the British-Indian imbalance in textiles had)...

By the late 1850's the Chinese have a trade <u>deficit</u> of 5 million ounces of silver

The emperor is incensed—not only from the loss of trade revenue, but also because of what the spread of opium addiction is doing to the Chinese workforce. The attitudes of the Westerners no doubt irk him as well—barbarians who refuse to kowtow and expect to be treated as equals of the Middle Kingdom. In the summer of 1839, he sends one of his most trusted commissioners to Guangdong to take stock of the situation and respond appropriately.

Soon after his arrival, Commissioner Lin quarantines all of the Westerners who are based in Guangdong, seizes all the opium they have in stock, and sets about destroying it, dumping it into a holding pond and mixing it with lime and salt. Then he pens a letter to be taken back to the British ruler (who at this time is the 20-year-old Queen Victoria). In it, he writes,

> There are those who smuggle opium to seduce the Chinese people and so cause the spread of the poison to all provinces. Such persons who only care to profit themselves, and disregard their harm to others, are not tolerated by the laws of Heaven and are unanimously hated by human beings. His Majesty the Emperor, upon hearing of this, is in a towering rage.... Let us ask, where is your conscience? I have heard that the smoking of opium is very strictly forbidden by your country; that is because the harm caused by opium is clearly understood. Since it is not permitted to do harm to your own country, then even less should you let it be passed on to the harm of other countries!

He goes on to say that anyone caught either selling or smoking opium in future will be executed.

It is unlikely that the letter ever finds its intended audience. The members of the Company are still operating with a great amount of independence and likely are confident they can sidestep their neophyte queen. One thing they do relate to her, and to the lords in her Parliament, is that the honor of Great Britain is impinged by having its citizens held captive and its ships detained in port.

Once the commissioner is assured that all opium stocks have been destroyed, the port is reopened. Henceforward, before an incoming ship can berth the captain will have to sign a bond stating that there is no opium on board. When the proud British refuse, the Chinese refuse to trade at all with them. For a time, they have to acquire their precious tea from a few American merchants who have no quibble abiding with China's demands. In fact, they find they can charge the Brits enough for tea to almost make up for the revenue lost in opium!

Meanwhile, British ships sit idle across the river mouth from Macao at Hong Kong, which is at this time nothing but a large protected bay. That is, until a particularly impudent British merchant ship arrives from India, sails straight up to Guangdong, signs the bond and takes on a load of tea. Two British naval ships chase after them. They will likely be too late to stop them, but they don't want other merchants, anxious to resume trade, to follow suit.

The Chinese, not understanding that the British navy ships are pursuing their own merchants, send 16 war junks out to block the navy's approach. When the British do not alter course, the Chinese open fire.

The first shots fired in what is known to history as the First Opium War are arrows shot from bows. They tear through the rigging of the British ships and fall upon empty decks. In the traditional Chinese style of naval warfare, a hail of arrows would disable the enemy's rigging and cause large numbers of casualties. The war junk would then ram into the disabled ship and its crew would grapple and board it. Once on board, they excelled at hand-to-hand combat. But these British ships have auxiliary steam power so are not fazed by the arrows. Their crews have no intention of engaging in hand combat. Safely below decks, they man the cannons....And unleash what is known as a broadside, where all of the cannons are synchronized to fire at once. They are not pointed at the enemy's rigging; they are pointed at the waterline. When a junk is torn open by such a blast, it begins immediately to sink.

The battle is a shocking humiliation for the Middle Kingdom, and it leads the British to further press their advantage. In the spring of the following year, they send a fleet north up the coast and capture the island of Chusan, which lies at the eastern point of the bay that leads to Hangzhou. They hold the island hostage and write their own letter to the Chinese ruler, listing these demands:

- Allow unfettered trade not only with Guangdong, but with five other major ports
- Officially cede us Hong Kong

- Compensate us for all the confiscated opium
- Recognize the British queen as the equal of the Chinese emperor, and treat our diplomats accordingly

Not receiving a reply, the British turn their sights again on Guangdong and sail a much larger fleet up the Pearl River, this time intent on forcing open trade rather than preventing it (and with no intention of signing any bond).

Two forts guard the Pearl River Delta narrows, but their outdated cannons are fix-mounted, and —unable to track the invader's maneuverable, iron-hulled steamships—much of their shot falls uselessly into the water. Once past the forts, British soldiers disembark and circle back to attack from behind. The Chinese defenders' 18th-century muskets are no match for modern British rifles.

The British get everything they ask for in the treaty that ends the First Opium War, signed in August 1842. It is the start of open season on China. The French and Americans both sign their own "unequal treaties" and the Russians and Germans start to move in, as well. From Shanghai to Macao, each of the opened port cities soon has a "concession" for each Western imperialist—a number of square blocks where the Westerners have complete *extraterritoriality* (where Chinese law does not apply).

Things go from bad to worse for the Qing Dynasty. Like the Mongols before them, the Qing are occupiers, having swept down from Manchuria. Though acculturated into China's dynastic tradition, they are distinguishable from their Han subjects. Women do not bind their feet. Men shave their heads except for a long ponytail. By the 19th century, corruption has become common in rural Manchu administrations, fostering enmity toward the outsiders. Now, humiliation by the barbarians only intensifies disloyalty among the common people.

In 1850, in a rural area not far from Guangdong, a man named Hong Xiuquan ("Shi-oh chun") declares that he is the brother of Jesus. He begins to blend a distorted version of Christianity with a sense of Han nationalism, and rapidly acquires followers intent on expelling the Manchus and bringing about a Heavenly Kingdom. They become known as the Taiping, which translates literally to "great peace."

It is quite the misnomer. The Taiping Rebellion will last 15 years. Over 25 million will be killed. Many Cantonese flee abroad, drawn to California and its gold rush or to work building the transcontinental railroad. The Taiping move north and then downriver along the Yangtze, where they capture the old imperial capital of Nanking and make it their own.

Overlapping with the Taiping Rebellion, the *Second* Opium War is fought. In the third year of the war, as combined British and French forces advance on Beijing, the emperor ignominiously evacuates the capital and flees to his hunting lodge on the other side of the Great Wall, leaving his brother in charge. He tries to frame his cowardice positively by publicizing that he will not let the actions of barbarians interfere with his hunting plans.

When the Europeans enter the city, they avoid the more impregnable Forbidden City and head instead for the Summer Palace, a place of great beauty to which the emperor and his retinue repair during the warmest months. It is a manicured setting of small lakes and island palaces filled with treasured works of art dating back to earlier dynasties.

Plunder is an important, expected component of the compensation for both British and French soldiers. The troops are set free to make off with whatever they can carry.

Prince Gong, who is an abler ruler than his brother, knows that he is out-gunned by the Europeans. He also correctly surmises that they have no intention of conquering China. He knows their core motivation is making money, not building empire. Though he regards them as barbarian in their morality, he knows they are the opposite in their technology, and he realizes that China can learn from them. For these reasons, he decides to accommodate them in China's midst, and possibly even put them to use.

Shortly before the emperor's departure, an advance delegation of about 20 Britons had been taken hostage. The prince now agrees to release them at once and pay an indemnity. He also allows the British and French to garrison troops in a quarter of the capital. They, along with the Russians and Americans, will be allowed to establish embassies. They all will be granted access to ten more ports and be allowed to navigate freely on the Yangtze River.

A formal agreement is signed and the invading forces prepare to withdraw. But on the morning when that withdrawal is to occur, columns of smoke begin to rise from northwest of the city. The beautiful Summer Palace is being destroyed.

When a detachment of imperial guards reaches the grounds, they find a message from the British commander. Not all of the 20 hostages had been returned alive. During their confinement, they were starved, deprived of water, taunted, and beaten. The commander has decided there must be punishment for this "horror and indignation." So he has ordered the entire 740-acre complex to be burned to the ground.

(8)

Though this event will blacken the relationship between the Chinese people and the British for decades, Prince Gong goes forward with his plan to work with them. He purchases British rifles for the Chinese troops, forms a force to attack the Taiping, and places a British officer in command. Within months, the 15-year rebellion is quashed.

By then, the emperor, never having returned to his capital, is dead at the age of 30. He has no surviving son with the empress, but before he took his last breath, the Number One Concubine had brought her young son to his bedside, where he deemed him the successor to the Dragon Throne.

Until the new emperor comes of age, the empress and the concubine will become a dual regency. The empress is only a pretty face, but the concubine has keen political acumen. While in the service of the emperor, she was addressed as the Noble Consort Yi. Now she takes the name of Cixi ("Suh-shi"). She is wisely wary of the Westerner's appetites and does not favor Prince Gong's openness to them. She will become his formidable adversary in the years to come.

While a tug-of-war between modernizers like Prince Gong and traditionalists like Cixi continued for another four-plus decades in China, in Japan the modernizers had already won.

For 250 years, it had been quite the opposite. The country had been a feudal assortment of warring samurai. Portuguese Jesuit missionaries had been highly active there in the later 16th century. Then, in 1603, centralized control was imposed by the Tokugawa Shogunate. (A shogunate is a dynasty where the ruler has the title of shogun, rather than emperor, because there already is a hereditary emperor, although he has no power whatsoever.)

The first Tokugawa shogun decreed there would be no more Jesuits, no more Christianity, no more foreigners, period!

It was soon decided that Western goods were not so bad as Western ideas, so an exception was made. The Protestant Dutch, being neither as evangelical as the Portuguese nor as pompous as the British, would be Japan's only conduit to the outside world. But they would be limited to a tiny island in the harbor of the port city of Nagasaki, and a short footbridge would be *their* only conduit to the Japanese home island.

Fast forward to 1853, and we have a high-tech American ship steaming its way into the harbor at Edo (modern-day Tokyo), where the Tokugawa are based. It carries a letter from President Millard Fillmore. He is smart enough to address it to the Emperor of Japan but deliver it to the shogun. In part, it reads,

> [T]he United States and Japan should live in friendship and have
> commercial intercourse with each other.... The Constitution and laws
> of the United States forbid all interference with the religious or political
> concerns of other nations.... We know that the ancient laws of your
> imperial majesty's government do not allow of foreign trade, except
> with the Chinese and the Dutch; but as the state of the world changes
> and new governments are formed, it seems to be wise, from time to time,
> to make new laws....

Fillmore also has two specific "requests." First, should American whalers that operate in the area be shipwrecked, that the Japanese treat them kindly and respect their property until they can be rescued. ("We are very much in earnest in this," Fillmore says.) Second, that American steamships be allowed to stop in Japan to supply themselves with coal and provisions. ("We are very desirous of this," he says.) He then concludes,

> These are the only objects for which I have sent Commodore Perry,
> with a powerful squadron, to pay a visit to your imperial majesty's
> renowned city of Edo: friendship, commerce, a supply of coal and
> provisions, and protection for our shipwrecked people.

As expected, the not-so-subtle reference to a powerful squadron precipitates much debate within the Tokugawa castle. One Lord Li sums up the prevailing sentiment: "There is a saying that when one is besieged in a castle, to raise the drawbridge is to imprison oneself."

The "castle" he refers to in this case is, of course, the Japanese homeland, for which the drawbridge is about to come down...

The shogun grants the Americans access to two ports, after which several other foreign industrialists come calling and are given similar privileges.

Rather than just passively acquiesce, modernizers in Japan have another idea. They have the benefit of seeing how the foreigners have treated the Chinese, taking a foot for every inch they are given, and they opt to become takers, themselves.

In 1867, a group of samurai oust the shogun. Don't imagine this group as traditional swordsmen. They are businessmen. Family businesses engaged in cottage industries like the brewing of sake or soy sauce had sprung up in Japan even before the arrival of the Americans.

The group rallies around (and exerts their influence upon) the new emperor, who was only one year old when Perry's ships came to Edo. And Japan begins a remarkable transition...

Samurai families start sending their most promising sons to Europe or Hawaii to study the ways of the Westerners. And they are enormously quick studies.

A constitution is written and a republican government created. A modern

the Meiji

...and the power behind the throne

banking system is established. A network of railroads is built. Factories are established by the government, then sold to the wealthiest families. By the 1890's, the country is fully industrialized. For going along with all these reforms, Emperor Mutsuhito will go down in Japanese history as the Meiji—the enlightened one.

China continues to go the other direction. Prince Gong has retreated from the public eye and the movement in favor of modernization drifts, leaderless. Cixi establishes herself as the de facto ruler, the Empress Dowager. As the British turn their Beijing legation into a little patch of home, with cricket grounds and a racecourse, no less, the empress smolders in the Forbidden City, averse to any break with tradition.

In Shanghai, in 1876, a British trading firm constructs a railroad from the American concession to their own. It doesn't last. Cixi, who detests the noise and smoke of the iron beast, orders it disassembled.

But she has graver worries. There has been a severe drought in northern China, and now people are starting to starve. The empire's population, the world's largest, exceeds 300 million, and the failed harvest can't keep pace.

As the drought continues into its second year, infanticide increases and fathers sell their grown daughters into prostitution. If anyone is caught stealing, they are placed in bamboo "hunger cages" suspended off the ground in the village square, denied food or water until they die of thirst. People resort to eating earth and boiling the thatch from their roofs.

China's First Great Famine lasts for three years. By the autumn of 1879, more than ten million people have died.

At the same time that many in China are starving, Queen Victoria is being celebrated as the Empress of India. The now 57-year-old queen makes her first appearance on the subcontinent, ceremonially affirming the Government of India Act, which was established back in 1858. That is the year that the British government officially took over from the British East India Company. After the sepoy's rebellion the year before, they felt they had to.

A sepoy was a member of an all-Indian British police force. When European industrialists took over a land, they had to be able to administrate it in the way they wished, despite being far outnumbered by the local population. To do this, they would create a local police force and afford them privileges to keep them happy.

Of course, the Indians had much to be *un*happy about: resentment over what the British were doing to their textile trade, high land taxes, disrespect for Indian traditions, and imposition of British social reforms. So there was a lot of pressure weighing on whatever happiness the sepoys derived from their privileged position. It all boiled over because of a rumor.

The force was issued new rifle cartridges, and it was rumored they had been greased with either cow or pork fat or a combination thereof, depending on whose story you heard. The cow is sacred to Hindus, and Muslims are prohibited from eating pork (which could be ingested, as these were paper cartridges that were typically licked in the process of loading), so sepoys of both religions were highly offended. Soldiers who refused to use the new cartridges were thrown in the brig, which made all of the others take exception and turn on their officers.

The mutiny spread from town to town. There were many cruel acts of carnage on both sides. The sepoys massacred women and children; the British summarily executed sepoys in the field, sometimes by strapping them over the mouths of cannons. Hostilities lasted for a year and half. In the end, the Company was told to back off while the Crown took over.

Another tactic industrialized nations used in their spheres of control was to employ both the carrot and the stick. There hence would be more British soldiers about and some stricter regulations, but the Crown would spend more time listening to the Indians' concerns than the Company ever had.

Indians employed a similar two-pronged approach in fighting for their rights. Terrorists bombed rail cars and bridges; meanwhile, an Indian National Congress met for the first time in 1885 to peacefully raise suggestions for more equitable cohabitation with the interlopers.

By the middle of the century, the interior of Africa is one place where no trade has yet occurred. As related in Chapter 6, African rivers are filled with rapids and difficult to navigate. But the industrialists now have smaller iron-hulled steamships with low drafts that can make their way inland. The obstacle that remains is mosquito-borne malaria.

Around 1850, the French discover that consuming quinine water makes the body unappealing to the mosquito. Quinine comes from the bark of a South American tree. It was discovered by the Spanish during the waning years of New Castille. This is the key that unlocks the last door.

But it isn't open season on Africa quite yet. Only a few adventurers are up to the task of penetrating the jungle of the central interior. One became famous: Dr. David Livingstone, an English humanitarian, comes to live among the poorest of the sub-Saharan peoples and share his medical knowledge. It is sadly ironic that the notoriety of this good man will lead to horrors inflicted on the very people he came to assist.

By 1871, no one has heard from Livingstone for five years. It is assumed he is either lost or dead. An American newspaper runs a contest offering a significant cash prize for anyone who can find him. A wealthy Welsh-American immigrant by the name of Henry Morton Stanley is the one to do it.

Stanley's escapade draws the attention of King Leopold II of Belgium, who hires him to survey the Congo River Basin.

For a king, Leopold is very much a man of the times. Unlike others of his rank who are tolerated or sidestepped by their country's industrialists, he is out front, seeking solutions to the overproduction issue. In addition to expanding markets, he ponders a different variable in the equation of capitalist success: raw materials.

Acquiring raw materials needed for production at the lowest possible cost has, of course, been an ongoing issue. But also, if *new* raw materials can be found, it will help ease the impact of overproduction. They can be fashioned into *new* products that might breathe new life into the local market.

Before describing the appalling behavior of the European industrialists in Africa, it is important to get into their minds. It should be a lesson for those alive today to look at how their misguided mindsets are formed: They do not zoom out and look at history from 30,000 feet; they are influenced by only their recent history. Their discovery of the new technology of industry makes them think

1. We are the most mentally advanced of the world's peoples.
2. Industry is progress, and progress is the God-given mission for humankind.
3. The natural resources of Earth exist to be used in the furtherance of this mission.

4.   If these resources exist where they are not being extracted and used to support industrial progress, then it is our duty as the most mentally advanced people to use our superior technology to extract them and put them to use.

A French economist will ultimately state this openly:

> A great part of the world is inhabited by barbarian tribes or savages [who] do not know how to exploit their land and its natural riches.... This state of the world implies for the civilized people a right of intervention.

Stanley returns from the Congo with the area mapped and having discovered the presence of huge forests of rubber trees. Outside these forests there are promising sites to dig for minerals, where ultimately diamonds and copper will be found. These three resources will prove invaluable in the years ahead: rubber for tires, diamonds for cutting machines, and copper for electrical wire.

Leopold immediately sends troops and administrators to establish an occupation. The interior of the Congo is vast—two million square kilometers. But as soon as the French and Portuguese establish camps only a short way inland along the Congo River, Leopold decides to act fast. It is he who calls the other European heads of state together and establishes the meeting in Berlin.

The great "Scramble for Africa" has begun. Leopold is given deference for his foresight in bringing all the European industrial powers together to hash out any conflicts up front. He stakes out his claim, then sits back to watch the proceedings.

Given their myopic view of history, the Europeans think of Africa only in its present, disastrous state. They do not think of that state as being caused by the recently-concluded era of the Atlantic Slave Trade and the post-abolition collapse of the economy. Instead, they attribute Africa's problems to their perception of its inhabitants as primitive. Therefore, in deciding how to divvy the continent up, they pay no heed at all to already-established African borders; they only focus on their own geographical needs, such as port and river access and the location of various resources.

The map at right shows the existing African borders. Compare these to the next map, which shows the borders of the European colonies that are eventually created.

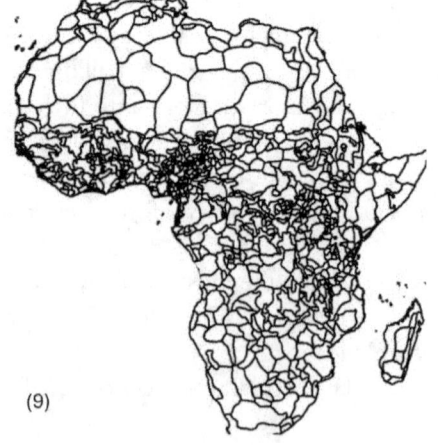

(9)

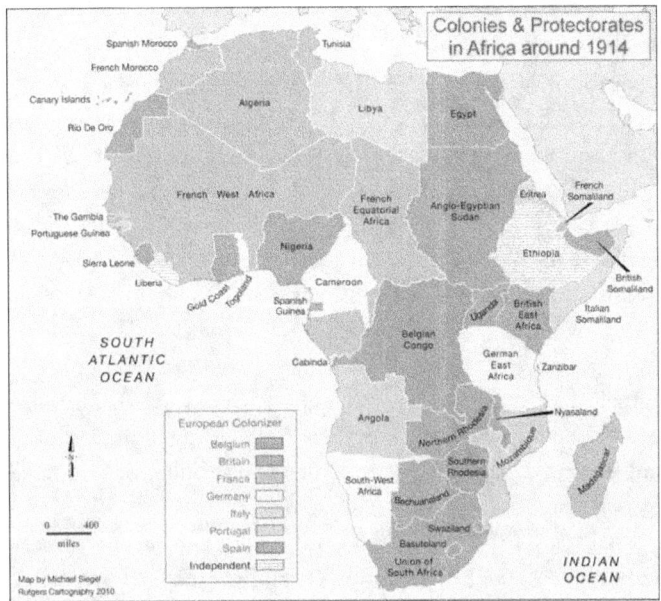

As you can see, in many cases multiple ethnicities are forced together while many single ethnicities are split across multiple colonies.

Aside from Liberia, which the Americans have already established as a "homeland" to which they have been deporting freed slaves, the entire continent is up for grabs.

(The Italians initially get Ethiopia out of the deal, but the Ethiopians have other ideas. Playing the British against the Italians, they are able to get hold of some advanced weaponry, which they use to successfully defend their mountainous domain.)

Recall that the slave trade left many bitter hatreds between neighbors because certain African nations had conducted raids to kidnap non-prisoners who never should have been enslaved. The strategy the British used in India of giving privileges to the sepoys and using them to control the larger Indian population now has a name: "divide and rule." In Africa, it is especially effective if an ethnicity that was wronged by its neighbors in the slave trade is now given privileged treatment in exchange for keeping those neighbors down.

And so the colonization of Africa exacerbates what the slave trade began. Hatreds from that era deepen. More than 100 years in the future, in Rwanda, they will erupt in genocide.

Whereas last time around, the Europeans dealt equally with African kings who were willing to engage in the trade of human beings, this time they enslave the very continent itself. Employing advanced industrial weaponry and the tactic of divide and rule, a minority of Europeans will master the African population and bend them to their will.

Nowhere is this more graphically illustrated than Leopold's Congo. He elevates one ethnic group to make them his *Force Publique*, charged with making regular rounds to villages to collect the rubber harvest. Every able-bodied villager, beginning at a very young age, is expected to take part in the harvest, and the quotas are quite aggressive.

Leopold does not rely on old hatreds alone to ensure the members of his force exert the requisite amount of pressure on the villagers. There are a number of rules. Rule number one: Force members are ordered to kill any villagers who do not fulfill their personal quota. To prove they did this, they are to cut off the hands of each villager killed. When they return to base, they must have either:

- an amount of rubber to match their quota, OR
- an amount of hands to make up for the shortfall.

Otherwise, *they* may be killed.

Leopold is very cognizant of expenses. No bullets are to be wasted. They are checked before members of the Force embark on their route, and reconciled with severed hands when they return. They had better return every bullet or else have a pair of hands to show for it.

Imagine you are a member of the *Force Publique* out on your route for a week. There are dangers in the jungle. Maybe you are threatened by a leopard or a nasty hyena. Or perhaps you are hungry (Leopold is keeping an eye on his expenses in feeding you, as well), and this tempts you to shoot an aardvark for your dinner.

Your week goes relatively well. You only have to kill one villager. As you turn back toward base, you realize that you have two hands in your bag, yet you used two bullets, which means you are two hands short. You don't want to kill any more villagers because you need all of them to harvest rubber; you'll only hurt yourself in the future. You don't want to start a war with your fellow *Force Publique* men; they will retaliate. What do you do?

The standard practice in this situation becomes to cut one hand from a villager for each number that you are short. It is important to cut only one hand, so that the worker still has one they can use to harvest rubber.

But that is only the beginning.

If you have read your Adam Smith, you certainly know the law of supply and demand. When demand is high for something that is difficult to supply, the price shoots up. Fear of punishment—perhaps *capital* punishment—for being caught short of hands makes the demand for hands by *Force Publique* men extremely high.

Next simple law of economics: When something demands a very high price, more people want to supply it. You know what's coming next... Hands begin to be harvested *before* they are needed. Jungle entrepreneurs terrorize villagers, taking away hands in their backpacks, then getting away to hideouts, where they can await the next member of the *Force Publique* to come by with a desperate look in their eyes. Leopold's callous greed has led to a proto-industrial market for human hands.

Leopold hid all this behind a sham organization called the International

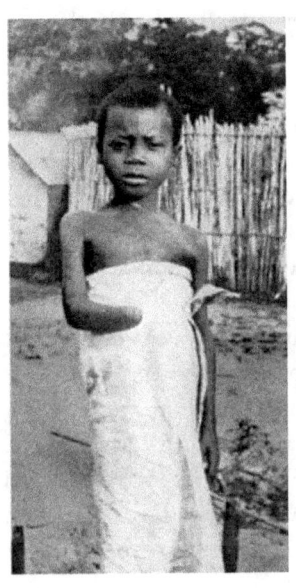

African Association, a nonprofit assumed to be doing humanitarian work. Even his subjects in Belgium had no idea what was going on. Unlike the other divisions established by the conference in Berlin, the Congo was not a government-sponsored colony; it was more like Leopold's private, two-million-square-kilometer estate.

Word did not get out about the atrocities in the Congo until the new century. It took 23 years to catch up to Leopold and transfer his holding to the Belgian government. He died the next year.

In addition to the human suffering, forced division of established political entities, and fomenting of antagonism between ethnic groups, Africa was stripped of its natural wealth and set up for continuing economic failure.

All of the rest of the world outside of the few industrialized nations was set up for some degree of economic failure, but Africa was in the worst shape. The extraction of natural resources came to dominate the economy, just as the extraction of human beings had dominated it in the prior century. But whereas before Africans were a part of that profiteering, now they are only the laborers in a trade run entirely by foreigners.

Latin America's setback from its encounter with the industrialists, though not as decimating, was just as enduring. Only *dependent* economies developed. Ruling *criollos* were in league with foreigners who came to extract resources. This alone made the ruling class very wealthy, so they had no incentive to develop industries of their own. They spent their newfound wealth on the foreigners' products, giving foreign economies the new markets that would relieve their overproduction. The *mestizo* workers who performed the hard labor in the mines and fields, however, were paid too little to afford the new manufactured goods.

Most of Latin America will suffer this extreme economic leveling many decades into the 20th century. The one exception will be Mexico, where a social revolution from 1910 to 1920 will achieve partial success, establishing an unstable democracy. They will also be successful in countering attempts by the United States to meddle in the revolution in order to protect American business interests.

After finally dispensing with slavery (although not with suppression of the rights of slaves' descendants), from the 1870's on, the USA expands apace. Railroads connect every corner of the country's original borders and soon stretch to the Pacific Coast. By the end of the century, the indigenous American population has been forced into scattered reservations and their young people sent to boarding schools with the objective of erasing their culture and indoctrinating them in the ways of their conquerors.

In 1898, the US starts a war with Spain. The Spanish have been mostly shut out of the Scramble for Africa, but they still hold Cuba, where local unrest provides an excuse for the Americans to get involved. Sensationalist news reporting about supposed atrocities committed by the Spanish rally the American public to support the war. But the real driver, behind the scenes, is—you guessed it—American business interests. Cuba is the world's leading producer of sugar. It has an economically dependent relationship controlled by American sugar distributors.

As part of the war, the Americans also attack the Spanish-held Philippine Islands. In the Philippines, where an active rebellion has been going on for some time, rebels are being rounded up and tossed in concentration camps. This is worse than anything going on in Cuba, but hasn't made the news since there is not any American agribusiness in the Philippines that needs protecting.

After American victory, Cuba becomes independent. Well, sort of: They have to get all of their trade deals and foreign policy decisions approved by the US. Technically, that makes them a *protectorate*, which is a nice way to say that they do not have full sovereignty. The US protects them from making bad decisions –like deciding to allow another industrialist country to edge in on the American sugar business.

The Philippines is handed over to American control. For a minute, the Filipinos embrace the Americans as their liberators, but then US president McKinley decides that he is not going to liberate them. Instead, the USA becomes their new overlord. So the Filipinos continue their rebellion against a new enemy. And the Americans start tossing Filipino rebels into the same concentration camps set up by the Spanish.

The Philippine-American War drags on for 14 years before the rebellion is finally put down. Over 50,000 Filipino lives are lost; two-thirds of these are civilians.

American leadership, encouraged by American business, had decided that the Philippines were important to them as a "stepping stone" to the great Chinese market.

Uncle Sam, stepping on the Philippines, carries American overproduction to a welcoming China.

Though not with the open arms portrayed in the image above, China is indeed opening up. Weakened by the Great Famine, it has gone on to suffer the ultimate indignity. It is preyed upon by a former tributary state: Japan.

As soon as its industry is up and running, Japan begins to modernize its military. It is an affront to the Chinese when Japan takes over Korea; it is the first time China has lost a tributary state to a different overlord. From there, the Japanese begin to meddle in Manchuria, the Qing Dynasty's ancestral home.

From 1894 to 1895, the Sino-Japanese war is fought. You can see in this illustration that it does not go well for the Chinese. Also note in the lower right corner how closely this development is being followed by a vulture-like flock of Western reporters...

(10)

Soundly defeated, China is made to cede the island of Taiwan to the Japanese and recognize the independence of Korea.

Now China is weak enough to embolden the industrialists to start negotiating how to divide it up. This was similar to what the industrialists did to Africa, but with two significant differences: First, they do not set up governing control. Instead, they expand bases where they have extraterritoriality. From these, they trade freely within a designated geographical *sphere of influence*. Second, where the industrialists' primary involvement in Africa is the extraction and removal of natural resources, in China it is relieving overproduction by selling manufactured goods to the huge Chinese population.

In the cartoon from L-R, Britain's Queen Victoria, Germany's Kaiser Wilhelm and Russia's Tsar Nicholas II prepare to carve while Japan ponders its slice and France peers over Russia's shoulder.

The British claim a sphere comprising Hong Kong and Guangdong, Tibet, and the Yangtze River Valley, including the area around Shanghai, Nanking, and Hangzhou. France's sphere extends northward from their colony of Indochina (present-day Vietnam, Cambodia, and Laos). Japan takes a piece of the mainland near Taiwan. Germany has the small province of Shandong, north of Nanking. Russia has all of the far north, from Xinjiang in the west across to Manchuria, which is also claimed by Japan. This eventually leads to the 1904–1905 Russo-Japanese War. Once again, Japan is victorious. Its defeat of a European power is a wake-up call as to just how far it has come (and how quickly it got there).

◇◇◇

As China's disastrous 19th century draws to a close, in Beijing, Empress Dowager Cixi worries that the Mandate of Heaven is about to be withdrawn. But there is one more fight left in her.

Cixi is not responsible for the peasant uprising that the foreigners call the Boxer Rebellion, and it will remain unclear whether or how actively she supports it. Like the Taiping, the Boxers are something of a cult. They call themselves the Righteous and Harmonious Fists and practice martial arts like kickboxing, which is where they get the "Boxer" label. Unlike the Taiping, they respect the Manchus and their leader. Their target is the foreigners and those Chinese who support them.

The Boxers don't fight like rebels in a war. They wear red bandanas and launch red balloons to announce their arrival in an area. They put up signs that say, "Barbarians out!" or, "Traitors die!" They pound their drums and march and drill, waging a mental war. Then they strike silently in the night, slitting a foreigner's throat, slaughtering Chinese converts in a Christian mission, or burning down the warehouse of a merchant who has gotten rich via foreign trade.

As they descend upon the capital in the summer of 1900, an international relief force begins marching inland from the port of Tianjin. In their separate compounds in the Legation Quarter, British, American, French, Japanese, German, Russian, Dutch, and Italian expatriates are quarantined for their own safety. They watch the red balloons float overhead and keep a lookout for movement in the surrounding streets. They listen to the drums and the footfall of the marchers. At night, they see the random flicker of torchlight.

Rumors circulate. Cixi is staying out at the Summer Palace, among the ruins, in restored quarters on one of the islands. Now word comes that she has arrived back in the Forbidden City with a small body of troops. Can it be good news? Or is she supporting the rebels?

While Boxers in Tianjin delay the relief force, the siege of the legations drags on for nearly two months, but finally the massive international force arrives. Reminiscent of the end of the Second Opium War, Cixi flees to the ancient capital of Xian in the west, leaving a prince behind to conduct negotiations.

It isn't until *18 months later* that Cixi and her court are borne by train(!) back to the capital and received with great ceremony at Beijing Railway Station. This is obviously a *new* Cixi. Immediately, she begins to implement sweeping reforms.

She sends her high officials to Japan and Europe to learn about Western law, government, and education. She orders an overhaul of the civil service examinations, downplaying Confucian text and calligraphy and expanding into engi-

145

neering and science. She even begins inviting ladies of the foreign community to garden parties at the Summer Palace.

...And in 1903, at the age of 68, she allows a Western-educated photographer to take this picture of her. Check out those nails!

Just before her death in 1908, Cixi installs the two-year-old Puyi, grandson of her favorite general and great-grandson of a previous emperor, as her successor. The child will be the last emperor of China. The modernizers have been busy since Cixi's return, and during the Puyi regency, they pull it all together.

The man they choose to lead them is Dr. Sun Yat-Sen. Sun grew up in Hawaii, receiving a Western education there and in Hong Kong. He became a revolutionary in the 1890's and was exiled to London for a time, then traveled widely in an attempt to attain financial support to overthrow the Qing.

Finally, on January 1, 1912, a provisional government of a new Republic of China is formed with Sun as president. The 6-year-old Puyi (with some help from his regents) abdicates on February 12. After more than 3,500 years, the history of the world's oldest empire is at its end. China's struggles, however, will continue.

CHAPTER TWELVE

A "War to End All Wars"
Sows the Seeds for Many More
(1913-1923)

It would not have taken an especially prescient futurist to envision a day when the cordial diplomacy of the industrialists, dictating the fates of the world's nonindustrialized peoples with the civility of swapping trading cards, would begin to break down. In fact, if you look closely at the cartoon on page 144, you may note a bit of tension between Kaiser Wilhelm (stabbing his knife somewhat aggressively) and his cousin, Queen Victoria.

Victoria passed away in 1901 after a 64-year reign, during which the British had built an industrial empire where "the sun never sets," possessing Australia and small bites of Central and South America, in addition to their longtime holdings in the Caribbean and significant swaths of Africa and Asia. But the advantage Britain had built from its head start in industry was no more. It was still heavily invested in older technology, while later entrants like the United States and Germany had taken the lead in innovations like electrification and the internal combustion engine.

The British were still the undisputed ruler of the waves. But there was no guarantee that would last either; Germany's navy was gaining on them, and this would cause a naval arms race to heat up as the new century progressed. The Germans had the smallest sphere of influence in China, but now they were adding several islands in the western Pacific and a chunk of New Guinea. To taunt the British, Wilhelm proclaimed that Germany was carving out its *own* "place in the sun."

Wilhelm had lately gotten under France's skin, as well, by granting German-occupied Alsace-Lorraine statehood. France had never gotten over losing the region to Germany, even though the Franco-Prussian War was now four decades in the past.

Perhaps to regain its self-assurance in the face of German irreverence, Britain reached out to take Russia under its wing and help it develop its industry, which had only begun to blossom late in the preceding century. Russia was ruled by an absolute monarch, Tsar Nicholas II of the Romanov Dynasty. He was eager to modernize the country after being embarrassed by losing the war with Japan in 1905. Public dissatisfaction over that loss had led to a mini-revolution later the same year. Nicholas was forced to accept the establishment of a parliamentary body known as the Duma. But before too long, he was getting all of his friends elected, so it was never a strong check on his actions.

Just as Britain could bolster its self-importance by assisting the Russians, Russia had its own place to turn where it could feel important: the Balkan Peninsula. There, it could play the big brother to its ethnic relatives, the Slavs, who had been swept up by feelings of nationalism, and, stuck between the Austrian and Turkish empires, were itching for independence.

The Balkans are a mix of both ethnicities and religions. Political borders had shifted continually over the last 400 years, ever since the Turks were driven back from Vienna. Ethnically, the Slavs were separate from the Romanians, Bulgarians, Albanians, and Greeks. Internally, they were divided by religion. The Slovenes and Croats, who were physically closer to the West, were Catholic. The Serbs, like most of the non-Slavs, were Orthodox Christian. The Bosnians, stuck in the middle, were Muslim, as were the Albanians.

Unexpectedly, it is in the thick of this stew of minor players—situated between two not-so-industrial, old-fashioned, non-colonial empires—where the coming conflagration is going to begin... (11)

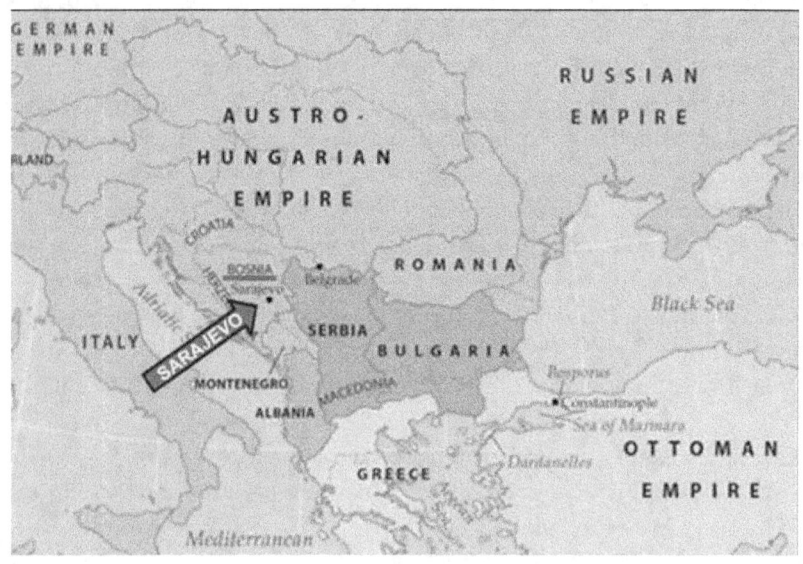

In 1875, a rebellion that began in Bosnia led to independence from the Turks for Serbia, Romania, and tiny Montenegro, but not for Bosnia itself. Instead, through an arrangement brokered by Russia, Bosnia was given to Austria, who merely occupied it for the next 30-plus years. The Austrians finally incorporated it into their empire in 1908. Now it is 1914, and the Serbs have become the leading advocate of unifying all of the Balkan Slavs into a new independent nation.

To counter the noise from the Serbs, the Austrian emperor, quite belatedly, decides to send his heir, Franz Ferdinand, to the Bosnian provincial capital of Sarajevo in order to formally welcome the Bosnians into the fold.

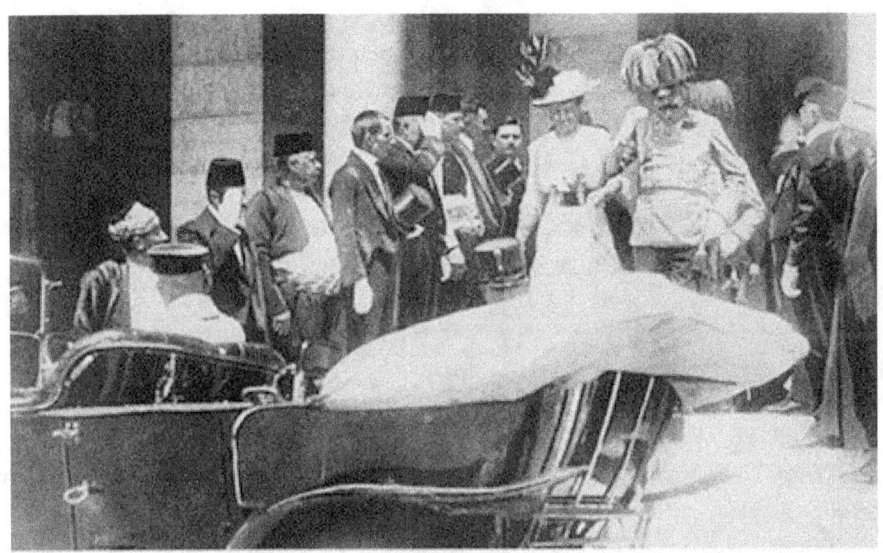

So here we have Franz and his wife, Sofie, on their way to the ceremony, all set to make the Bosnians feel proud to be part of such a fine empire. Franz even went for the fancy headdress with a full round of ostrich feathers this morning. The streets are crowded and, among the crowds, there are members of a pan-Slavic Serbian terrorist organization called the Black Hand. One of them tosses a bomb at their car, but it bounces off that folded canvas top.

Despite the bomb exploding under the next car in the motorcade, Franz stays on schedule and gives a little speech in the first planned ceremony. After that, the couple alters their schedule to stop by the hospital to see how those wounded in the explosion are doing. Then it is back into the car for one last ride. This time, the car happens to stall right in front of another assassin, who steps up and shoots them both.

Austria has no problem pinning the assassination on the Black Hand, and it turns its ire toward Serbia, who it thinks may be shielding the organization. Meanwhile, Germany pledges to support Austria, should there be any trouble with the Serbs.

The six major industrial powers had by this time aligned themselves into two "teams" of alliances. Britain and France had long ago signed an Entente Cordiale (cordial agreement) and had recently expanded this into a Triple Entente that included Russia. Germany, beginning to feel hemmed in on all sides, had drawn close to Austria, and they had added Italy. This evened things up three-on-three, each country promising to come to the aide of either of the others if they were ever attacked.

Nationalism, as the primary cause of World War One, cut two ways. There was the Slavs' yearning for nationhood that lit the spark of Franz Ferdinand's assassination. But that act would never have erupted into worldwide war without the extreme nationalist pride of those who had already achieved their own nations: France, which had started spreading nationalism in the Napoleonic Wars; Germany and Italy, who had recently unified; and Britain, with its long, proud history of parliamentarianism. The exclusivity of the imperialist club created an overabundance of hubris all around. This was the powder that threatened to explode, given any spark. If ever a war should result, both Germany and Britain were sure they would come out on top. In fact, Britain, in its heart of hearts, may have wished for a war to erupt, if only to put the upstart Germans in their place.

Four weeks pass before Austria throws down the gauntlet to the Serbs. On July 23, 1914, it issues an ultimatum: Serbia must suppress all anti-Austrian propaganda and root out all Serbian nationalist organizations. The clincher is that it must also allow Austrian officials access inside Serbia in order to conduct their own investigation of terrorist activity.

As expected, Serbia replies that it cannot allow Austria to conduct an internal investigation. Austria immediately suspends diplomatic relations with Serbia, and Serbia begins to mobilize troops to the Austrian border.

Russia attempts to persuade Austria to modify the terms of its ultimatum. The Austrians refuse and declare war on Serbia. In response, Russia begins to mobilize its troops, but not just to the Austrian border—to the German border, as well.

On August 1st, Germany declares war on Russia and on August 3rd, it attacks...

...Belgium. It marches its troops through Luxembourg and attacks Belgium.

Throughout the years of France's simmering desire for revenge, it has been slowly adding troops to the Maginot Line, a line of continuous fortification that stretches all along the border of Alsace-Lorraine, from Luxembourg to Switzerland. As it prepared for the war it knew was inevitable, Germany looked at the map of Europe and considered the following:

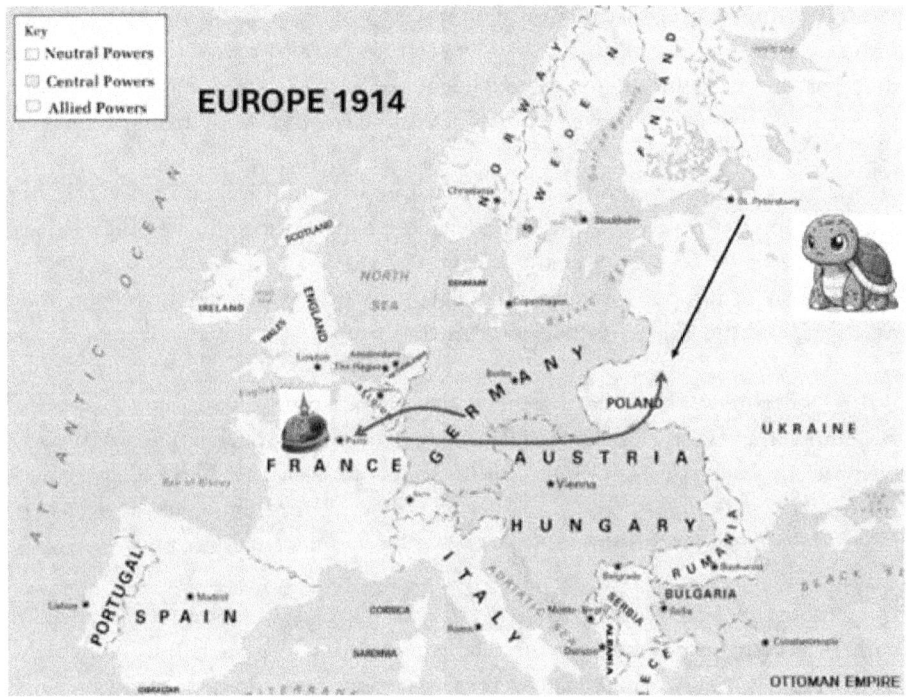

EUROPE 1914

1. Given the Triple Entente: If we are at war with Russia, we are at war with France.
2. We don't want to be fighting a war on two fronts.
3. Russia has a huge army, but it will mobilize slowly, due to its inferior railroads; we may not have to face them for a month.
4. A month is not enough time to break through the Maginot Line and reach Paris.
5. If, instead, we march through Belgium, we can surprise the French; with our allies, the Italians, attacking from the south, we will force them to surrender.
6. We have the best railroads in Europe. We can leave a small occupying force behind, then we can scoot our forces back east in time to meet the Russians at our border.

Confident in the success of this plan, the kaiser told his troops they would be home by the time the leaves began to fall.

But three things didn't happen according to script:

1. France and Italy had recently conducted negotiations pertaining to a dispute about their national borders. France had settled by relinquishing land to

the Italians; the details of the negotiation were not made public. Turns out what France got out of the deal was a promise from Italy to renege on the promise they had made to Germany about attacking France, should war begin. When Germany attacked, Italy stayed put and said it was withdrawing from its alliance.

2.   Belgium proved to be a significant obstacle. Germany thought they might simply get out of the way and let them pass through, but they denied them passage. They were prepared to fight the Belgians if need be, but figured they could quickly be overrun. But Belgian resistance was much tougher than expected, and the Germans lost precious time.

3.   Germany knew that Britain had made a promise eons ago to support Belgium if they were ever attacked. But they figured the British would not want to become embroiled in a war on the continent just to honor a moldy old agreement with a (so they thought) two-bit player like Belgium. But Britain, just as over-confident, saw it as an opportunity...

Before the German army could get to Paris, the French forces were reinforced with Brits who shipped across the English Channel. Together, they launched a counterattack. The Germans dug defensive trenches to hold their position. Then they launched an attack further to the north and west. So the French and British dug trenches and held their position. This back-and-forth dance continued all the way until it reached a dead end at the North Sea coast.

So for four more long years, this Western Front of the war would remain pretty much unchanged, with neither side able to advance. The defensive standoff was a result of two inventions of the previous century, one low-tech and one high: barbed wire, invented in the USA, where it played a major role in taming the Western frontier; and the machine gun, a British invention that played a large part in subduing nonindustrialized peoples around the world.

Barbed wire would be strung some yards ahead of the lead trench, where it hampered any attackers. Machine guns placed at the top of the trench could be aimed via periscope, keeping the operators from being exposed. The result was a lot of this >>>

Lives were wasted uselessly in order to gain forward progress that could be measured in yards, only to be lost again as the enemy countered with its own futile advance.

Of course, there was other technology applied in an effort to break the stalemate: Cannisters of poisonous gas were tossed at the enemy. This only led to gas masks becoming standard equipment.

Bigger and bigger guns rolled off the industrial assembly lines and were dispatched to the field. So underground bunkers were dug into the sides of trenches, where bombardments could be waited out.

The constant shelling only inflicted PTSD and devasted the terrain, turning idyllic farms and woodlands into a landscape that resembled the moon more than Earth...

The belligerent nations were shocked by what their industry wrought. They had expected a war like the glorious campaigns of the past. They had gone into battle outfitted for one. The French had worn smart blue uniforms with red pants. No one initially wore helmets. They had ridden horses.

Now, horses could be found rotting in the muck with their sides blasted open. Rats crawled everywhere. Despite putting down "billy boards" to walk upon, the water in the trenches permeated boots and led to cases of "trench foot," where the feet would numb and turn color and start to swell and decay.

Young men who marched into war with visions of glory and confident of a reasonably quick victory returned physically and mentally maimed. Unlike in wars to come, home fronts were mostly spared from first-person exposure, but abhorrence to accounts of the slaughter and the evidence of it that came home led to a worldwide movement for pacifism. It was humankind's moment of youthful idealism. People assured themselves, optimistically, that this was but a hard lesson learned. Now that the world had seen what industrialized warfare was like, no one would ever let it happen again.

After Italy's defection, Germany and Austria shopped around for a replacement and were able to convince the Ottoman Turks to join their side. Britain, France, and Russia promised Italy that if it joined *their* side, it would be rewarded with a chunk of Austrian territory once the war was won. This opened up another front in the Alps and forced Austria to fight on two fronts.

Of course, Germany, too, was now engaged on both fronts. It not only had to fight the Russians on its own border; it also had to bail out the Austrians, who were being driven inward by the Russians. In the East, the sides were not able to dig in like on the Western Front; there was too much front to cover. But the fighting was just as unproductive, with neither side able to gain the advantage for long.

Further east, the Turks struck at the Russians from their border in the Caucasus Mountain region. After being repelled by the Russians, they blamed it on Armenian spies. The Armenians were one of many not-so-happy ethnic nationalities within the Turkish Empire. Embittered by their defeat, the Turks began systematically slaughtering them.

Another unhappy ethnic nationality under control of the Turks, the Arabs, took advantage of the war to revolt. The British were happy to offer their assistance.

Called the Great War in its time, "World War One" is an accurate historical label, as fighting indeed spread even farther beyond Europe's borders. Britain had formed an alliance with Japan back in 1902 to check Russian expansion in China. The Japanese were happy to help the British in their present cause by pouncing on Germany's western Pacific islands and kicking them out of China's Shandong Province.

The British also coerced their colonies to fight. Australians kicked the Germans out of New Guinea. At a cost of a great number of lives, Kenyans in British East Africa took over German East Africa (modern-day Tanzania). The other German colonies in Africa, too, eventually fell to the British and French.

By the end of 1916, Germany had begun to push into Russia. Russia had no shortage of men to sacrifice, but it did have a shortage of guns. It couldn't supply them fast enough. This did not stop it from sending its troops into battle, however. Those at the rear of an attack would be sent forward empty-handed until they could pick up a gun from a fallen comrade ahead of them.

The Russian populace was beginning to suffer, as well, with food shortages. With the Turks now fighting against them, they could not get shipments of food and supplies through their Black Sea ports.

On the other side of Europe, the British had set up a naval blockade across the North Sea to prevent food and supplies from reaching Germany. Germany countered this by dispatching a fleet of submarines into those waters (its famous U-boats, short for *Unterseeboot*).

The United States had wisely kept out of the war, content to watch the European powers destroy each other while at the same time getting rich supplying both sides with war materials. Now, with the British blockade in place, that trade became decidedly one-sided. The USA had been financing the cash-strapped belligerents, and the debt it was owed by Britain and France began to pile up much faster than what it was owed by Germany. Would it ever recover that mounting debt if Germany won the war?

Germany's U-boats also began to interfere with American trade. They even attacked passenger liners that they suspected were carrying war supplies. Inevitably, American lives were lost, and American sentiment, which at first had been divided, began to tip the scale in the same direction as those British and French IOU's did: toward support for Britain and France.

But getting behind those two entailed getting behind Russia, as well, and that presented a moral issue for some (American president Woodrow Wilson among them) because Russia was an autocracy. That, however, was about to change.

Over the winter of 1916-17, Nicholas II managed to upset just about every segment of Russian society...

If you were a soldier, you didn't like him because he sent you into a meat-grinder of a war without a gun.

If you were a peasant, you didn't like him because the retreating Russian army was instructed to engage in "slash and burn," leaving a trail of desolation behind them, destroying crops so the advancing Germans couldn't eat them (and therefore neither could you).

If you were a noble, you didn't like him because he spent all his time away at the front and you didn't trust the tsarina, who you felt was falling under the spell of a shady character named Rasputin.

The faith-healer Rasputin was a fixture at court until his assassination by a cabal of noblemen in late December 1916.

If you were a factory worker, you didn't like him because he had made the Duma into a joke and his war was causing shortages, first in supplies, and now, more seriously, in bread.

When, in February, the government begins to implement food rationing, workers in St. Petersburg, the capital, begin to walk off their jobs.

The Russian Revolution has begun. As a social revolution, it will progress in stages very similar to those of the French Revolution.

Day by day, more workers join the others in the streets as urgent cables try to reach the tsar at the front. Nicholas, seemingly irritated by the interruption, orders soldiers to fire upon the protestors. Initially, a few dozen protestors are killed, but in the coming days the soldiers begin to refuse their orders. One garrison's soldiers turn and fire upon their officers instead. (Recall how the National Guard in Paris, called in to put down the storming of the Bastille, joined the people doing the storming.)

Finally realizing the seriousness of the situation, Nicholas boards a train to return to the capital. But the tracks have been blocked some kilometers out of town. There he sits, stuck on the tracks in the middle of nowhere, while messages from his closest advisers are relayed from the city. They tell him the only way to keep the peace is to abdicate. He feels he has no choice but to do as they say.

News of the tsar's abdication is greeted with great fanfare. A coalition of workers and soldiers form what is known as the St. Petersburg Soviet. A "soviet" is a people's assembly. Sessions are open to all. Anyone can get up on the dais and speak. Anyone in attendance can vote. It is direct democracy, in practice for the first time since the Athenians debated and voted on their issues in the marketplace.

A provisional government (PG) is put in place with liberal representatives (factory owners, etc.) drawn from the Duma. A dual authority is declared, where power will be shared between the PG and the Soviet.

Full democratic elections are promised to elect a constituent assembly tasked with writing a constitution. A giddy sense of optimism is pervasive. People feel something new and special is being created. They call each other "Comrade." (Recall how the Parisians, at the pinnacle of their optimism, called each other "Citizen.")

It seems the revolution is already a success, with hardly any blood spilled. But we know what comes next. We've seen this movie before.

Just about the time that the tsar is abdicating, American intelligence receives notice from the British that they have intercepted an encoded telegram purported to be from the German foreign secretary to the German embassy in Mexico. It outlines a plan to invite the Mexican government to ally with Germany and attack the United States. It promises that, if the war is won, Mexico can take back the land from California to Texas that it lost to the US in the Mexican-American War of the previous century.

The Wilson administration has been going round and round with the Germans about limiting their U-boat activity, with promises being made and broken. The timing of the telegram coincides with Germany cutting off all further negotiation and resuming unlimited submarine warfare.

Everything seems to be moving the US toward joining the war. Russia has toppled its tsar and is talking about democracy. Furthermore, because of the instability in Russia, there is great concern on the part of the British and French that Russia might collapse in surrender to the Germans or, before that can happen, negotiate a way out of the war altogether. Which is what some in the Soviet are calling for.

If Russia falls, it will be over for Britain and France. It is all a numbers game. With the current amount of German troops at the Western Front, the defense of France will hold. But if the majority of troops on the Eastern Front were free to be transferred west, the balance would tip and Paris would be toast.

On the other hand, if fresh *American* troops could be injected into the Western Front, then it would be the Germans going into full retreat.

On March 1, the contents of the German foreign secretary's telegram are divulged to the American press. With cries of "Extra! Extra!" on the streets, the American public is aroused enough to support sending its young men to the trenches. On April 2, Wilson goes before a joint session of Congress to ask for a Declaration of War. America will "make the world safe for democracy," he says.

The race is on. It will take until October to get the first American soldiers enlisted, trained, shipped to France, and deployed to the front. Where will Russia be by then?

Back to our flu analogy for social revolutions: Russia has gone through the initial pain, then the seemingly quick recovery and the burst of optimism that comes with it. So what signs of the illness still lurk below the surface?

The royal family has been placed under house arrest. Its supporters in the Duma who did not make it into the provisional government are at large. The foreign minister privately reassures Russia's allies that Russia will stay in the war until its completion. The communication is intercepted and angers many in the public, especially the radicals in the Soviet.

When the French Revolution was at this point and they were celebrating on the Champs de Mars, Maximilien Robespierre was in the crowd, but he wasn't celebrating. Robespierre has a Russian parallel.

As the news from Russia spread west across Europe, Vladimir Lenin reads of it in a coffee house in Switzerland. He has been abroad since 1905, when he was exiled for his participation in the revolution of that year.

Karl Marx spent time in Swiss coffee shops. It is where his theories on communism became fully developed. The location is also fruitful for coalescing Lenin's own philosophy. He believes entirely in the communist ideal—in the end product—but has come to the realization that he disagrees with Marx about how to get there.

Whereas Marx said the revolution had to be led from the bottom, by the proletariat, Lenin thinks that a trained group of educated revolutionaries deployed to rally the workers can make the revolution happen now. If only he can get to St. Petersburg...

Germany would like to help.

The German leaders know Lenin is trouble. They know he is a rabble-rouser. They know if they can just pop an invisibility cloak on him and shake him loose in St. Petersburg, it will be like dropping a chain-reaction bomb in the streets of the Russian capital.

So they go to him, smuggle him into a sealed train car, and send him on his way.

Before Lenin even leaves St. Petersburg's Finland Station, he delivers a speech he has been working on en route. It becomes known as his April Theses, the heart of which is:

Down with the war!
Down with the Provisional Government!
Down with the petty-bourgeois leadership of the Petrograd Soviet!

158

Petrograd, "Peter's City," is a secularized version of St. Petersburg. Lenin is down on the current leaders of the Soviet because they support the workers' unions, which are trying to get reform laws passed. Like Marx, he does not want the workers making incremental progress by negotiating with owners. He wants them upset enough to rise up when he calls for a communist revolution.

Within the Soviet's communist bloc, he butts heads with by-the-book Marxists who are willing to wait for workers to develop class-consciousness. But, through the force of his personality (here, he is quite different from Robespierre), he will begin to gather a sizable minority of converts. He does this by employing the propagandist's trick of stating a lie with authority (if you say a lie often enough, it is sure to become true). He calls his faction the Bolsheviks, which means "the majority." He calls the real communist majority faction (the pure Marxists) the Mensheviks, which means—you guessed it—"the minority."

In June, a failed military offensive against Austria results in nearly half a million Russian casualties, which plays right into Lenin's anti-war message. As the summer heats up, the Bolsheviks stir up a series of violent strikes and protests, calling for an end to the war. The police crack down hard on the protestors. Lenin is forced to flee to Finland, but as discontent increases, so do the numbers who call themselves Bolsheviks.

The majority party that holds the leadership of the Soviet, the one that Lenin called "petty-bourgeois," which supports the unions and reform laws, is called the Social Revolutionaries (SRs). Politically, the summer protests shift the mood of the country to the left. Within the PG, the ruling coalition of liberals has collapsed, and the SR's now have control of that branch of authority, too.

Out on the front, this angers a general by the name of Kornilov. The military has been struggling with deserters and he would like to reinstitute capital punishment for the offense. The SR's, who are friends of the working-class soldiers, oppose this. Now, with news of their ascendancy in the PG, the general is keen to rid the capital of those dang socialists. So he turns a battalion of his soldiers around and begins to march on St. Petersburg.

With this news, the PG is all in a tizzy. There aren't enough police to stop Kornilov. Panic builds as his troops move closer.

But there is an undercover group inside the city that has been hoarding guns: the Bolshevik Red Guards. Lenin knew a time would come when he would need to use force to effect the revolution, so one of the first things he did once he hit town was to begin forming his muscle group.

And so the Bolsheviks save the day. With the Red Guards swelling the ranks of the police, they are able to get Kornilov to stand down.

With the People now looking up to the Bolsheviks as the heroes of the Kornilov Affair, it is safe for Lenin to return. And by October, the Bolshevik faction has truly become the majority, not just within the communist bloc, but in the Soviet overall. Of Lenin's April Theses, check off the one on the bottom.

Moving up the list from bottom to top, we come to: Down with the provisional government!! In the first week of November, the PG takes its last action: It shuts down all the Bolshevik newspapers. In response, the Bolsheviks announce the dissolution of the PG. The Red Guards lead the coup. Check off number two.

The All-Russian Congress of Soviets convenes and deems that local Soviets spread all across Russia are now the government of the country, with the Petrograd Soviet at their head and Lenin as chairman. He immediately issues two decrees: The Decree on Land says that private ownership of land is abolished. The Decree on Peace says there will be a cease-fire, beginning negotiations with Germany as soon as possible.

As the Bolsheviks were attracting converts over the summer by fanning the people's discontent, the war was not the only thing they could point to. There was also the failure of the PG to schedule the promised democratic elections of a constituent assembly so that work on a constitution could begin. Lenin feels he must act on this while the Bolshevik triumph is still fresh in the public's mind. So before November is over, the election is held. Forty-four million people turn out, which is a significant percentage of the adult population. But when the votes are counted, the Bolsheviks finish a distant second behind the SRs.

Lenin schedules the first meeting of the assembly for mid-January. This buys him some time before he knows he will lose control, as the SR majority will be able to substantially determine the design of the future Russian government.

On December 15, the Russian–German armistice occurs. Though the first wave of American troops are now active on the Western Front, their impact is not yet felt, for a roughly equivalent number of British and French troops have had to be diverted to Italy to repel a big push south by the Austrians.

Early in the morning of a day in January 1918, the Russian Revolution moves into its high fever phase. The first meeting of the constituent assembly was the day before and had continued long into the night. None of the Bolsheviks' proposals fared well. Now, as the delegates return to continue their work, they find the building surrounded by the Red Guards.

Lenin has shut them down. He previously claimed that the highest form of democracy should elevate the interests of the working class. He now claims that it is the Bolsheviks who best know what the workers want, and they have no need of an elected assembly to tell them otherwise.

What the People want (spoken by an upper-middle-class revolutionary). There is that fever-phase language again.

Robespierre: "Our people don't want to go backward...."

Lenin: "When one makes a Revolution... *one must always go forward—or go back.* He who now talks about the 'freedom of the press' goes backward, and halts our headlong course toward Socialism."

Lenin establishes the All-Russian Extraordinary Commission for Combating Counter-Revolution (the Cheka). This secret police force will utilize terror and violence in seeking out traitors to be branded as **enemies of the revolution.**

Whether they are enemies of Russia's Revolution or not, there are now plenty of enemies of Lenin. There are the royalist conservatives in the countryside who are about to lose their estates to Lenin's Decree on Land. There are the SR's who just had their democratically earned mandate as the ruling party taken away. There are the anti-socialist liberals who supported the PG. There are the Mensheviks, who disagree with Lenin's approach (even more now that they see where it is going).

Lenin knows all this, and he immediately begins to prepare for civil war. The peasants are now forced to turn most of what they produce over to the Bolshevik leaders so it can be used to feed a Red Army. Farmers are pressured to inform on their neighbors if they try to hold back any amount over the meager limit for themselves.

In March, the Treaty of Brest-Litovsk is signed, outlining the terms of the surrender to Germany. They are harsh. Russia will lose one million square miles of land. With it will go a third of its population, a majority of its coal and oil, and much of its industry. Worried that Germany will have access to these resources, British, American, and Japanese troops make plans to move into Russia.

Throughout the spring and early summer of 1918, as the American troop build-up in France reaches full strength, the Germans also pour in troops from the former Eastern Front. Unlike the Americans, however, they are war weary. Their commanders send them again and again on major offensives (German command figuring they have one chance to win the war now, before the Americans can send even more fresh troops).

For the first time in nearly four years, there is appreciable movement of the front. In early June, the Germans push all the way to the Marne River, less than 100 kilometers from Paris.

But combined French and American forces are able to halt the advance. There will be more surges by the Germans, but with less and less success. In August, they will begin to retreat.

Back east, the Arabs have won their revolt against the Turks, and now smaller scattered internal revolts are finding success within Austria's empire. In October, the Austrian emperor sues for peace.

Soon after, with his allies gone, his own soldiers exhausted, and some in the navy beginning to mutiny, Kaiser Wilhelm decides to call it quits. An armistice is arranged for the eleventh hour of the eleventh day of the eleventh month. Wilhelm splits for the Netherlands, leaving Germany in a leadership vacuum, with multiple groups pointing fingers, blaming each other for the country's defeat.

Since January, President Wilson has been working on a peace plan. He calls it the Fourteen Points. Wilson is an idealist and a planner. He sees clearly what he feels must be done. He isn't especially accommodating of other perspectives. But now, with the Americans being looked up to as the ones who came to the rescue, Europeans are ready to receive him with open arms. He arrives in Paris before Christmas to great fanfare...

The peace conference will begin in mid-January. Wilson's goal is more than the usual spoils of war and punishment. It is nothing short of achieving lasting worldwide peace— assurance that humankind will never let this happen again.

The peacemakers are led by the Big Four: the US, Britain, France, and Italy. The first basic question before them is how—and how much—to punish Germany. With the kaiser gone, Germany has set up a democratic republic, and for a second the question is raised whether the struggling democracy should be punished for the sins of its forerunners. But only for a second. France, especially, is focused on keeping Germany down once and for all. Even they worry, however, about what may happen if they go too far and push Germany into a corner. One word defines that worry: Bolshevism.

Russia's former allies know little about the details of what is happening there. News sources are sketchy at best. One incident in particular is fogged in attempted secrecy. After Brest- Litovsk, Lenin moved the capital to Moscow to be farther away from the new frontier. The Romanov royal family was moved nearly 2,000 kilometers farther east, into a home in the town of Yekaterinburg. One day, they were called into a room to pose for a family photograph.

It wasn't this one. No photographer ever arrived. Instead, they were all either shot or bludgeoned to death and their bodies tossed down a mine shaft.

An important concept championed in Wilson's Fourteen Points is *self-determination*, an idea that went entirely against the concept of imperialism: A people should be able to determine their own geo-political fate.

The naked idealism of introducing such a concept at this time was bound to shake the world up. Perhaps it could be successfully applied to out-of-fashion empires like the Austrians and the Turks, but would the industrial-imperialists accept it? Even Wilson had no intention of having the United States let go of the Philippines, which they had so recently subdued at great cost (mostly to the Filipinos).

And what about the effect on the colonized peoples, themselves? Wilson was not only all the rage in Paris; his message of self-determination had made its way around the world and he was beginning to gain near-savior status in the colonies. One example: A young Vietnamese man who had come to Paris and was doing a stint as a kitchen assistant at the Ritz sent Wilson a petition, hoping the conference would result in freeing his country from the French. It was ignored. One day that man, whose name was Ho Chi Minh, would found the Vietnamese Communist Party, which four later American presidents would have to tangle with.

Self-determination conflicted with the old notion of the "spoils of war." Victors who felt that the war was not their fault and had lost lives winning it felt they should gain something. Traditionally, they would gain territory. France had been waiting over 40 years to avenge the Franco-Prussian War, so getting back Alsace-Lorraine was, to them, a clear assumption.

There were also practical considerations of security. A big one was the Rhineland, the area of Germany west of the Rhine River, which was where most of their industry was. France was adamant that Germany not be left capable of starting another war. If the Rhineland was returned to the Germans, they may soon be building up their military again.

In his idealism, Wilson would have had the people of Alsace-Lorraine vote whether they would like to be German or French (and thought they might opt to remain German now that nearly 50 years had passed). He was wise enough not to even broach this with the French, but he held firm on only a short occupation of the Rhineland by French troops. They settled for a ten-year phase-out after five years up front.

Wilson disagreed with giving German-speaking Tyrol, an Austrian alpine province, to Italy, but he let it go. He also disagreed with giving the German-speaking edges of Bohemia to the new nation of Czechoslovakia. He let that go, as well. Poland was put back on the map after disappearing into Germany with Brest-Litovsk. He agreed the Poles should have a corridor to the sea (even though it split East Prussia from the rest of Germany), but he made sure the Poles would receive the minimal amount of acreage from this German-speaking area.

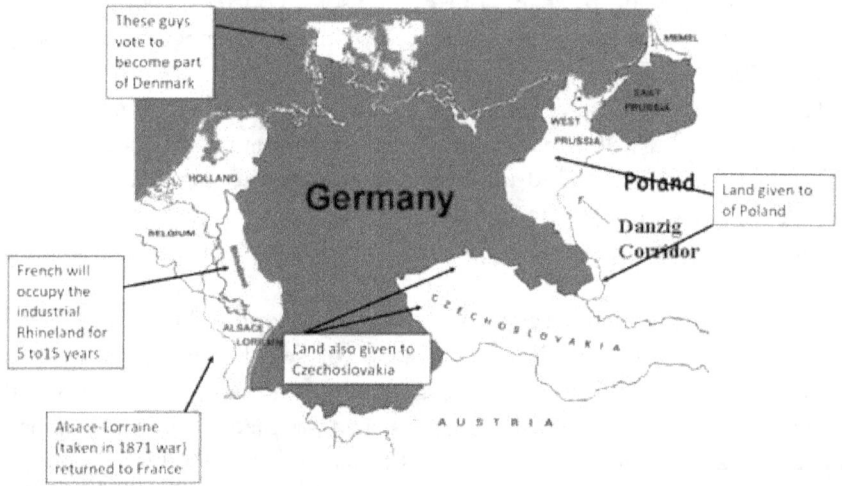

Wilson's 14th point was his dearest: the establishment of a League of Nations, a body containing representatives of all the world's nations, with the sole mission of keeping the peace. It would be an open forum where all diplomacy took place. All the nations of the world would form a single group with no subset alliances and no secret agreements being made. Forced to operate against his controlling nature, Wilson was only able to bear the less-than-perfect solutions to the issues above by keeping his eyes on the ultimate prize, which was the League.

The leaders of the Big Four did think long and hard about what to *charge* Germany and Austria for the war. Wilson wanted a bill for reparations rather than indemnities. In other words, the defeated powers would pay for the repair work necessitated by the destruction of the war rather than being monetarily penalized for starting it.

Once again, with an eye toward fending off any Bolshevist uprising, the Big Four tried to limit the amounts charged to what could be paid without causing utter economic ruin. Still, Germany ended up with a bill of nearly 2.7 *trillion* American dollars, adjusted for 2020-level inflation.

The IOU the Germans had to sign began with the words,

> Germany accepts the responsibility of Germany and her allies for causing all the loss and damage to which the Allied and Associated Governments and their nationals have been subjected as a consequence of the war imposed upon them by the aggression of Germany and her allies.

It will later be labeled the "Guilt Clause," and a rising Hitler will use it to whip up public indignation.

Fifty-two percent of the reparations were slated to go to France, which had lost the most—8,000 square miles of farmland wiped out, 1.5 million head of livestock killed, 300,000 homes and 6,000 factories destroyed, coal mines vandalized by retreating Germans. Twenty-eight percent would go to Britain, which had contributed the most materiel (though much of that was now owed as debt to the Americans).

Japan was intent on including a racial equality clause in the heading of the treaty. As the lone non-White industrial-imperialist, it felt it was being disrespected. This feeling was immediately validated when both Australia and New Zealand attacked the proposed clause, fearing it would lead to legal challenges against their restrictions on Asian immigration.

Wilson, too, was determined to keep the clause out, as he thought it would keep West Coast congressmen from voting to ratify the treaty. This would take some wheeling and dealing and cause him to once again sacrifice his ideal of self-determination. This time, however, it would have dire long-term consequences...

China had sent 100,000 laborers to France to dig trenches, which freed up that many soldiers to serve in combat. At home, the new Chinese republic was struggling. Between imperialist spheres of influence and lands controlled by warlords, Sun Yat-Sen had been unable to build a functioning republic. Now, a second government had been established at Guangdong, with a second president. Neither leader could get away to Paris, but both sent delegates.

Despite the chaos at home, the Chinese delegates were optimistic. They were reformers, eager to bring China into the modern world. They revered President Wilson, were emboldened by the promise of self-determination, and looked forward to China's becoming a member of the League of Nations. As compensation for their efforts on the Western Front, they began by asking for an end to extraterritoriality and for full control of China's railroad system.

And of course, they looked forward to the return of Shandong, the German sphere of influence that had been liberated early in the war by the Japanese. Though small, Shandong's geographical location was important, halfway between Shanghai and Beijing, spanning the Yellow River and the Grand Canal. It also had important cultural significance: It was the birthplace of Confucius.

The issue of Shandong was so important to the Chinese reformers that they scheduled a massive celebration in Beijing's Tiananmen Square on the evening of May 4, the date the news from Paris was expected. When word did arrive, the celebration morphed into a protest. Wilson had let them down. To appease the Japanese for leaving out the racial equality clause, he told them they could keep Shandong.

One of the reformers in the crowd that evening who felt the blow of disappointment was a young man named Mao Zedong. Later that summer, Lenin's foreign minister would offer to give up Russia's sphere of influence in China. Though it never happened, it left a positive impression at the time, and it helped turn the admiration of the Chinese reformers away from the West and to their north—toward Russia. The following year, the Chinese Communist Party was formed. As of the moment that just passed, the Chinese were still celebrating every May 4 in Tiananmen Square, where the troops in review pass before Mao's huge portrait, hung prominently before the entrance to the Forbidden City.

Officially, Shandong was to be a League of Nations *mandate*. A mandate was given to an industrial-imperialist power for a time, with the intention to prepare the native population for self-governance. If, until now, self-determination had been viewed by colonies as the end of imperialism, these "mandates" for those who "were not ready for self-governance" sounded an awful lot like... more imperialism.

All of Germany's colonies became mandates. Their African colonies were split between Britain and France. New Guinea went to Britain. Their Pacific islands went to Japan.

Technically, countries were not supposed to put military bases in their mandates, but Japan put them in its islands, where they would remain and be used in World War Two.

Japan's military budget would quadruple in the 1930's. Point Four of the Fourteen Points addressed militarism. It said that all countries would reduce their armaments to the minimal amount required for defense. Except for severe limita-

166

tions imposed upon Germany, no one else ever complied.

In the end, Serbia got exactly what the Black Hand was after when they murdered Franz Joseph and his wife. The new nation of Yugoslavia (Union of the Slavs) was created by joining Serbia and Montenegro to Bosnia, Croatia, and Slovenia.

The northern Slavs also made out well, with the Czechs and Slovaks forming their own new nation. Some of the north also went to Poland. Romania held onto Transylvania. The Austria that remained was a small, landlocked country.

In June, the treaty was ready for signatures. The ceremony was conducted in the Hall of Mirrors at the Palace of Versailles, for which reason it is known to history as the Treaty of Versailles.

When Wilson returned to the States in July to start selling the treaty to Congress, the fate of the nationalities of the Turkish Empire was still up in the air. He instructed the other three of the Big Four to follow the mandate model. As in the Scramble for Africa, new borders were drawn without regard for traditional ones.

The native Arabs wanted to establish a nation of Syria using its traditional borders, which would include the Turkish provinces of Palestine and Mosul. Instead, to accommodate French and British horse-swapping, it was split into three. A smaller Syria was given to the French. Palestine received its own mandate, going to the British. Kurdish-majority Mosul was pasted together with Persian-majority Baghdad and Arab Basra to form another British mandate, which they called Mesopotamia. The natives called it Iraq.

Back in the US, Wilson, a Democrat, was having difficulty convincing a Republican-majority Congress to ratify the treaty. The Republicans of the time were highly isolationist; the idea of being in the League scared them off. Meanwhile, the intractable Wilson would not entertain the slightest modification.

Giving up on direct negotiations with Congress, Wilson took his message on the road to the American people. He embarked on a grueling tour by rail that ended up destroying his health. He returned to Washington in late September and, days later, suffered a stroke.

In March, a coalition of moderates from both parties put forward a version of the treaty with amendments. They had the votes but, from his sickbed, Wilson encouraged others in his party to vote against it. It went down in defeat. Though it was the brainchild of the American president, the United States would never become a member of the League of Nations.

By the summer of 1920, the Russian Civil War was drawing to a close. Once hostilities completed, it had killed four times as many Russians as the Great War and brought widespread economic hardship and famine.

To the common peasant, one army sweeping through must have been indistinguishable from the next. Loosely speaking, it was the Whites against the Reds. The Whites, though, were nothing close to an organized alliance. They were anyone who opposed the Bolsheviks: Menshevik communists, anti-communists, liberal republicans, conservative monarchists, British, Japanese, and American troops left over from the Great War, nationalists from the Baltic countries and Ukraine.

One would think that with so much opposition, the minority Bolsheviks were bound to fail. But due to forced enlistment, there were more Red soldiers than White. Lenin framed the conflict as a Russian nationalist struggle against foreigners, which put the force of patriotism on their side. They held the center of the country, while the Whites were scattered around the perimeter. By August, it was clear the Reds were going to win.

The new Russian Empire that the Reds inherited was christened the Union of Soviet Socialist Republics (USSR). Non-Russian nationalities at the periphery became their own subservient Soviet Socialist Republics (SSRs). By the eastern border with the Turks, tiny Armenia became one of them.

This was all the Armenians had left after the Turkish nationalist revolutionary Mustafa Kemal Ataturk took over the defeated Turkish Empire just as it was about to be doled out as mandates to Britain, France, and Italy. A portion had been left for the Armenians. For a second, they were the only Asians about to score their own country. But then Ataturk comes along and kicks out all of the above in order to create the fully Turkish nation of Turkey. He sets up a new capital at Ankara, well back from the European frontier.

With the deposition of the sultan, Ottoman rule is ended. The new nation will not only be a republic; it will be a secular one. This is significant. On a wider scale, the removal of the sultan is also the removal of the caliph. For the first time in its 1,300-year history, there will be no single spiritual head of a *Dār al-Islam*.

Much has changed in the nine years leading up to 1923, yet much has remained the same. If history was a storybook, the horrors of the Great War and the idealism generated in reaction to it would have put an end to the Era of

New Imperialism. As with the French Revolution, the genie of change has been mostly stuffed back in the bottle, but not quite. While the peacemakers were still hard at work in Paris in April 1919, violent protests against the British occupation of Egypt had begun. It became the first colony of the era to successfully agitate for independence, which the British granted in 1922.

India, too, was becoming restless. Many Indian troops died in the Great War due to failures of the British command made in their attempt to take Mesopotamia from the Ottomans. This led to unrest in the Indian Punjab, where, in 1919, a British commander ordered troops to fire on a peaceful assembly that included women and children. It became known as the Massacre at Amritsar. Not long in the future, a young activist by the name of Mohandas Gandhi would time one of his peoples' great acts of protest with the anniversary of that incident.

But any spread of decolonization will remain decades away. The Fourteen Points called for "fair adjustment of colonial claims, giving equal consideration to the natives of the colony," but not a single colony was set free. The mandates in the Middle East effectively created new colonies. Arabs who successfully battled the Turks compared the fate of their nationalist dreams to those of the Europeans, who *did* gain nations, and rightly felt they were the victims of prejudice.

Neither was any sphere of influence or claim of extraterritoriality renounced. In China, the positive glow around Wilson's idealism was extinguished. The up-and-coming leaders of the new nation were practically wrapped and delivered to the communist Russians. Chinese communism would one day cross the border to Vietnam, where Ho Chi Minh, who had also felt that rejection, would lead its spread.

Both sides of Wilson's deal with Japan, rejecting the racial equality clause and allowing the Japanese to stay in China and the German islands, would come back to bite the US. Distrust and hatred of the West would energize Japan's continued imperialism, and it already had its first footholds in Shandong and the islands.

Finally, there was Germany. It was backed into a corner after all, or at least enough so that a populist demagogue could make it seem that way to the German people. He would not be the Bolshevik the Big Four had feared, but would instead come from the other end of the political spectrum. And where a functioning League of Nations may have been able to change the outcome, due to several flaws—no enforcement, lack of central organization, no commitment by key players (following the example of the absent United States)—it would be helpless to contain the threat.

As Edward House, Wilson's primary adviser in the first months of the conference, told the president,

If after establishing the League we are so stupid as to let Germany train and arm a large army and again become a menace to the world, we would deserve the fate which such folly would bring upon us.

CHAPTER THIRTEEN

Worldwide Depression Begins a Backlash Against Democracy
(1924-1936)

In January 1924, Lenin dies of a stroke. It is his third. Bedridden for some time, he has had plenty of time to dictate orders and dispense advice regarding his legacy. The two comrades he had worked most closely with were Leon Trotsky and Josef Stalin. As he nears death, he warns others that Stalin, the current party secretary, may not be the wisest choice for his successor. His warning is not heeded.

Stalin will go on to be, by many measures, the biggest mass murderer in history. He will also oversee the building of a centrally-planned economy that will steer the Soviet Union through the Great Depression and have them emerge from World War Two as one of the world's two great superpowers.

Given the goal of complete economic leveling, the purely communist economy must go through a process of collectivization and redistribution. Agricultural output must essentially be pooled, then distributed equally across the nation. This is similar to what Lenin instituted to supply his troops during the civil war, but on an even grander scale, across the world's largest nation by area.

The Soviet Union comprises one-sixth of Earth's land surface, and, under Stalin, 94% of that land becomes owned by the government. If you are a farmer who resists relinquishing your quota of output for collectivization, if you are lucky you will be deported; more likely, you will be shot.

Then there is the fate of the Ukrainians... Ukraine is the largest center of wheat production in the entire USSR. The Ukrainians are a proud people, many of whom fought against the Reds in the civil war. When Stalin hears that only 60% of the Ukrainian quota has been met, he suspects that it is being deliberately withheld. As punishment, he sends troops to take out all the remaining grain they can find and imposes a blockade to keep the people in. Seven million starve in what has been called the Ukrainian Genocide.

Another way Stalin might kill you is to send you to one of the *gulags*, a constellation of concentration camps spread across the vast, often frozen, region of northern Siberia. There, you would support the growing economy with your slave labor. Due to the intensity of the work, the harshness of the climate, and the sparseness of your care, average life expectancy is one winter. Despite the turnover rate, at one point, the camps are estimated to contain 10% of the country's population.

Finally, there is the most straightforward method of murder: Stalin's daily purges. At night, he sits in his study, going over lists of people, checking off those he wishes eliminated, then giving the list to his henchmen to carry out the murders before daylight. He is intensely paranoid, so he often comes up with a list of 50 or so. Some nights, if he can only find ten names he recognizes, he scrawls at the bottom of the list, "Find twenty more."

Stalin's purges have a long reach. Leon Trotsky, his rival to succeed Lenin and an early critic, is eventually exiled. While living in a villa in Mexico in 1940, he will become the victim of a home invasion in which he is attacked with an ice axe and dies of his injuries a day later.

Going back to our model of social revolutions, it would seem that the Russian Revolution, unlike the French, will remain in its high fever phase, that its citizens (er, comrades) will not soon be entering their convalescence. But remember that convalescence does not mean achieving the goal; rather, it means continuing to cede one's freedom, this time to a nurturing caretaker. And who would appear more nurturing than the grandfatherly figure above? While Stalin does his dirty work behind the scenes, this is the image presented to the Russian people.

ПОД ЗНАМЕНЕМ ЛЕНИНА, ПОД ВОДИТЕЛЬСТВОМ СТАЛИНА, ВПЕРЕД К ПОБЕДЕ КОММУНИЗМА!

The image has been carefully crafted, and it appears everywhere. Films show Stalin surrounded by children. They show him attending an evening performance of the ballet or an opera. Often the performance is a premiere of a new work... all about Russia's great revolution and Stalin's part in it. That part is exaggerated, of course. He is portrayed as working closely with Lenin, as if he was the great man's obvious choice to succeed him.

The work of the image-crafters is a success in that it brainwashes enough of the population to enable the dictatorship, while those who are intelligent enough to see past the ruse are suppressed by fear of becoming one of its victims.

This is what is known as a personality cult.

The Russian Revolution is not the only event to give rise to this new concept. Stalin's ascent to power coincides with that of Benito Mussolini of Italy, although the personality projected by Mussolini is the antithesis of Stalin's grandfatherly persona. Italy has not gone through a social revolution. It is not in need of convalescence; according to Mussolini it needs to wake up!—to remember its glorious history, to rise up and reclaim its preeminence.

In his youth, Mussolini leaned toward communism, but his experiences in the Great War turned him away from class concerns and toward a fanatical nationalism. "Class reveals itself as a collection of interests," he says, "but the nation is a *history* of sentiments, traditions, language, culture, and race."

These beliefs lead him to create a new political movement. While he sees communism as promoting loyalty to the proletariat class over the individual, his movement instead promotes loyalty to the *nation* over the individual. He calls it fascism.

Fascism comes from the word *fasces*, which, fittingly, was a symbol of national power from Italy's glorious past as the center of the Roman Empire. A fasces is simply a group of sticks bound tightly around an axe. The sticks represent individuals; the binding is the nation. A stick is only a stick without the binding. Bound together, the sticks are powerful and wield the axe, symbolic of the movement's martial nature.

In fascism, Mussolini explains, "the State determines the moral code of the country, and enforces order, discipline and obedience according to it." Thus cultural values are determined by the government. Conflicting minority cultural values are banned. "The State is an absolute, whereas all individuals are relative, only to be considered in their relation to the State."

Although fascism shuns individualism, there is one individual who *becomes* the nation, is symbolic of and synonymous with it, and that is the leader to whom the personality cult swears allegiance.

The public personality created by Mussolini exudes pride, martialism, sternness. His speeches are highly animated. His chin juts out and his whole upper body rears stiffly back. He sways from side to side, then pauses after a point with his arms folded, nodding seriously. He has Lenin's ability to fire up a crowd.

Cowed by Mussolini, the Italian king appoints him prime minister. It takes him three years to gradually erode the country's democratic institutions. By 1925, the fascists have control of the country under his dictatorship.

If the United States made out well supplying the belligerent nations during the war, it does even better afterward. It costs Europe even more to rebuild from the war than it did to fight it. American industry is happy to oblige.

Before the war, the US was well on its way, along with Germany, to rise to the top of the heap of world-dominating industrialist nations. Now, with Germany stripped of its colonies and military power, with its industrial heartland occupied and its reparations debt to pay, the US sits alone atop that heap. The only other industrialist nation to come out of the war better than before is Japan, who may now be the Americans' nearest competition.

In American politics, the isolationist Republicans, who now hold the presidency as well as Congress, are focused on supporting business, and the American public, glad to be free of the war, on being consumers. In 1920, after a 70-year struggle, American women had finally been granted the right to vote. In the cities, women carry their newfound freedom through to social norms, as well. Both hair and dress length shorten. Many begin to smoke in public. Rather than entertain suitors playing the piano in the parlor, they go out on dates to jazz clubs.

The new form of music is an invention of Black Americans, who have begun a steady migration north, east and west to escape continuing persecution and terrorism in the former slave states of the South. From newly Black-majority neighborhoods in cities like New York and Chicago, the music, and lively new forms of dance that accompany it, spread to Paris and Berlin and Tokyo.

US Economy: Roaring along...

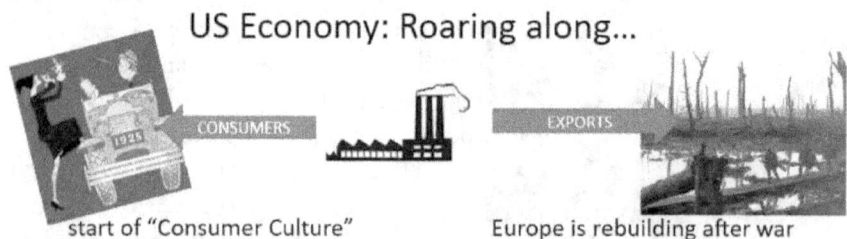

start of "Consumer Culture"   Europe is rebuilding after war

Between American consumerism and European rebuilding, there seems to be a constant supply of fuel for the American economy... until there isn't.

The first segment of the economy to falter is farming. The rural central Great Plains and South have not experienced the same rise in standard of living that the cities have. The Northeast, industrial Midwest, and West Coast have been electrified; the rest of the country has not. At first, areas where the war was fought, particularly France, were in desperate need of American food exports. But in Europe, agriculture is the quickest segment of the economy to return to form, so in the mid-1920's, the price of American food exports plunges.

Not everyone in the richer parts of the country is on the firmest of economic footing, either. The Federal Reserve, a branch of the American government that is not controlled by either Congress or the president and is responsible for setting the country's base interest rates on loans, has kept rates low, which means there is a lot of "easy money" around. Merchants make it even easier to buy stuff by offering layaway plans.

The boom in business to this point has made the government flush with money from tax receipts. That, in turn, has allowed it to loan money to Germany, which Germany has depended upon in order to make its reparation payments. But as European industry starts to recover in the second half of the decade, there is suddenly much less demand for American goods. Overproduction rears its head, causing prices to fall.

At first this is welcomed at the retail level, where they make even more of those layaway sales. But with manufacturing profits down, the government's tax receipts are down, and it can no longer lend money to Germany. Soon Germany starts to default on its payments, which curbs British and French spending even more, and we're into a downward spiral...

Later in decade: Manufacturing declines, too...

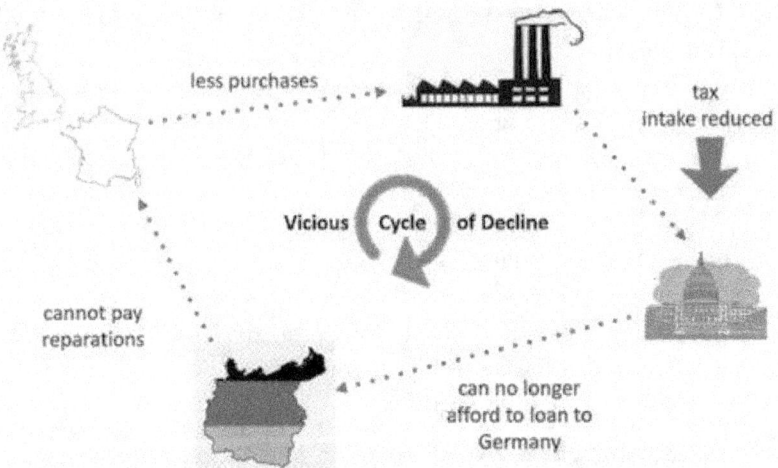

On "Main Street" in the US, retailers and banks are both overextended and unable to recoup their loans. Consumers can't make their payments. Wall Street (the financial markets) has already come to Main Street: Many first-time stock buyers have been rushing to buy shares on *margin*, the stock market equivalent of layaway. Only worse. For when a stock you buy on margin falls a certain percentage, a *margin call* occurs, forcing sale of the stock at the loss. And here we have another downward spiral: An abundance of margin calls weighs on the market, and prices across the market fall even more...

The US is already technically in a recession when the bottom falls out of the stock market in October 1929. The Great Depression has begun, and the world's economic depressions, like its wars, are now shared by all.

In Japan, the years of struggle that ensue lead the military to take control. At first, they only exercise their influence on the civilian government, convincing it that military spending and imperialist expansion are what the economy needs. They have a weak next-door neighbor who will be easy to take advantage of....

China remained fragmented. In 1926, the north had fallen under control of a military warlord, forcing Sun Yat-Sen's successor, Chiang Kai-shek, to move his capital south to Nanking.

The following year, as Chiang is preparing his army to retake Beijing, he orchestrates a purge of the communists within its ranks. This becomes known as the Shanghai Massacre. It is effectively the beginning of the Chinese Civil War.

Chiang's anti-communist followers become known as the Nationalists. By the end of 1928, they have resecured Beijing, but their hold on faraway Manchuria remains tenuous.

In 1931, the Japanese military sets up a "false flag" incident at the Korea/Manchuria border, blowing up some railroad track and blaming it on the Chinese. They use this as an excuse to invade and conquer Manchuria, converting it into the puppet state of Manchukuo. They even recruit the now–25-year-old Puyi, the last emperor of China, whom they make into the provincial governor.

The next year, the military assassinates the prime minister and takes over the Japanese government directly.

Japan's extreme nationalism had many similarities with Mussolini's fascism, as indicated in the following excerpts from the *Cardinal Principles of the National Entity of Japan*, recorded later in the decade:

> -The entire nation serves the Emperor, united in mind.... Offering our
> lives to the Emperor does not mean self-sacrifice; it is the casting aside
> of our "little selves" to live in his grace. We must sweep aside the
> corruption of the spirit... that comes from being obsessed with one's
> self, and instead return to the pure state of mind that belongs to us
> as subjects, and thereby deeply understand the great principle of loyalty.

-Our nation has adapted the good elements of the advanced education seen among European and American nations. However, [this has led to] an infiltration of individualistic concepts. The only course open to us is to make clear the true nature of our national identity, and to strive to [eliminate] individualistic ideas.

Like in fascism, there is a shedding of individualism as one is absorbed into the greatness of the nation-state. But in Japan's case, the state is embodied in the emperor, who is only a figurehead; the actual leaders shed their individualism, as well, in order to pull the levers of power in anonymity.

This was in keeping with both Japan's feudal history (where the shogun ruled in the name of the emperor) and the Meiji Restoration (where the samurai oligarchy was actually in charge). In all of these cases, it was important to keep the emperor foremost in the peoples' minds, as Japan had had a single hereditary line of emperors purported to be descended from the goddess of the sun. Many Japanese people would have been surprised to know what little power their emperor actually had.

Japan's overtaking of Manchuria is the first act of open defiance of the Covenant of the League of Nations. When a report by a multi-nation commission is finally released criticizing Japan, the Japanese simply withdraw from the League.

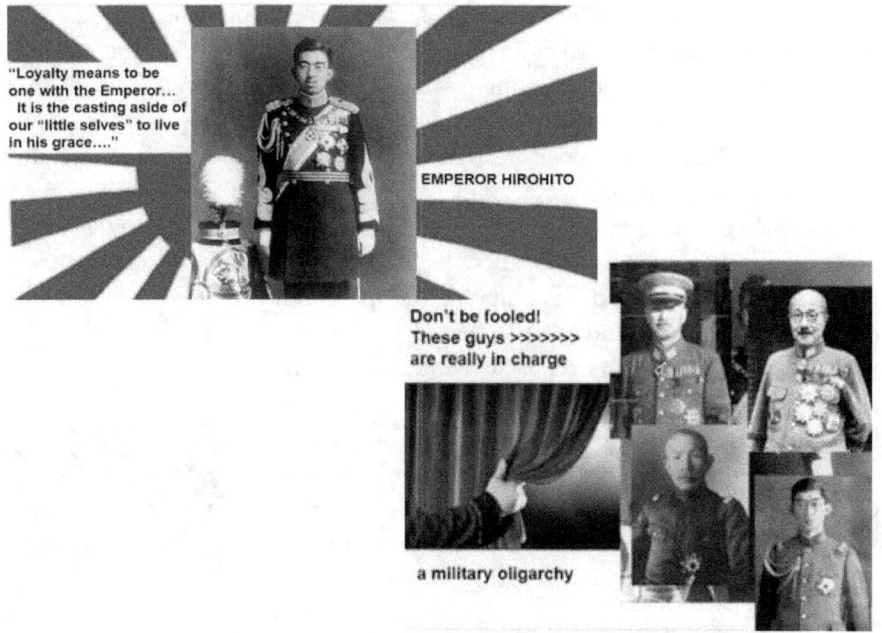

"Loyalty means to be one with the Emperor... It is the casting aside of our "little selves" to live in his grace...."

EMPEROR HIROHITO

Don't be fooled! These guys >>>>>>> are really in charge

a military oligarchy

◇◇◇

The Great Depression plunges all Europe into that state of instability the peacemakers in Paris had feared for Germany. In Britain, a Labor government comes to power, but there is still plenty of labor unrest; there are minority movements of both fascists and communists. On top of this, there are colonial disturbances. In the British mandate of Palestine, Jewish immigration creates tension. The Zionist movement, a three-decade-old response to Jewish persecution in Eastern Europe and Russia, calls for the creation of a Jewish homeland there. Britain endorsed the idea back in 1917, which hasn't helped relations with their Arab Palestinian "charges."

Also throughout the 1920's, Britain has had to deal with a thorn in its side in India. His name is Mohandas Gandhi, better known today as Mahatma Gandhi, *Mahatma* being an honorific meaning "great soul." Gandhi received a law degree in London and practiced in the large Indian community in South Africa, where he organized a civil resistance movement against the White minority government. He returned to India in 1914. From the time of the 1919 Massacre at Amritsar, he begins putting pressure on the British occupiers.

In response to the unrest leading to the massacre, the British extend a wartime security act that gives extrajudicial power to the police. Gandhi's response is to call for a "day of prayer and fasting," which is his euphemism for a general strike. Indian workers of all types fail to report to their jobs on the same day. Since Indian workers run everything—the trains, the telephone and telegraph systems, every line of service—everything in the country more or less stops. It puts the British in panic mode for a day, but more importantly, it elevates Gandhi in the minds of freedom-desiring Indians of all castes and all religions. Soon, he is famously appearing in his one-piece of homespun cloth, leading rallies where great bonfires are set, onto which people throw their British-imported clothes. As the boycott of British textiles continues, the spinning wheel becomes the symbol of Indian self-reliance and independence.

In 1930, as the British struggle with the Depression at home, Gandhi directly defies their law by extending that self-reliance to another commodity. The British have imposed a monopoly on the making of salt, so Gandhi plans what becomes known as the Salt March. He will walk 240 miles from an inland ashram to the sea, where he will make his own salt.

Gandhi in his homespun cloth, by his spinning wheel.

He schedules the march so that it will complete on the anniversary of the Massacre at Amritsar. He makes sure that the media is notified. Over the course of the walk, he gathers followers who join with him so that it becomes a larger and larger procession. Along the publicized route, Indians sit spinning their spinning wheels. Once he reaches the shore, he wades into the ocean that bears India's name and brings from it a bucket of its water, from which he proceeds to make salt.

After the enormously successful publicity of the march, Indians living near the ocean now begin to make their own salt. They are arrested, of course, and oftentimes beaten in the process. That is where Gandhi employs his key "weapon": civil resistance—*satyagraha*, he calls it, which literally means "love force." The idea is to disobey an unjust law in order to provoke a response from the authorities. Then, when faced with arrest or violent crackdown, you remain nonviolent. It is important to get the media's attention so that the general public can witness your dignified pacifism in the face of oppression, belittling those who are doing the oppressing. The technique will be successfully emulated three decades later by Martin Luther King in the American Civil Rights Movement.

Gandhi's organization is able to inspire a unified response that spreads across the subcontinent and gains international attention, condemning the British. Since the days of Queen Victoria, India has been Britain's "jewel in the crown." Now its hold on that precious gem is teetering. Gandhi is invited to London to discuss India's "possible independence."

For Gandhi, there is much to be discussed, not just with the colonial overlords, but among his own brain trust. Gandhi is a Hindu. One-third of Indians are Muslims, and the Muslim representative of that brain trust, Muhammad Ali Jinna, is concerned about how the two religious groups will share an independent India.

Meanwhile, the rest of the world is not standing still. As much as it would like to ignore them, Europe's fascists are becoming an even bigger headache.

In Germany before the Depression, the Nazi (National Socialist) Party was an extremist outlier. They made the news—the so-called "brownshirts" brawled in the back alleys with communists; Hitler railed against the Jews and others who he claimed had "sold out" Germany by surrendering in the Great War—but they never polled very well. In 1930, as Germany descended into seriously hard times, that changed.

Modern Americans, with natural national bias, often look down on Germans of the 1930's. How, they think, could they have ever been so stupid or ignorant to be deluded by a madman like Adolf Hitler?

It was not a matter of lacking intelligence; many of the elite actually facilitated Hitler's rise to power. Ignorance certainly played a large part, but how many Americans are exempt from its reach in this passing moment, similar as it is to a moment in 1930? We underestimate the persuasive power of effective demagogues combined with effective propaganda at our peril.

Hitler, like Mussolini, was an extraordinary demagogue, which is to say that he understood how the human mind reacted to certain stimuli. He knew he must interpret the listener's world for them as a simple duality of Us and what is good versus Them and what is bad. He spoke of a past that had been lost and made it seem so much brighter than what it actually may have been, and he promised a return to it. His promises were deliberately vague, but his targets specific, both external (the Versailles peacemakers) and internal (communists, Jews, the ineffective democratic government). He knew how to appeal to a crowd's base emotions. His speeches had lots of pauses and low points, from which they rose into highs of righteous anger.

Equally talented was his consummate propagandist, Joseph Goebbels. Goebbels pioneered the mass proliferation of disinformation. He created a Nazi press and heavily utilized radio broadcasts. If particular Nazi behavior was criticized, he would accuse the opposition parties of the same, more loudly, before the criticism could spread. Where Nazi policies were commonly held to be suspect, he would present them as if they reflected majority opinion. His propaganda machine repeated the same messages endlessly, though in slightly varying form. He recruited talented filmmakers like Leni Riefenstahl to glorify the Nazi cause. He made sure Hitler's public rallies were professionally staged. The crowd would be deliberately kept waiting while military music blared and huge banners of swastikas rippled in the breeze. As their leader finally came to the stage, his uniformed followers would salute him and chant "Heil, Hitler!" Then, later, as darkness fell, there may be a torchlight parade.

So ignorance can certainly be understood. But not all were ignorant of Hitler's penchant for authoritarianism, and many of those who were aware of it did not favor it. Their mistake was thinking that they could control it. They still gave him their support, some grudgingly, others eagerly. They *enabled* his rise. He could not have succeeded without them.

In 1930, the Nazis won 18% of the seats in the Reichstag (the German parliament). Two years later, with the economy in free fall, they took 37%, more than any other party. They were a rowdy bunch, and a huge pain in the neck for Germany's octogenarian president, Paul von Hindenburg.

Von Hindenburg is one who enables Hitler begrudgingly. In January 1933, in a vain attempt to pacify the Nazis, he makes Hitler his right-hand man by appointing him chancellor, a position that directed the day-to-day running of the executive government.

There are those in less radical conservative parties who give support to Hitler despite their misgivings, hoping they can ride the Nazi wave of conservatism to new majorities once the public's infatuation with him passes. But the support that keeps the Nazis strong, and makes them stronger, comes specifically from big business.

To enable a sweeping package of propaganda as grand as that put together by Goebbels, of course, requires a lot of financial backing. Early in 1933, the party finds itself drained of funds and unable to continue with it.

On February 22, Hitler arranges a secret meeting with Germany's largest corporations to pitch why they should support him. Krupp, the country's largest arms manufacturer, is an easy sell, as the restrictions of the Versailles Treaty are weighing heavily on its business. But Hitler is also able to convince the mega-conglomerate IG Farben and others that Germany's democratic government will never be their friend, unlike him, who would eliminate the trade unions, put an end to the communist threat once and for all, and return Germany to greatness. Goebbels' coffers are soon full again, and just in time...

On February 27, in the middle of the night, the Reichstag building is destroyed by a fire. Evidence of arson is strong. Hitler accuses the communists. More than likely, it was the Nazis, themselves.

As chancellor, Hitler is able to declare martial law. He immediately starts rounding up communists. The first concentration camp is opened at Dachau to contain them.

Supplied with this concrete threat from one of Hitler's targeted "Them," the Nazis are poised to attract more gullible listeners to the "Us" side. As the pool of corporate donations begins to flow in, Goebbels' propaganda machine kicks into even higher gear. In the next election, the Nazis take majority control of the Reichstag.

In August of the following year, President von Hindenburg dies. Under an obscure clause in the constitution, and with support of the military, Hitler is able to become the next president. Under another legal loophole, his first action is to abolish the presidency and declare himself *Führer*—absolute leader of Germany.

Hitler has legally disassembled Germany's democracy; he has completed his rise to Führer entirely through constitutional means.

In the USA, President Herbert Hoover instituted two policies that exacerbated the downward spiral of the Depression within the US. He famously said, "Prosperity cannot be restored by raids upon the public treasury." So in order to shore up the government budget, which was hurting from the decline in tax intake, he persuaded the Federal Reserve to *raise* interest rates.

This tightening of credit, of course, reduced consumption, hurting businesses even more. Hoover slapped tariffs on imports, hoping to focus what little consumption there was on American goods, but that only resulted in a trade war, which dried up American exports.

The US begins 1933 with a new president, Franklin Roosevelt. From the moment he takes office, he reverses tack completely. He removes the tariffs and even forgives international loans in order to increase exports. Then he severs the connection between the American dollar and the price of gold, allowing the government to increase the money supply in order to boost consumption. Finally, he expands government spending in a big way, creating a myriad of new government agencies in charge of public works (like electrifying the parts of the country that lagged behind).

The latter is inspired by the recent work of British economist, John Maynard Keynes, who says that governments should only work on tightening their belts when the economy is strong. But in a cycle of overproduction, when businesses are laying off workers, the government can become the employer of last resort.

Despite these actions, the most Roosevelt is able to accomplish is to stop the bleeding. Unemployment in the US falls from the level it was when he took office, but remains stubbornly high. It is nothing like the good old days, when the country was supplying a war and its recovery. They won't have long to wait for those days to return...

Rollercoaster capitalism is in the lowest trough of its 150-year history. Despite the anti–laissez-faire modifications of Keynesian economics, it still seems that the only escape will be the same one the industrialists began to employ in the late 1800's: more imperialism.

Wilson's plan for peace had not ended imperialism, but it did give it a bad name. It led to the use of euphemisms like "mandate." It caused the British to consider independence for their biggest prize (India), and to actually grant it to less valuable ones (Egypt and Iraq).

The fascist/nationalist governments, however, have no qualms. In fact, imperialism is a part of their mission. Whereas the communist objective is to spread an ideology across the world, the fascist/nationalist objective is to spread a nationality.

In 1935, Italy attacks Ethiopia from its neighboring colony of Somaliland. It is a blatant, unprovoked attack on a sovereign state, and the League of Nations is powerless to stop it.

While this distraction is going on, Hitler begins quietly to defy the Versailles Treaty's provision against German rearmament. Then, not so quietly, on March 7, 1936, he marches troops into the Rhineland, where an occupying French presence remains. He later writes in his journal,

> The 48 hours after the march into the Rhineland were the most nerve-racking in my life. If the French had [met us], we would have had to withdraw with our tail between our legs; for the military resources [we had] would have been wholly inadequate...

It is one of those intersections where one path of history may have been quite different than the one taken. With French inaction, Hitler is emboldened. It is a pattern that will continue.

The Americans, too, seem to be focused on not getting involved. An isolationist US Congress passes legislation that directly counters the three things that got the US involved in the Great War: allowing belligerent nations to buy on credit, shipping arms to them, and letting foolhardy American citizens travel to the war zone. It states that

- Nations at war must pay for all goods in cash
- Nations at war cannot buy arms
- The president must warn Americans to stay off ships that may be subject to attack

But war will find all eventually.

CHAPTER FOURTEEN

A War Against Humanity
(1937-1945)

In December 1937, Japan full-out attacks China, kicking off World War Two in the Pacific. During the raid on the capital of Nanking, two American oil tankers are inadvertently bombed, as is a gunboat that is trying to evacuate diplomatic staff. The boat sinks and three of the staff are killed. The Japanese apologize. Congress pressures President Roosevelt to unconditionally accept the apology.

The war with Japan puts China's own civil war on temporary hold. After being beaten back in the Shanghai Massacre, the communists had regrouped in the south. From October 1934 to October 1935, Mao Zedong made a name for himself by leading the First Red Army on a 9,000-kilometer trek in a wide semicircle to the West in order to meet up with other forces in Yanan, west of Beijing. This became known as the Long March. It positively exposed many in the countryside to the communists. The party would go on to distinguish itself fighting valiantly against the Japanese over the next eight years.

After subduing most of China, gaining control of the entire east from Manchuria down to Guangdong, Japan set its eyes on other resource-rich areas to the south. The military leadership called the expanded Japanese sphere of influence a "Greater East Asia Co-Prosperity Sphere," portraying the Japanese as liberators from Western dominance and sloganeering "Asia for the Asians."

The propagandists left no stone unturned. A publication for children showed a map of the region with cartoon Western imperialists peering greedily from the edges. The enlarged caption read, "Look! America, England, the Netherlands and others have been keeping us down and doing bad things to us in Greater East Asia." It went on to present the Japanese as coming to the rescue. A Japanese soldier on horseback salutes a group of children, with the caption:

> Our commander, strong Japanese commander, is riding on horseback,
> clip-clop, clip-clop. When we saluted him, the commander saluted us
> back, smiling brightly from atop his horse. Our commander, kind-hearted
> Japanese commander.

The reality was quite different. After the surrender of Nanking in early 1938, Chinese troops were tied up and used for bayonet practice. Some were burned or buried alive. Soldiers went door-to-door, seeking women to rape. The victims were usually killed afterward, often in brutal ways best not described. It fell to a German Nazi who lived in the city at the time to establish an "International Safety Zone" to which women could flee.

More than 300,000 were murdered during the occupation. It was just the start of a vicious killing spree against military prisoners and ordinary citizens alike that would kill more than ten million throughout the so-called "Co-Prosperity Sphere" under Japanese expansion.

◇◇◇

German expansion begins with Hitler's annexation of his birthplace, Austria, in March 1938. A sizable percentage of the population of the small country looks on this favorably, so it is convenient for the French and British to look the other way. They also have an excuse to stay on the sidelines when, in October, Hitler announces his intention to annex the German-speaking edges of Czechoslovakia. After all, back in 1919, Wilson proposed letting the region vote on whether to become German or Czech. But this time, they toughen up and say …Let's talk about it.

British Prime Minister Neville Chamberlain flies to Munich to meet Hitler on his home ground (Munich is the city where he first burst on the scene with his Nazi Party 18 years before). He tells Hitler he can only acquire the region if he promises to be a good boy from now on. Back in London, he pops off the plane, waves Hitler's signature for the press photographers, and proclaims to have achieved "peace for our time."

I have achieved peace for our time

Well, he didn't achieve that. But he did achieve two things: Adding the word "appeasement" to the vocabulary of high school students and World War Two history buffs everywhere; and becoming one of the better-known

(12)

laughingstocks of world history, leading his party to lose seats at the next election and paving the way for the rise of Winston Churchill.

The following March, Hitler takes over the rest of Czechoslovakia.

While French and British leaders were ignoring or appeasing Hitler, Stalin decides to make a straight-up deal with him. In late August, the world learns that the two have signed a "Nonaggression Pact." Promising openly not to attack each other, they secretly make plans to split up Poland, which has the unfortunate luck of being located between them.

World War Two in Europe begins on September 1, 1939, when the Germans, copying Japan's strategy employed in Manchuria, stage a "false flag" operation. Some German soldiers put on Polish army uniforms and fake a Polish attack on a radio transmitter.

Britain and France declare war on Germany two days later, but by then Poland is already lost. Behind the scenes, German military strategists have been busy plotting a new kind of war made possible by advancements in two technologies introduced in the later parts of World War One.

The first advancement is air power. In the previous war, planes were initially used only as reconnaissance and in those legendary "dogfights," individual one-on-one air battles where flying "aces" mostly died but sometimes gained glory. In World War Two, they will be an integrated part of the ground battle tactics.

The second advancement is armored tanks. Toward the end of World War One, the British pioneered an "anti-trench machine" that could roll right over barbed wire and repel machine-gun fire. But early tanks were death traps that flipped over easily and nearly asphyxiated their occupants with exhaust, so they failed in their mission to break the war's stalemate. In World War Two, much improved, they were to become the stars of the ground battle.

Planes would drop paratroopers behind the enemy to disable communication lines and head off reinforcements. A smokescreen would be created at the enemy's weakest point, and a column of tanks would penetrate that point, followed by ground troops. Once past the lines, the tanks would fan out and circle back to attack from behind.

The Germans called their new style of war the blitzkrieg, literally "lightning war." It was an apt title. In Poland, they showed the world that the new war would be the antithesis of the war on the World War One Western Front. Fronts would zoom ahead before one's eyes. On September 17, Poland's capital, Warsaw, falls to the Germans. Meanwhile, Russian troops occupy the eastern half of the country.

After blitzing Poland, Hitler waits so long before his next move that people begin to call it the "Phony War." Then, bam! In April 1940, the blitzkrieg flashes again, this time in two directions. To the north, Denmark falls on April 9 and Norway on June 7. To the west, the Netherlands falls on May 15 and Belgium on May 28.

The German advance pushes rapidly across northern France, with British and French soldiers in desperate retreat. Nearly the entire remaining British army becomes trapped on the beach at Dunkirk.

In one of his first actions as the new prime minister, Churchill authorizes an innovative rescue plan. He calls on all British citizens with capable watercraft to take their boats across the English Channel, pick up as many soldiers as possible, and bring them home to safety.

Amazingly, it works. Nearly everyone is rescued. From the jaws of absolute defeat, Churchill has wrested a moral victory. His people have saved their army to be ready to fight again in the future. He celebrates the feat with a famous speech to Parliament's House of Commons on June 18, four days after the fall of Paris: "Let us therefore brace ourselves to our duties, and so bear ourselves that, if the British Empire and its Commonwealth last for 1,000 years, men will still say, 'This was their finest hour.'"

His call for them to brace themselves comes just in time, for on July 10, about 350 German bombers descend over the British homeland. It is only the first wave of a sustained bombardment that will last until early November.

Churchill's trademark 'V' for Victory

On January 19, 1915, in the quiet seaside town of Yarmouth, 72-year-old Martha Taylor became the first English person killed by a bomb. It was dropped from a German zeppelin. This may have been the first time civilians were deliberately targeted in war. A few thousand more citizens would become bomb victims during the Great War, but as in most of the wars before it, the war was almost entirely directed away from the general population.

Not so in World War Two. This was a new kind of war, much of which would be directed squarely at civilians. The Japanese military would direct nationalist hatred against those in the lands they occupied. The Nazis would direct antisemetic and ideological hatred against those in their own country and in the lands they conquered. All sides would strategically target the enemy's citizenry with the intention of breaking down morale and causing the populace to pressure its leaders to surrender. The latter began with the Battle of Britain.

The Germans initially try to take out military targets and hobble the Royal Air Force (RAF) in preparation for a planned seaborne invasion. But after nearly two months of facing stiff resistance from the RAF, Hitler's patience wears thin and he begins to direct his bombers to pound British cities. In London, the raids send residents underground to catch whatever rest they can in subway tunnels or church crypts. Speeches by Churchill and the king do their best to stiffen citizens' resolve. Ubiquitous posters echo a similar theme: "Your courage, your cheerfulness, your resolution WILL BRING US VICTORY."

Tens of thousands of tons of bombs are dropped. Miraculously, the dome of St. Paul's Cathedral survives.

News from the continent is grim. Germany, Italy and Japan have declared themselves the "Axis Powers." Hungary, Romania, and Bulgaria have sided with them. A fascist dictator has taken control in Spain. The Soviets occupy Finland and their half of Poland. Sweden, Switzerland, and Portugal remain neutral. Only Greece and Yugoslavia continue to resist the Axis. Survival of the British on their small island may soon be Europe's last hope for freedom.

On the morning of November 2, Britons wake up realizing that, for the first time since early September, their night was unbroken by air raid sirens. The resolve of the citizenry and of the Royal Air Force has outlasted Hitler's determination to crush them. These won't be the last bombs to fall, but for the next few months, Hitler will be occupied with other issues.

The Italians have begun to fail on two fronts. In Africa, from their colony of Libya, they have pressed into Egypt, where British troops are based. Now the British not only repel them, but have them on the run. In the Balkans, the Italians attack Greece from Albania, but get nowhere. In the spring, Hitler diverts some German troops to both of these fronts. In Africa, the front reverses again as the Germans drive deep into Egypt. Meanwhile, a sizable detachment of German troops drives south from Austria to capture Yugoslavia and Greece, putting all of southeastern Europe in Axis hands.

On the single night of May 10 to 11, 1941, German bombers drop over 700 tons of bombs on Britain, at least 80,000 of them incendiaries (designed to start fires on the ground). But this isn't a resumption of the Battle of Britain; it is more like a fit of anger at Britain's stubborn refusal to fold. Because shortly afterward, Hitler launches a totally new plan: He breaks the Nonaggression Pact he'd signed with Stalin and mounts a ground invasion of the USSR.

German troops from Poland advance in three directions: toward St. Petersburg, which has been renamed Leningrad; toward Moscow; and to the southeast toward Volgograd, which has been renamed Stalingrad. It will be the bloodiest campaign of the war, with huge numbers of both military and civilian casualties.

In August, Roosevelt and Churchill arrange a secret meeting on a ship some miles northeast of Newfoundland. Despite continuing isolationist resistance at home, Roosevelt is planning for the US to enter the war. Together, he and Churchill draw up plans for what they will do when they win.

They are following the precedent set by Woodrow Wilson, designing the postwar peace even before the first American fighter is killed. They create a document called the Atlantic Charter. In addition to Wilsonian objectives like collective security, disarmament, freedom of the seas, and self-determination, they add economic cooperation. Thus, it will be a model not only for the United Nations, but for the World Bank and the International Monetary Fund (IMF), as well.

Before they go their separate ways, Roosevelt tells Churchill something that would rile the isolationists in Congress if they heard it: "We will [do] everything [to] force an incident." The next month, in that same North Atlantic, when a German submarine fires on an American ship, Roosevelt gives orders to shoot at German subs on sight. As far as he is concerned, the Americans have joined the war.

Back in the fall of 1940, when the Japanese took over the French colony of Indochina, the US tried to make a statement by cutting off all trade with them. Trade between nations, though, is one of the better ways to keep the peace. In this case, ending trade was an especially bad move for peace because the US was Japan's principal supplier of oil. Needing oil desperately to lubricate their imperialist expansion, the Japanese military was forced to look elsewhere.

The Dutch East Indies had significant oil reserves, and they were just a hop and a skip from Indochina. Unfortunately, that hop was over the American Philippines. Thus, Japan started laying some plans: They would first attack the Philippines. From there, they would move on to take the Indies for their oil, as well as British Malaya for its rubber. But to ensure that this key strategy was a success, they felt they needed to concurrently attack the American naval base at Pearl Harbor in Hawaii in order to keep the US from coming across the ocean to interfere.

On December 7 and 8, 1941, the Japanese put their plan into action. At Pearl Harbor, they are able to cripple 300 planes and sink 18 ships, but none of these are aircraft carriers, which will be of the most strategic importance in the war. All of the carriers from the base happen to be out on patrol that morning. This will be a great help to the Americans later on, but for now, aside from bringing the Americans into the war against them, Japan's plans are a success. By early spring, Malaya, the Indies, and the Philippines are all in Japanese hands, and they have their sights set on Australia.

At the same time that the US declares war on Japan, it also declares war on Germany, but it will be nearly a year before the first American troops make it across the Atlantic. Hitler, meanwhile, has begun to implement his "Final Solution": genocide of the Jewish people. This begins with in-field executions by special killing squads that follow the troops into Soviet-held Poland and the USSR. The first victims are simply shot. Eventually, the squads employ mobile gassing vans. Just days after the attack on Pearl Harbor, the first of seven dedicated killing centers opens in Poland. As distinguished from concentration camps, the killing centers will be like factories of death, their sole purpose being to process living bodies in and dead bodies out.

In Russia, the Germans have begun to lay siege to Leningrad. The city survives the hard Russian winter, but the siege continues deep into 1942. One woman writes in her journal, "Everyone is shriveled, their breasts sunken in, their stomachs enormous and, instead of arms and legs, just bones poke out through wrinkles."

While taking Leningrad and Moscow is key to achieving a Soviet surrender, the push toward Stalingrad is key to Germany winning the war. It would give them access to the resource-rich Caucasus Mountains, position them to invade oil-rich Iran, and open up a connection to potential allies Syria and Iraq.

But here, Hitler makes a choice that military historians will second-guess. Things may have turned out differently if he had directed his troops to skirt around the city of Stalingrad. Is it because the city is named for his rival that Hitler is obsessed with conquering it? The Germans attack the city in August 1942. They will still be fighting within it, house-to-house, come winter.

If pushing through the Caucasus to the Middle East will bring Germany ulti-mate victory, conquering Australia will do the same for Japan. If Australia falls, the Japanese will control maritime movement between the Indian and Pacific oceans.

In May 1942, US Marines in landing crafts hit the beach at Guadalcanal Island, liberating it and opening up access to the Coral Sea, which lies off the northeast Australian coast.

The Battle of the Coral Sea, fought exclusively by carrier-launched planes, is the turning point of the war in the Pacific. Australia is saved; the Japanese sweep is halted. From here on, the lasso the Japanese have cast out to encompass most of the islands of the western Pacific will gradually shrink.

It will be a long and painful process. Japanese society has been indoctrinated in the "Way of the Warrior," a discipline that downplays the self and prepares to "meet death with perfect calmness." Those who surrender are considered inferior. Willing to sacrifice their "little selves" for their emperor, kamikaze pilots are willing to crash their planes into American aircraft carriers. To defend each island possession, the Japanese are willing to fight to the death.

Against such determined defense, liberation of every island becomes an enormous task for American Marines. Once an island is taken, they must "island hop" to the next, until they at last come within reach of the Japanese homeland.

As the Americans claw their way through the Pacific tropics, until February 1943 the Germans and Russians claw their way through the frozen rubble of Stalingrad in winter. More than 840,000 German soldiers die there. The Russians lose more than one million, but they eventually reassert control of the city and begin to push the Germans back westward.

After losing troop strength during their engagements in the Balkans and North Africa, the astounding losses in Stalingrad are too much for the Germans to sustain. From this point on, they will be in retreat, not only in Europe, but in Africa as well. Throughout the spring of 1943, they are chased from the western bank of the Nile back to the center of the North African coast. At the other end of the Mediterranean, the British had liberated Morocco, where American troops had started arriving in November 1942. Together, they press eastward, and now the pincers close on the Germans in Tunisia.

From here, it is only a short hop to Sicily, which is in Allied hands by mid-August. In Rome, Mussolini resigns. A new government throws him in prison and initiates a formal surrender. But German troops come to bail out the Italian fascists a third time. They rescue Mussolini and secret him away in the north of the country.

Since the prior century, Iran had been split into two spheres of imperialist influence, with the Russians in the north and the British in the south. Now, with its precious oil fields safe from German invasion, it is to Iran that the "Big Three" leaders –Roosevelt, Stalin and Churchill—come to discuss how to finish the war in Europe and transition to peace. They discuss what a postwar occupation of Germany might look like and how to prevent yet another occurrence of territorial aggression by Germany or anyone else. Roosevelt and Churchill introduce Stalin to their idea for the UN.

As for what is needed to get to that point, Stalin is adamant that a western front be opened up in order to reduce the toll on Russian troops. Roosevelt supports him, and they are eventually able to convince Churchill to back a seaborne invasion of occupied France launched from Britain. British, American, and Canadian troops would take part. A date is set, known only to the highest level of command. The many participants would know it only as D-Day.

Throughout the spring of 1944, as British and American forces push north up the Italian Peninsula and the Soviets push westward, the D-Day invasion forces prepare. The German shore defenses know an invasion is coming. For soldiers on both sides of the English Channel, the date is the only unknown.

In the early morning of June 4, 160,000 Allied soldiers huddle in their landing crafts. They are headed for five beachheads spread across a 50-mile stretch of Normandy coastline.

There are 2,500 such landing craft. They will keep coming over the next five days, eventually unloading 54,000 vehicles, over 100,000 tons of materiel, and 325,000 men onto the beaches.

Many of those men will not make it off the sand and into the shelter of the undergrowth. In a way, it is like storming the enemy trenches in World War One. But the attackers also deploy 700 warships with long-range artillery that can fire across the beaches at the German defenses, and they send planes to circle behind those defenses and drop paratroopers. Due to the sheer numbers of attackers, the coastal defenses are eventually overrun. From here on, the Germans will be fighting a war on three fronts: the east, the south, and the west, each drawing inexorably inward.

There is another front drawing in upon Germany: the sky. The sky war that began with Germany's pounding of Britain in 1940 is now being won by the combined British and American Strategic Air Command. Since February, four months ahead of the D-Day invasion, SAC bombers have been targeting every major German city. The campaign will continue for another 11 months, leaving much of Germany's urban landscape in ruins. Three hundred thousand civilians will die and another 7.5 million will be made homeless.

Scientists on both sides of the conflict had been at work developing weapons of mass destruction and death. According to physicist Albert Einstein's 1939 letter to President Roosevelt, the Nazis had already begun work on harnessing nuclear energy for a weapon even before the invasion of Poland. In August 1942, Roosevelt combined multiple research programs into the Manhattan Project, a top-secret program tasked with developing a nuclear bomb before the Nazis did. In January of the next year, a secret laboratory opened in a remote stretch of Native American land in New Mexico.

It will be June 1945 before a bomb can be built and successfully tested. By then, both Hitler and Mussolini will be dead (as will be Roosevelt, from a stroke) and the war in Europe over.

It is apparent that Roosevelt is ailing when the Big Three meet once again in Yalta, Ukraine, in February. The Russian forces are less than 100 miles from Berlin, and American, British and French troops are at Germany's western border. It is time to get down to the business of carving up Germany for occupation and determining how to get the liberated countries back on their feet.

Poland is a big question. The Soviets are once again in possession of the eastern half of the country (the part they took in 1939 before the Germans stole it from them), and Stalin doesn't want to give it back. After being attacked twice by Germany in the last 30 years, he says his country needs a buffer zone. The three leaders come up with a solution to make everyone happy, including the Poles: Just shove the country over to the left on the map. Stalin gets to keep his piece, and the Poles get equal-sized bits of Germany to make up for it.

Then there is the question of who is going to govern the country. The Soviets have just installed a communist Polish government in the part they occupy. There is also a democratic Polish government-in-exile in London. Possession being nine-tenths of any negotiation, Churchill and Roosevelt agree to hand power to the communist government that is already in Poland, as long as Stalin promises to orchestrate democratic elections for a new government soon.

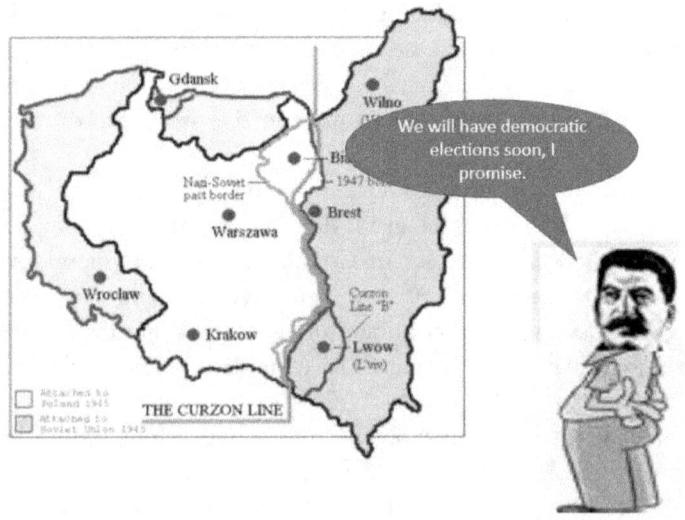

...Yeah, right.

◇◇◇

April 1945 is an eventful month. Roosevelt dies on the 12th and is succeeded by his vice president, Harry Truman. On the 25th, American and Russian soldiers meet at Germany's Elbe River, and the UN Charter is drafted in San Francisco. On the 28th, the Italian opposition catches up to Mussolini in his mountain hideaway. He and his mistress are killed and their bodies hung upside-down in a village square, where those who have suffered under his rule are free to mutilate them with clubs. On the 30th, in his underground Berlin bunker, Hitler and his mistress opt for a more dignified exit and shoot each other.

The European Axis Powers surrender on May 8. That leaves the Japanese. The Americans take Okinawa, the last in the chain of islands that has led them within reach of the Japanese homeland.

As was done in Germany, bombers now regularly pound major Japanese cities. On one night in March, American incendiary bombs destroy 16 square miles of central Tokyo. Tens of thousands of civilians are thought to have died, with nearly one million left homeless.

As the raids continue into the summer, Japanese leadership becomes severely concerned about what it mildly terms "the domestic situation." The fear is that food shortages will soon lead people to rebel. Emperor Hirohito, whose suggestions are typically ignored by the military, puts together a peace proposal in which he can remain emperor and there will be no occupation of Japan. His adviser proposes it be forwarded to Stalin as an intermediary, rather than directly to the United States.

At 5:29am Mountain Standard Time on July 16, 1945, at Los Alamos, New Mexico, the first atomic bomb is detonated. It is a stunning success. American president Harry Truman has just arrived in Potsdam, in suburban Berlin, to meet with Churchill and Stalin. When he receives a terse message that "test exceeded expectations," he knows he has inherited an incredible power, greater than that held by any human being to date.

In Potsdam, a date is set for the Soviets to join the assault on the Japanese homeland, beginning with an invasion of Manchuria. This will provide some welcome relief to the Americans. In a letter to his wife, Truman writes, "I've gotten what I came for – Stalin goes to war [against Japan] August 15.... I'll say that we'll end the war a year sooner now, and think of the kids who won't be killed!"

But the situation in Europe has taught Truman that any involvement with Stalin is not without its challenges. Germany has been divided into four zones of occupation, with the Americans, Russians, British, and French each overseeing a zone. All of the occupied countries to the west of Germany are in the process of taking back their own control, but to the east, the Soviets are reticent to withdraw and have begun to prop up minority communist factions.

In exchange for his support against Japan, Stalin asks for a concession of some territory from China. Will it end there? Will the US have to share the occupation of Japan with the Soviets? Truman's letter seems to conflict with his diary entry later that evening: "Believe Japs will fold up before Russia comes in. I am sure they will when Manhattan appears over their homeland."

Stalin and Truman seem to be gaming each other. In a meeting later in the week, Stalin, who earlier informed Truman of his being contacted by Emperor Hirohito, brushes off the peace proposal as "unclear." Is he withholding information because a peace would prevent him from getting his hands on the land in China? Meanwhile, in another letter to his wife some days later, Truman seems to muse about the bomb as a power he holds over Stalin: "[He] doesn't know it, but I have an ace in the hole."

Truman discusses the matter privately with Churchill, and they decide to tell Stalin about the bomb.

They draft an ultimatum directed to the Japanese emperor. It promises "utter devastation of the Japanese homeland" unless Japan unconditionally surrenders. The terms are that Japan will be occupied until there is "convincing proof that [their] war-making power is destroyed" and "freedom of speech, of religion, and of thought, as well as respect for the fundamental human rights [are] established" by a new Japanese government. There will also be war crime trials for the military leadership.

On July 25, the night before the ultimatum is completed and approved, Truman writes in his diary, "The target will be a purely military one and we will issue a warning statement asking the Japs to surrender and save lives."

But as to that: According to David Lilienthal, chairman of the US Atomic Energy Commission, who visited with Truman a few evenings before, the president told him,

> I don't think we ought to use this thing unless we absolutely have to....
> You have got to understand that this isn't a military weapon. It is
> used to wipe out women and children and unarmed people, and
> not for military uses.

And as to the "Japs" surrendering to save lives: Immediately after that statement in his diary, Truman writes, "I'm sure they will not do that, but we will have given them the chance."

The bomb that is dropped on Hiroshima on August 6 kills 95% of the people within its half-mile epicenter as radiation destroys their cells. Buildings up to a mile-and-a-half away collapse from the bomb's radiated shock wave and the winds of up to 600 miles per hour that it generates. There are people whose eyes are blown out by the shock and those over two miles away whose skin is severely burned. Well over 100,000 die, either in the blast or soon after it, or will die well after it from the lingering effects of radiation.

News trickles in to Tokyo over the next 48 hours. In a meeting with the military leadership on August 8, Emperor Hirohito expresses that the war must end.

Japan, too, has been working to develop a nuclear bomb, but they are well behind. Their scientists know enough to respect the enormous complexity involved. For that reason, they suspect that the Americans cannot yet have others available.

They do not have long to wait for their suspicion to be proven wrong. On the morning of August 9, a second bomb destroys Nagasaki, and tens of thousands more people die, with tens of thousands more to follow from its effects.

Japan surrenders, asking for one condition: that the emperor be allowed to remain. With respect to the strength of the land's long imperial tradition, the condition is granted with the understanding that the emperor will exercise no more power over the people's democracy than he has had over the military for the last 15 years.

Of the 72 million human beings whose lives were ended during World War Two, 47 million were civilians. The innocent victims of Hiroshima and Nagasaki were only the last. Humanity has never again entertained the naïve notion that there could be a war that ends all wars. There has been a tacit acceptance that where there is war, civilians will die—at least as part of collateral damage, but often as direct targets.

Hiroshima

Dresden

(13)

In a way, the peace after World War Two will be a do-over of the failures of the peace after World War One:

- The flaws of the League of Nations will be addressed and a better organization, the United Nations, built in its place.
- Wilson's other great ideal, respect for self-determination, will at last blossom into an era of decolonization.
- Rather than heap more misery on the citizens of the pulverized cities of Germany and Japan in the form of reparations payments, the victors will instead provide money and support to them.

But this peace will be fraught with its own flaws. Not only are any qualms about attacking civilians erased, but two diametrically opposed ideologies are staring each other down, and each will soon be armed with the power to destroy the world.

CHAPTER FIFTEEN

The "Free World" Battles Authoritarian Communism, Even as it Impedes "Third World" Sovereignty
(1946-1976)

At this point, an alternate history might be written in which the capitalist industrial-imperialists face up to the errors of their ways, free all their colonies, and help them on their way to becoming industrialists themselves.

One might begin this ideal history by stating that, by the end of 1945, there were 51 member states in the UN, and by the end of 1976, there were 103. It could be added that the IMF and the World Bank were created to provide loans and assistance to these developing nations.

Everything in the above paragraph is true. But in reality, the imperialists were reticent to let go of their colonial possessions—some more than others—and even when they did ostensibly let go, they often tried to convert the relationship from outright political ownership of the nation to simple corporate ownership of the economy (á la the dependent relationships already established in Latin America). The IMF and the World Bank, meanwhile, were often used as cattle prods to force developing nations to do the developed world's bidding.

The USA starts off setting a good example by freeing the Philippines in time for it to become one of the original 51 signatories of the UN Charter. But the Dutch refuse to release the East Indies, and the French refuse to release Indochina. In both places, the native population, having suffered considerable losses against the Japanese, keeps its armies intact and turns them against its colonial overlords.

The British drop a couple of hot potatoes: India and Palestine.

In India, it is becoming clear that a quarter of the country's population (its Muslims) are not going to quietly assume the role of minor partner to the Hindus in an independent India.

There is danger, too, in Gandhi granting too much of a role to the Muslims. India's ancient mystic foundation, with its emphasis on tolerance, had supported a wide religious/cultural diversity throughout its history. But then came the British occupation, with its attendant persecutions. And just as the Catholics of classical

Rome fought persecution by establishing strict orthodoxy with no tolerance of other beliefs, Hindu nationalists begin to fight British persecution by lessening Hinduism's traditional tolerance of Muslims.

Gandhi, with great reluctance, gives in to a plan for two new nations to gain simultaneous sovereignty on August 15, 1947: India and Pakistan. Two of his closest friends will become the new countries' first prime ministers. Their closeness does not prevent an explosion of carnage from befalling the subcontinent.

The problem is that nearly every corner of the land contains both Hindu and Muslim families. The largest Muslim majorities are in the northwest and northeast. The solution is to split Pakistan into east and west sections 2,000 kilometers apart. The next task is to move the minority Hindus out of Pakistan and the minority Muslims out of India.

And so begins what is, at this time, the largest migration of human beings in history. As expected, it is not without incident. Clashes occur where migration paths cross. Muslims who choose to remain in India are attacked. Leaders on both sides are powerless to stop the rioting. Cities like Delhi and Kolkata, which contain large Muslim minorities, are set aflame.

Finally, only Gandhi, the great purveyor of nonviolence, can bring calm. As he has done many times before in protest against the British, he begins to fast. On the *sixth* day of his fast, surrounded by political leaders from both countries, the news is conveyed to him that rioting has stopped in all major cities, and he is persuaded to take some nourishment.

As he recovers, Gandhi makes plans to continue promoting peace with a visit to Pakistan, but he is assassinated only a couple of weeks later –by a Hindu nationalist who opposed his openness to the Muslims.

And then there is the trouble brewing in Palestine...

Recall Abraham/Ibrahim, the legendary patriarch of the Hebrews and Arabs who is supposed to have flourished in the Middle East in the 2nd millennium BCE. The people known in the 20th and 21st centuries as the Jews and the Palestinians have both been genetically traced to the Canaanites, who lived along the eastern shore of the Mediterranean during the Axial Age. Later, the area came to be dominated by the Jewish people from their kingdoms of Israel and Judah, located in what, centuries later, became the central and northern portions of the British mandate of Palestine. Arab people, the ancestors of modern Palestinians, occupied kingdoms that lay inland from Israel/Judah, east of the Jordan River.

Next, recall how much of the Jewish population was massacred in two uprisings against the Romans in the 1st and 2nd centuries CE. The result was that the Jews went from majority to minority status in the area after many survivors of these brutally-suppressed uprisings fled in the Jewish Diaspora.

Recall how, more recently, the Zionist movement of the early 20th century began a stream of Jewish emigration back to Palestine. After the genocide of more than six million European Jews by the Nazis in World War Two, that stream rapidly became a flood.

Once again, as in India, the British overlords can see that this situation will lead to an outcome they do not want to be responsible for. So they turn to the new United Nations to help with their withdrawal. The result is a plan that maps out how Palestine can be split between Jews returning to their ancient homeland and Arabs who have long since moved into the areas the ancient Jews vacated.

First, the UN lops off all of the land east of the Jordan River, which becomes the Arab nation of Transjordan (later shortened to simply "Jordan"). It declares the city of Jerusalem (holy to all three Abrahamic religions) an international zone to be shared by all. So far, so good. But then they split the rest into Jewish-owned and Arab-owned areas. Just as in India, this is not a simple division into two. There are multiple mostly-unconnected pieces. Two tiny corridors, which the Jews must hop across, connect the Arab pieces. Also as in India, real life is not so simple; there are Arabs living in the Jewish bits and vice versa.

The UN General Assembly passes the plan, and the Jews approve. The Arabs don't, reasoning that the percentage of land apportioned to them is less than their percentage of the population. The British, not wanting any part of the argument, bolt for home. And there's war.

The Jews win the war, rather convincingly, and declare the independent nation of Israel. The Arab Palestinians would have been better off with the original plan. There will be no independent nation of Palestine. In the south, a narrow strip known as Gaza is added to Egypt. The land between Jerusalem and the Jordan River is added to Jordan. Jerusalem, itself, is split into east and west halves, each with definite owners. There will be no sharing. Instead, hatred will fester.

In 1946, in Harry Truman's home state of Missouri, smack in the geographical center of the United States, Winston Churchill made a famous speech in which he said that in Europe, "from Stettin on the Baltic to Trieste on the Adriatic, an *iron curtain* has descended across the continent."

The Soviets had continued to hang on to the half of Europe that its forces had liberated from the Nazis. Churchill was in the US to make a pitch to integrate British and American military and intelligence organizations. That particular idea wasn't received too well, but his warning about Stalin and the Soviets was spot on. He may have been the first to acknowledge that what was soon to be called "the Cold War" had already begun.

"Cold," as opposed to "hot," only meant there would not be any direct conflict between the capitalist USA and the communist USSR. There would be plenty of war going on around the world between capitalists and communists. There would be plenty of involvement in those wars between Americans and Soviets; they just would not be firing the guns. They would, though, be manufacturing those guns, and handing them to the side they wanted to win. They would also be supplying those sides with military intelligence.

These wars would be called proxy wars, borrowing a term more common to corporate shareholder meetings, where small-time investors mail in their votes to be cast at the meeting by a proxy. Only in this case, it's the big-time investors using the little guys as the proxies. Like how the Americans and Soviets began to use the Greeks in 1947.

The Greek Civil War had been going on since liberation from the Nazis in 1944. The communists were fighting to keep the Greek king from being reinstated.

Greece was the only European country behind Churchill's iron curtain that wasn't occupied by the Soviets. That was because they had been liberated by the British, who came up from the Aegean Sea. But now, the British feel tapped out militarily (which is why Churchill had been in Missouri looking for American help), so they are preparing to pull out their troops and leave the Greeks on their own.

This causes Truman to make a commitment, and he makes it cover a lot more than the immediate situation. He says that the USA will "support free peoples who are resisting attempted subjugation by armed minorities or by outside pressures."

That's a big commitment. It is the first outright declaration that the USA is going to be the world's policeman.

Truman then gets more specific to the current situation in Europe. With regard to communism, his policy will be "containment." In other words, the US will not interfere with European nations that currently have communist governments with Moscow pulling their puppet strings. But it will quarantine communism like a viral disease and take actions to prevent its spread. Those actions will amount to supplying materiel, intelligence, and battlefield strategy, all of which immediately start flowing to the royalist, anti-communist Greeks.

Here is a map of Europe, with a lasso tossed around the puppet states in which communism will be contained:

A month after Truman gets things going in Greece, the North Atlantic Treaty Organization (NATO) is formed. It includes the US, Canada, and the countries to the west of the quarantined ones, with the exception of fascist Spain; neutral Switzerland, Sweden, and Finland; and still-recovering West Germany and Austria. NATO is an old-fashioned alliance that says, "If you attack me, you're attacking all of us. (And, by the way, Mr. World Policeman USA with the Big Bomb is one of us.)" Now that the teams are set, it's game on...

Right away, the US starts sending money to its old and new European friends who are most beat-up by the war, and it is new friend West Germany that needs it the most. Stalin is following all of this with interest, of course. Since a tiny part of West Germany, known as West Berlin, sits right in the middle of communist East Germany, he is concerned that an improving economy there will begin to attract defectors from his side of town. So he fashions a little lasso of his own and tosses it around West Berlin.

This is not the more permanent Berlin Wall that will come along 12 years from now. It is a very quickly-formed blockade of simple barriers, with sentry-guarded crossing gates at key points of entry. The blockade encircles the French, British and American parts:

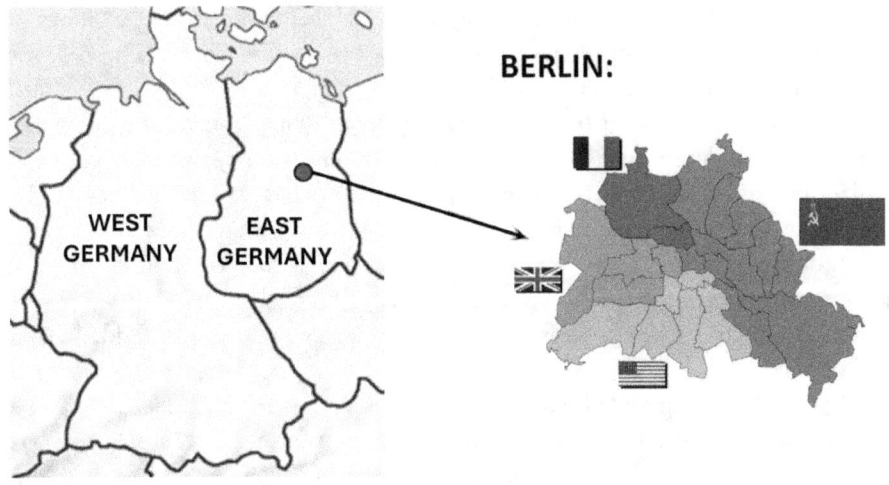

BERLIN:

Not only are freedom-seeking East Berliners being kept out of the west side of town; supplies from the NATO countries are also prevented entry. Which makes the situation critical for the West Berliners.

Truman doesn't hesitate at all before making his counter-move. Just two days after the blockade goes up, American planes are taking off 'round the clock from airfields in West Germany. Over the course of the next *two years*, the planes will make 278,000 airdrops into West Berlin, totaling 2.3 million tons of food, fuel, and supplies. Finally, in May 1949, Stalin gives up and pulls down the barriers.

West Berliners awaiting another drop

So far, 1949 is a good year for the NATO team. But on the other side of Eurasia, there is cause for concern in what has become a second proxy war: the Chinese Civil War.

Mao Zedong, having garnered noteriaty during the Long March, is now at the head of the communist army. After their courageous performance against the Japanese, the communists win the majority of popular support. With morale high, their troops have a string of successes on the battlefield.

Meanwhile, Chiang Kai-shek has not been the greatest representative of "free peoples." In fact, the Chinese are not free at all. They suffer not only from the war, but also from a corrupt government that has sapped the economy while profiting its members. Furthermore, Chiang's military is beginning to look so incompetent that, without injecting actual boots-on-the-ground support, it's likely that this proxy war will be lost.

Truman and his brain trust briefly consider reaching out to Mao to make some accommodation just to keep him from getting too cozy with Stalin, then realize that ship has sailed (back on May 4, 1919). They wonder if they might be able to put together a third force, maybe have their spies seek out some still-undefeated warlord who might fare better against the communists (but fat chance anyone like that would be any better than Chiang). Ultimately, they decide to double down on what seems their only choice: spend more on added arms shipments.

Then, while Truman is focused on all the bad news from China, even worse news comes from the USSR: In August, the Soviets successfully test their own atom bomb. It is a shock. Americans and their allies figured it would happen one of these days, but they thought their advantage would last much longer.

It's a new game now, and when good news comes in October that the capitalists have won the first proxy war in Greece, no one is in the mood to rejoice.

Any celebration would have been brief, anyway: The capitalists' 1–0 lead in the proxy wars lasts even less time than their lead in having the biggest bomb did: In December, Chiang's forces give up and flee the mainland for Taiwan. China has fallen to the communists.

The United Nations was designed to be dominated by the World War Two victors: the United States, the Soviet Union, and Great Britain, with the addition of the two allies who were liberated, France and China. These five nations would be permanent members of the UN Security Council, the body that has primary responsibility for maintaining international peace. Importantly, each of the five would have veto power over any council resolution. (There were also six nonpermanent members elected to two-year terms on the council. This was expanded to ten nonpermanent members in 1965. None of these members have veto power.)

Six months after the communist victory in China, in June 1950, the tiny "Republic of China" on the island of Taiwan continued to fill China's seat on the Security Council. Meanwhile, in Mao's vast mainland "People's Republic of China," change had been constant.

China may have been bankrupt and devastated by 22 years of constant war, but under Mao's leadership, the Communist Party was focused and enervated. No other newly-sovereign, formerly-imperialized country would pursue modernization so aggressively.

Mao rolled out a party organization that canvassed the entire nation down to the most remote precinct. Local leaders called meetings to explain the party vision, its specific goals, and the process for achieving those goals. Highly positive propaganda was everywhere.

The government did not just accentuate positives; it offered them. The work units to which people were assigned also gave them free education and health care. The government's first major legislation made women the legal equals of men. Since the time of Confucius, all marriages had been arranged, and women had been subjected to the three obediences: obedience to the father until wed, to the husband until his death, and then to the eldest son. Overnight, the new government ended nearly 2,500 years of tradition.

Very early in his reign as the leader of the world's largest nation, Mao has done a masterful job of winning the People's allegiance. In doing so, he has invested his words with tremendous power. From this point on, he will be able to state a directive and his word will disseminate down and outward through the party and propaganda infrastructure to every corner of China. He will have a habit of giving an initiative a name, underlying it with slogans, and just tossing it out there. Like a rock falling into a vast, calm sea, ripples of empowerment will spread outward as the initiative gains its own life.

Mao knew that in order to support an industrial economy, he would first have to boost agricultural production to sufficiently feed what was, at that time, a quarter of the world's population. Much of the rural population was going hungry. To address this, Mao called on peasants everywhere to seize land from their landlords.

Very quickly, the communist ideal of land redistribution was implemented. Peasants organized themselves and called huge meetings, hauling their landlords before the crowd. Local leaders encouraged them to humiliate the landlords, who would be put upon a makeshift stage, bound, and denounced. Usually, they were beaten.

It was impossible, of course, to control how every last acre of land was redistributed. In many cases—probably more than 100,000—landlords were killed.

But the ultimate objective was successful. With more land, the peasants could grow more food. Widespread hunger was eliminated, and for the first time since the early Qing Dynasty, China had a firm agricultural foundation.

The early success of Chinese communism influenced the spread of communism to neighboring Korea. The Soviets had first introduced it during the regional occupations at the end of World War Two, when the USA occupied Japan and the USSR occupied Manchuria. Lying between the two, the Korean Peninsula had been split along an arbitrary line at 38 degrees latitude, with the Soviets to the North and the Americans to the South.

In June 1950, a North Korean communist army crossed the 38th parallel into the South. It was the first crisis to fall upon the new UN Security Council. It just so happened that, only days before, the USSR had boycotted the council in protest because its demand to have the communist People's Republic of China replace Taiwan's Republic of China on the council had been rejected by the US, Great Britain, and France.

The Soviet boycott was convenient for the other members of the council, as the USSR would have vetoed any move to intervene in Korea. As it was, the others were able to arrange for a special UN force to go to war on the side of the South Koreans.

As UN troops began to push north of the 38th parallel, Mao became concerned about where this development on his border might lead, so he called up the Chinese army to intervene on the side of the North Koreans. They crossed the border in October.

Most of the UN troops were supplied by the US. Hence, Mao's first named initiative became "Resist America and Aid Korea." As winter descended on the north of China, the call went out that the Chinese should give whatever money they could to support the brave Chinese troops.

And those donations began to flood in—from everywhere in the country. Some who could afford it actually donated their entire paychecks.

By the spring, Chinese and North Korean troops had pushed the UN troops back across the 38th parallel. The war became a stalemate. Peace negotiations began. Korea was split into North and South, with a narrow "demilitarized zone" in between, as it remains today.

The Chinese, as a unified people, were swollen with pride. They had fought a world superpower and its allies to a standstill.

It wasn't until July 1953 that the ink dried on the Korean peace agreement. By then, Stalin had died, leaving the USSR in a state of transitional leadership. In the USA, there was a new president: Dwight Eisenhower, the general who had overseen the European theater in World War Two.

The US also had a new weapon in its nuclear arsenal: the hydrogen bomb. The explosive force of a hydrogen bomb can be up to 1,000 times that of the bomb dropped on Hiroshima.

Eisenhower's tenure as American president would be marked by heavy reliance on the Central Intelligence Agency (CIA) to support the aims of US proxies. Those proxies' opponents would *not* always be communist, but they *would* always be interfering with American business interests.

To date, the Americans' record of supporting "free peoples" is not unblemished; in Greece—their one proxy victory—they helped to reinstate a king. In Iran in 1953, they drop all pretense of being out to support freedom and orchestrate a coup to remove a democratically-elected prime minister.

The USSR had withdrawn from their Iranian *sphere of influence* seven years before, after the USA chastised it in front of the UN for "interfering with a sovereign nation." This was quite the height of hypocrisy, as Russia's departure left the British, and eventually the Americans, too, in control of most of the country's oil production. These relationships helped enrich the family of the shah of Iran but prevented the country from developing a fully-industrial economy of its own.

207

By the start of the next decade, representatives in Iran's parliament were calling for full nationalization of the country's oil industry (moving it into the hands of *Iranian* companies). When a newly-elected prime minister begins to make concrete plans for this to happen, CIA agents help foment a coup and he is arrested. A Western-friendly general from the Iranian army is installed in his place, and life for British and American oil interests continues as before.

A year later, the CIA is at it again, this time in Guatemala. Guatemala had established democracy in 1944, after a popular uprising ousted a military dictator. Now, ten years later, they have had their first democratic transfer of power. But the new Guatemalan president has begun to institute land reforms that threaten property owned by American agribusiness giant United Fruit Company.

UFC is a former legal client of Secretary of State John Foster Dulles, whose brother, Allen Dulles, is the CIA director. With the CIA's help, Guatemala is returned to a military dictatorship and the reforms are halted.

By 1955, the Soviets have successfully tested their own hydrogen bomb. They also have finished playing musical chairs with their dictators and settled for the long haul on one Nikita Khrushchev. The juxtaposition of the H-bomb news with video of Khrushchev caught in his habit of banging his shoe on the table during angry speeches is a bit unsettling.

In 1956 in Mao's new China, the first fault lines of public dissatisfaction begin to show…

After the enormous success of the Resist America campaign, with the country still bathed in the glow of proud patriotism, Mao encouraged the peasants to begin to form cooperatives with each other. Very soon, two-thirds of rural China had complied with his wishes, and everyone was happy with the results.

It worked out so well that Mao accelerated his plans, moving the country to the next step: collectivization. Local party officials were responsible for forming collectives. They used a propaganda campaign of "everyone is doing it" to pressure people to join. In a collective, you signed over all of your private property, your tools and animals included, to the government. The government in Beijing dictated how much grain could be retained by the collective. The rest was sold—at low prices—for the government to redistribute to the cities. Within months, all peasants had given in. But they were no longer happy.

Mao senses that the honeymoon period is over. At the same time, he is disturbed by the rise of elites within the party who might eventually challenge him. He can also see that the collectives have not really increased production.

To address these things, Mao rolls out his "Let 100 Flowers Bloom" campaign. He calls upon the people, at all levels, to express themselves with constructive criticism. Rather than be held back by the constant barrage of government propaganda, with its singular messages, ever-present in government-sponsored films and stage productions, he asks that people "Let 100 flowers bloom in the arts" and "Let 100 schools of thought contend in science."

The people have bottled up their feelings of frustration, and suddenly the cork is pulled out. Soon, the walls of the major universities are covered with posters asking for change.

Those in the various descending ranks of the administration suddenly find themselves criticized by ordinary people, and they are quick to voice their own displeasure with the campaign. The reaction is so intense that it leads Mao to completely reverse course. In the spring of 1957, all of the blooms die. Mao publishes an article calling all those who spoke out during the 100 Flowers campaign "rightists," a term for enemies of communism, and begins his "Anti-Rightist" campaign.

"Struggle meetings" are called, where rightists are forced to sit at the front and be denounced by their colleagues. If they are not sent away to a hard labor camp, at a minimum, they lose their position, along with any hope of finding a similar one. They are ostracized. Their neighbors refer to them afterward as "done for."

Mao's action is the most consequential flip-flop in the history of politics. At this point, only reputations are ruined. Unlike the landlords who endured similar humiliation years before, no one is killed. But because Mao's reversal has made the price of dissent so clear to the Chinese people, it will soon lead to far more deaths than the land redistribution program did, and Mao, no tyrant the likes of Stalin or Hitler, will become responsible for more total deaths than either of them...

By 1958, China's industrial output has more than doubled that of 1953, but Mao is still unsatisfied. His next campaign will be the most ambitious to date. He calls this one the "Great Leap Forward." The Great Leap he hopes to achieve is to become the industrial equal of the United States in 15 years.

Once again, the entire country is mobilized with positive propaganda. People shout slogans while they work from dawn into the night. On a visit to the countryside by train, Mao looks out the window and reads a passing banner aloud: "People's communes are good." A reporter overhears and quotes him. The news spreads virally that Mao wants people's communes to be formed. Soon they are forming all across the country. (It is reminiscent of a long-ago Tang emperor who was overheard casually admiring a woman's tiny feet.)

Multiple villages combine into larger people's communes. The division between nuclear families dissolves, as parents go off to their manual labor and those whose job it is to raise the children take care of them collectively.

One of the tasks of every people's commune is to manufacture steel. The people round up everything made of iron or steel—their cooking implements, their bedframes, whatever can be found—and melt it all down in homemade charcoal-fueled furnaces kept continually alight.

Though the work is exhausting, the people are generally excited, thinking they are launching China ahead in the world. But no amount of enthusiasm can make up for the fact that they are simply amateurs trying to make homemade steel. The pots and pans they create crack and fall apart when heated. After all that work, the only thing they have done is destroy all of their kitchenware, tools, bedframes, etc., so they have no iron or steel remaining.

But the primary goal of every people's commune is to increase agricultural output. Rallying to the slogan "The corn will grow higher the more you desire," communes set goals for production and report them to the party bureaucracy.

Each commune tries to outdo those nearby, leading them to set higher and higher goals. Unfortunately, as the slogan indicates, it is literally wishful thinking.

The trouble begins when this commune-to-commune competition with its number inflation progresses from inflating *goals* to inflating *actual production*.

Mao himself pays visits to the rural communes. Once the people know he is coming, they put together a display for him, perhaps by moving grain in from neighboring areas and putting it all in one field.

It is not just the local accountants and administrators who become aware of the discrepancies with reality; anyone who reasons carefully about the numbers versus the visual evidence can tell the amounts are inflated. But nearly everyone is afraid to speak out. Those who do are accused of being rightists. In 1959, it was only two years on from Mao's sudden reversal of the 100 Flowers campaign.

As a result, when representatives from the government come to collect the commune's contribution, they apply the percentage on numbers that are too high. Suppose the reported number is ten tons and 50% is supposed to go to the government. What if the actual number is only five?

As the communes boost their numbers higher and higher, the party takes more and more grain, leaving the peasants with nothing to eat. Meanwhile, after all has gone to feed the cities or has been sent away as payment for the country's debts, there is enough left over to rot in warehouses.

China's Second Great Famine, lasting from 1959 to 1961, eclipses its 19th-century famine. As many as 50 million people die across China, despite there being plenty that could have fed them.

Mao will be responsible for yet more deaths to come. There will be one more campaign. He will initiate it as innocently as the others, then sit back as its ripples spread of their own accord, the whole country upheaved by the power of his word.

◇◇◇

In Europe in 1955, Khrushchev is instrumental in putting together the Warsaw Pact, a counter-alliance that includes the USSR and all its Eastern European puppets. Countries in neither alliance begin to be called the "Third World." The term carries an imperialist connotation, as if the Third World is of lesser importance—only a playing field for Cold War scheming and manipulation. But the very next year will give a glimpse of a new world order, in which a Third World country can rise to be a player, itself.

Egyptian president Gemal Nasser wants to build a dam across the Nile. The US, competing for influence against the Soviets in this strategic midpoint of the Arab world, offers to help fund it. But when Nasser gives diplomatic recognition to communist China and announces an arms deal with communist Czechoslovakia, American Secretary of State Dulles gets angry and withdraws the offer.

Instead of letting it pass or going begging to the other side, Nasser makes a calculated move. Egypt has been a sovereign nation since 1922, but the Suez Canal, which passes through it, remains under the control of the British and the French, who worked together to build it. Now, Nasser says it is time for Egypt to nationalize the canal and start charging for all the traffic going through it.

This gets Britain and France so riled up that they turn to Israel and persuade it to start a war. The Egyptians are already hassling the Israeli army along their shared border, so Israel is cool with this. As Israeli forces drive into the desert of the Sinai Peninsula and the Egyptian military responds, the British and French use the fighting's proximity to the canal as an excuse to come in and "protect it."

The British and French seem to think this is 1914, but they are not the main players anymore. Neither they nor the Israelis have informed the US about their plan. This ticks off Eisenhower, who immediately threatens them all with economic sanctions if they do not back down. The US joins with the USSR and others in the UN to pass a resolution calling for a cease-fire.

Israel pulls back its troops, and Britain and France go home with their tails between their legs. The British prime minister is chagrined enough to resign. France is a bit more huffy about it; it has been fighting independence-seekers in its nearby colony of Algeria and still mistrusts Nasser, whom it suspects of supplying arms to the Algerian freedom fighters.

The incident underlines how only the two superpowers run things now. But more importantly, Egypt has won. It has taken back a valuable economic resource within its sovereign borders. Other Third World nations will be emboldened by Nasser's example.

211

Two years later, in Iraq, nationalist military officer Abdel Karim Qasim over-throws the Iraqi king and puts an end to the sweetheart deals the king had made with American and British oil companies. In 1960, Qasim will be instrumental in the founding of the Organization of the Petroleum Exporting Countries (OPEC). Member states Iraq, Iran, Saudi Arabia, Kuwait, and Venezuela will find strength in numbers. Ultimately, they will use that strength to weaponize the world's most valuable resource, turning the tables on the imperialists.

◇◇◇

On the other side of Africa, a man named Kwame Nkrumah is now the leader of an independent Ghana. He had studied the methods of Gandhi and rallied Ghanaians to take part in a campaign of civil disobedience against the British. Over the next decade, 32 other new sovereign nations will be added to the map of Africa. As soon as each is free of its colonizers, the two superpowers cozy up to it with dubious offers of economic assistance.

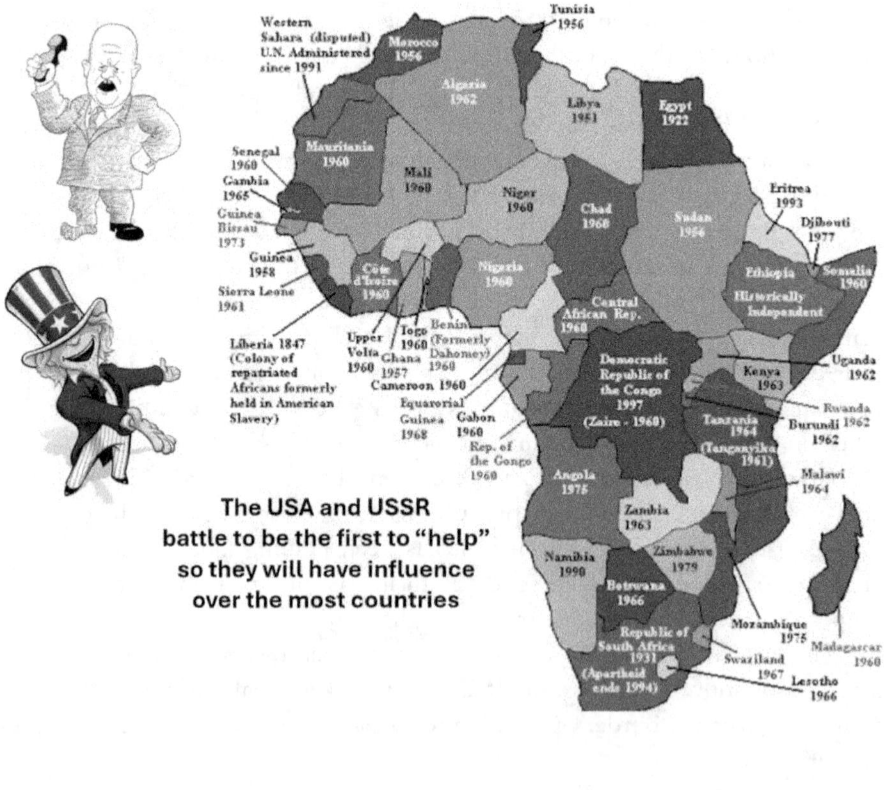

Western Sahara (disputed) U.N. Administered since 1991

Tunisia 1956
Morocco 1956
Algeria 1962
Libya 1951
Egypt 1922

Senegal 1960
Mauritania 1960
Gambia 1965
Guinea Bissau 1973
Guinea 1958
Sierra Leone 1961
Mali 1960
Niger 1960
Chad 1960
Sudan 1956
Eritrea 1993
Djibouti 1977
Ethiopia 1960
Somalia 1960 Historically Independent

Liberia 1847 (Colony of repatriated Africans formerly held in American Slavery)
Upper Volta 1960
Togo 1960
Ghana 1957
Benin (Formerly Dahomey) 1960
Côte d'Ivoire 1960
Nigeria 1960
Central African Rep. 1960
Cameroon 1960
Equatorial Guinea 1968
Gabon 1960
Rep. of the Congo 1960
Democratic Republic of the Congo 1997 (Zaire - 1960)
Kenya 1963
Uganda 1962
Rwanda 1962
Burundi 1962
Tanzania 1964 (Tanganyika 1961)
Angola 1975
Zambia 1963
Zimbabwe 1979
Malawi 1964
Namibia 1990
Botswana 1966
Mozambique 1975
Madagascar 1960
Republic of South Africa 1931 (Apartheid ends 1994)
Swaziland 1967
Lesotho 1966

The USA and USSR battle to be the first to "help" so they will have influence over the most countries

212

Whether or not a former colony had to agitate or even war for its independence had to do with the size of its White population. If the number of European emigrants was significant, it would often mean war, as was the case in Algeria (vs. France) and Kenya (vs. Britain).

In those two countries, the majority Arab and Black populations were able to wrest back control. In the Republic of South Africa, which also had a large emigrant White population, independence had been granted way back in 1931, but to a *White* government that persecuted the Black population, denying them rights via its policy of *apartheid* (from the Dutch for "segregation").

The wave of freedom that washed over the continent in the early 1960's had inspired the Black people of South Africa to begin to agitate for their rights. But in 1964, their leader, Nelson Mandela, is imprisoned. He will remain so for the next 26 years.

Meanwhile, Black Americans have been doing much better. Martin Luther King was but the most famous of a host of civil rights leaders who had been active in courtrooms and in carefully orchestrated public action since World War Two. The movement had gained momentum throughout the 1950's and early 1960's, making headway in integration of schools and public transportation. In 1964, the same year as Mandela's imprisonment, the first federal civil rights legislation is passed to protect Black Americans' right to vote.

The year 1964 was significant to Americans for another reason, though they did not know just how much at the time...

Ten years before, after fighting against the French for nine years, the forces of Vietnamese communist leader Ho Chi Minh had finally won their country's independence. The potential creation of a new communist country set off an alarm within the intelligence corridors of the US government. Its representatives were halfway around the world in no time, before the French and Vietnamese could even get their pens out to sign a peace agreement.

The US brokered an arrangement in which Vietnam would be temporarily split into northern and southern halves, with Ho Chi Minh as the provisional ruler of the North and TBD to be provisional ruler of the South. Nationwide democratic elections were set to occur two years out, in 1956. The idea, encouraged by the US, was to give people time to move if necessary to whichever half of the country suited them.

The US had some difficulty choosing a leader to back for the South, eventually settling on Ngo Dinh Diem (pronounced "Ziem"). Once again, the Americans were not necessarily backing "free peoples." Diem had his own secret police with extrajudicial power. He was a Catholic who persecuted Buddhists, one of whom, in a famous incident, set himself on fire on a busy Saigon Street corner.

The Americans turned a blind eye to most of this. They liked Diem's being a Catholic because he was able to promote mass migration of Catholics from the North to the South, and the South needed all the votes it could get, as Ho was enormously popular among those who remained in the North.

Diem's unpopularity led to communist guerillas popping up in the South. They had recruited many Buddhists and ethnic minorities. Diem labeled them the Viet Cong to distinguish them from Ho's Viet Minh.

As things turned out, the Americans made sure the 1956 elections didn't happen, because they knew their side was going to lose. Ho tried to come to a reconciliation with Diem directly. Negotiations went nowhere. Despite this, and despite the repeated urging of the Viet Cong, Ho was reluctant to take up arms again. He did, however, begin to construct a supply route through the dense jungle along the Cambodian border en route to the South.

In October 1957, an even bigger alarm goes off in the halls of American government, and immediately after in the American press and populace. There was a Soviet satellite in orbit around Earth called Sputnik. This was a major wake-up call for the Americans: It was the first time the US had lagged behind the USSR in a technology related to national security.

Americans were treated to all manner of convenient *household* technology. The US economy was the envy of the world, still far ahead of the Soviets. Most households had a television, through which President Eisenhower addressed the nation as a lame duck at the end of his second term, warning all to beware of the growth of what he termed the "military-industrial complex." (It is somewhat concerning when your president warns you about something you thought he was in control of.)

Television had helped the handsome 43-year-old John F. Kennedy get elected. The US had started its own satellite program in 1958 and, in May 1961, just a few months into his presidency, Kennedy made a rousing speech, committing the US to getting a man on the moon before the new decade was out.

In part, the speech was meant as a distraction from an embarrassing failure that had occurred just the month before. Kennedy had let holdovers from the Eisenhower administration in the CIA talk him into supporting an anti-communist rebellion in Cuba. The island nation, just 90 miles offshore from America's Florida Keys, had become communist in 1959, when rebels led by Fidel Castro ousted Fulgencio Batista. Batista had been maintaining a decades-old dependent economic relationship that supported the American sugar business. In April 1961, a band of Cuban exiles with American support mounted a naval invasion at Cuba's Bay of Pigs. It failed miserably.

Watching from Russia, Khrushchev gauges what he sees as Kennedy's youthful inexperience. He takes advantage later that summer by quite suddenly constructing a wall around West Berlin. Unlike in 1947, there is no attempt this time to keep supplies from West Berliners. It is a very solid wall, however, under constant surveillance, with guardhouses at checkpoints where sentries are ready to shoot East Berliners on sight, should they try to escape to the West. It rather starkly exposes how citizens of the Warsaw Pact countries are de facto prisoners.

Then, a little over a year later, in October 1962, American air reconnaissance over Cuba comes back with some disturbing photos showing newly-installed launching pads that could easily accommodate nuclear missiles. And it just so happens that there is also a convoy of Soviet ships on its way across the Atlantic, headed straight for Cuba. It is assumed those ships are carrying missiles for placement on the launchers. They would be pointed directly at US cities along the East Coast.

So Kennedy is closeted day and night in secret meetings with his advisers as the ships steam ever closer. This is the inevitable confrontation that no one has wanted ever since the Soviets reached nuclear parity with their development of the H-bomb.

Ultimately, Kennedy orders a naval blockade around Cuba. He also informs the UN and makes a televised address to the American people in which he says,

> I call upon Chairman Khrushchev to halt and eliminate this...
> reckless...threat to world peace.... He has an opportunity now
> to move the world back from the abyss of destruction.

He also secretly pledges to remove American nuclear missiles from Turkey.

As the world is still here, it obviously works. And it helps Kennedy gain the traction he needs in future dealings with Khrushchev.

It is uncertain how much traction Kennedy ever gains with the CIA, however. In February, its fingerprints are all over the assassination of Iraqi Prime Minister Abdel Karim Qasim, who had killed American oil deals and helped to found OPEC. The coup puts the Ba'ath Party in power. It will still be there 16 years later, when their candidate, Saddam Hussein, takes over the country.

The following November, Kennedy is perturbed to learn, after the fact, of American involvement in one more murder of a foreign leader: Ngo Dinh Diem is gunned down by his own generals, who have lost faith in him. It is perhaps for the best, but, unlike the Qasim assassination, it happens in the spotlight of the world's attention, heaping bad PR on the US. It also leaves Kennedy with a leadership vacuum in the South that will be difficult to fill.

He won't be there to fill it, however. Three weeks later, he is himself assassinated at a campaign event by a former member of the "Fair Play for Cuba" committee.

The next US president is Lyndon Johnson. Like Kennedy, Johnson is a big believer in the "Domino Theory," which warns that once any small country in Asia falls to the communists, it will cause another in the region to fall, and that will cause another, and so on. Under Kennedy, US involvement in Vietnam had deepened into full proxy war status, with the South Vietnamese army depending heavily on US supplies and the leadership of American advisers. Now, with the South going through a rotating door of ineffective leaders, Johnson privately feels like only full American involvement can keep this wobbling domino from falling.

One day in August 1964, Johnson announces to the American public that, overnight, the North Vietnamese fired torpedoes at an American gunboat innocently patrolling in the Gulf of Tonkin. He uses this as a reason to ask Congress to grant him war powers. The resulting Gulf of Tonkin Resolution grants the president power to "take all necessary measures... to prevent further aggression."

It will never be clear exactly what happened that night in the gulf. As a navy pilot who had been flying overhead later reported, "I had the best seat in the house to watch that event, and our destroyers were just shooting at phantom targets.... There was nothing there but black water and American fire power."

No matter. This is no longer a proxy war. The USA is about to have boots on the ground.

In 1966, Mao announces his last campaign: the Great Proletariat Cultural Revolution. It will reprise some of his ideas for the 100 Flowers campaign. He is once again inviting constructive criticism of the party (some of which will be directed at those in the higher ranks who have begun to doubt him as a result of the failure of the Great Leap Forward). The key difference this go-round will be the audience at whom the invitation to levy criticism is directed: the youth who have no memory of the past.

Mao tells the upcoming generation that they will never build a strong, communist China without first destroying the "Four Olds": Old Ideas, Old Culture, Old Habits, and Old Customs. As with everything else he has rolled out, he stands back and lets the campaign take on a life of its own.

Many other elements of the campaign are familiar. There is a propaganda blitz that shames nonconformists. Mao's words are published in a little red book that every high school student keeps closer at hand than any of their schoolwork. Students wear uniforms with the same red scarves, which makes them feel like a unified army striving to bring about a purely communist nation.

216

Students broke from their regular studies to go outside and write da-zi-bao, banners that criticized specific examples of the old ways

(14)

Senior students might become members of the Red Guards, charged with organizing attacks on the old ways. "Struggle meetings," an old favorite of Mao's, are back in style. In her memoir, *Red Scarf Girl*, Ji Li Jiang describes the older students leading her and her classmates to a target in the neighborhood. A corner grocer has a sign above his store that reads, "The Great Prosperity Market." Based on their understanding of Mao's little red book, the Red Guards decide that since "great prosperity" indicates making a lot of money, it promotes a form of exploitation; therefore it is part of the Four Olds and should be destroyed. In a joyful spirit, the students tear down the sign and smash it before hauling the owner into the street for an impromptu struggle meeting, making him kneel on the asphalt in the hot sun while they lecture and humiliate him.

Red Guards are zealous about their new responsibilities. In cities across the country, they do not just destroy shop signs. They burn books on great bonfires. They raid museums and destroy priceless cultural artifacts. They take struggle meetings too far and allow their targets to die from beatings, dehydration, and heatstroke.

Students of college age are sent to the countryside for "reeducation," where they squander their university years working as peasants.

Much of the country's educated class is eliminated. Some of its greatest scientific minds are tossed into solitary confinement and forgotten. Many of them would die.

This wildfire spreads across China for nearly a decade. Finally, in September 1976, Mao suffers his third heart attack of that year and dies. The Central Committee of the Communist Party deems the Cultural Revolution over. In an assessment five years later, they will declare it a "severe setback" for the party. But in 1976, Mao lies in state at the Great Hall of the People in Tiananmen Square, and crowds of the People wait for hours to pay their respects.

Much of the anti-capitalist vitriol of the Cultural Revolution was, of course, directed at the USA. As Americans tuned in to their nightly newscasts, they could see Chinese youth setting effigies of Uncle Sam aflame. They also saw more and more footage of Vietnam: American soldiers fighting a strange new kind of war in jungle terrain half a world away. There was a souring of the national mood. The innocent times of the 1950's and early 1960's seemed to have died with their young president.

Before long, events in the Middle East also begin to negatively affect Americans. In 1967, Egypt's President Nasser moves troops into the extreme south of Israel to cut off its access to the Red Sea. The resulting war, with Israel facing off against five Arab nations, proves the vast superiority of an Israeli military that benefits greatly from US support. It is over in six days, by which time Israel occupies the entire Sinai Peninsula up to the Suez Canal. It has also moved into the Golan Heights of Syria, as well as the West Bank—the part of Jordan that lies west of the Jordan River. Continuing occupation of these areas leads to the rise of the Palestine Liberation Organization (PLO), which pledges to destroy Israel.

In 1973, Egypt and Syria attack Israel, beginning the three-week Yom Kippur War. After another Israeli victory, OPEC decides to retaliate against those who gave the Israelis support—the US, the UK, Canada, and Japan—by beginning an oil embargo. In the US, shortages occur and motorists line up for hours to gas up. The resulting inflation is permanent. Americans will never again be able to fill their tanks for pocket change.

Poor choices by the American government have caused the USA to lose favor in the Middle East. Twenty years earlier, American involvement in the overthrow of a democratically elected prime minister who wanted to nationalize Iranian oil had led to the formation of OPEC. Now the American public is footing the bill. The debt to Iran, though, has not yet been fully paid.

Similar dubious choices have caused the USA to lose favor in its own hemisphere. Because of Latin America's history of severe economic leveling going back to the days of *criollo*-led revolutions and imperialist-driven dependent economies, nearly all Latin American governments at this time support the rich and hold down the poor. This leads many poor majorities to embrace socialism. In 1973, the US applies the playbook it used two decades before in Guatemala to oust another democratically-elected leader in Chile.

The Chileans have elected a socialist, Salvadore Allende, as president, and the US fears, without any strong evidence, that the country might be falling into the Soviet orbit. They help put a military man in power instead. His name is Augusto Pinochet, and he will become the biggest butcher in a long string of right-wing Latin American dictators.

As world policeman, the US has not garnered a very good reputation. US foreign policy is a far cry from the support for "free peoples" avowed by Harry Truman over three decades before. The government has been making deals with the devil, often to oppose communism, but just as often only to preserve American business interests.

Now, in Vietnam, the US has gotten itself into an actual "hot" war. The war will last about as long as China's Cultural Revolution, overlapping with nine of its eleven years. From 1964 to 1975, nearly seven million tons of American bombs are dropped on Vietnam and on Cambodia, through which the Viet Minh army travels en route to the South. One million Vietnamese soldiers and two million Vietnamese civilians die in the war. Others suffer long-term effects from Agent Orange, a defoliant sprayed on dense terrain where Viet Cong guerillas often hide.

The US institutes a draft in 1969, and nearly 60,000 American soldiers are lost. More than that flee to Canada in protest. Draft cards are burned and anti-war protests erupt across the nation. Four student protestors on the campus of Ohio's Kent State University are shot dead by the National Guard.

Two American presidents, Johnson and Richard Nixon, have their legacies blackened by a war that—despite costing not only American lives, but also over $20 billion dollars per year—could not be won. In the South Vietnamese capital of Saigon on the final day of April 1975, the last American helicopter departs from the roof of the US embassy in ignominious defeat.

Soon, the capital has fallen to the North Vietnamese. It will be renamed Ho Chi Minh City, after a man who long ago worked as a kitchen assistant at the

Paris Ritz Hotel at a time when that city was abuzz with hopes for an everlasting peace.

CHAPTER SIXTEEN

Democracy and Capitalism Win This Round, But Deals With the Devil Come Due in the Middle East
(1977-2023)

On the final day of 1977, in Tehran, Iran, American president Jimmy Carter raises a glass to Shah Mohammed Reza Pahlavi. Carter describes Iran as "an island of stability in one of the most troubled areas of the world."

It has been 24 years since the American CIA orchestrated the arrest of Iran's prime minister in order to free Pahlavi to continue to personally benefit from Iran's dependent economic relationship with the US and Britain. Even though Iran has since become a member of OPEC, Pahlavi thinks that if he does right by the Americans, they will continue to have his back. He will need all the support he can get in the year ahead.

Since 1963, Pahlavi has aggressively pushed Iran toward modernization. The result is increased industrialization and urbanization, accompanied by shifting social values. Secularization of the court system and liberalization of laws pertaining to women have angered religious conservatives. Secularization of the education system has angered the *ulama*, the elite corps of traditional Muslim scholars. When the highest-ranking of the *ulama*, the Ayatollah Ruhollah Khomeini, began to stir up trouble, Pahlavi had him exiled.

Perhaps in response to Carter's visit, Khomeini, who has been living next door in Iraq, begins to find his voice again. When rumors spread that an Iranian press editorial attacking him was written by the government, conservative protestors in Tehran begin to attack symbols of the monarchy. A number of protestors are killed in clashes with Pahlavi's security force.

An escalating cycle of protests and violent responses continues throughout 1978. By December, millions are calling for removal of the shah, to be replaced by the ayatollah.

There is no CIA coming to the rescue this time. The shah and his family pack up and head to Egypt "for vacation," leaving the prime minister to face down the mob. The PM declares martial law. The ayatollah says to ignore him. The army says it is sitting this one out, and the government collapses.

With the success of the revolution, Iran's modernization is thrown into reverse. Over the next year, the constitution is overhauled. The country becomes a theocracy, and a highly conservative one at that. Women's lives, in particular, are greatly changed, as stringently-enforced laws dictate that they must cover their hair and body at all times when in public.

In late October, Shah Pahlavi is admitted refuge in the United States. In response, on November 4, 1979, student protestors storm the US embassy in Tehran, blindfold the staff, and declare them hostages to be held until the shah is extradited. The US will hold firm, and the hostages will not be returned until 1981(!), held 444 days in total.

So this is how the US and Britain's 1953 deal with the devil begins to be paid. The events of 1979 will ripple through the coming years of world history. Pahlavi's modernization program and years of alignment with the West have positioned Iran to become a force in the Middle East, and now Khomeini's social revolution has made them the West's enemy.

But 1979 is also the year that the USSR makes a critical error. The Russians no doubt enjoyed seeing the Americans get sucked into actual fighting in Vietnam, where Soviet weaponry supplied to the North Vietnamese had helped defeat them. Now the same situation, with roles reversed, is about to play out in Afghanistan.

A communist government has already come to power in Afghanistan, but now it is being threatened by a group of hardcore conservative Islamic insurgents that shares the same values as the ayatollah next door. They call themselves the Mujahideen. Even though they seem cut from the same cloth as the USA's enemies in Iran, the Mujahideen check the one required box labeled "not communist," so they absolutely qualify for US weaponry and intelligence support.

The war drags on for a decade, with huge costs to the USSR in money and lives (and, of course, an even greater one for Afghan civilians). But the Americans have once again made a shady deal, and the debt they accumulate will cost them dearly.

Americans did make good on Kennedy's pledge to put a man on the moon by the end of the 1960's. They did so six times between 1969 and 1972. Those missions were enabled by huge mainframe computers that took up an entire room. By the end of this chapter, people will wear an equivalent amount of computing power on their wrist. Spacecraft will rove the surface of Mars. Thousands of satellites will orbit Earth, along with two full-time manned space stations.

Over 500 of those satellites and one of those space stations will belong to China. Which is quite amazing, because in 1979, very few families in China even had a refrigerator. More than half lived in outright poverty.

China's amazing economic turnaround begins when Deng Xiaoping takes control of the Chinese Communist Party in December 1978. He is not Mao's chosen successor; his economic policies will be diametrically opposed to Mao's.

Deng once said, "It doesn't matter whether a cat is black or white as long as it catches mice." He meant that it didn't matter what method China used to industrialize, as long as it allowed them to quickly catch up to the Americans.

Or perhaps he meant that it didn't matter if China became capitalist; they could still call themselves communist.

Or perhaps he meant that it didn't matter whether China was communist or capitalist; he would still sic the cats on anyone who didn't play by the government's rules.

All would apply to the China that Deng's policies craft over the next 11 years.

One of Deng's first actions is to impose the One Child Policy. Though Mao already overturned Chinese tradition by elevating the status of women, this did not stamp out the deeply-ingrained importance of the first-born son. Thus, the One Child Policy is quite the sacrifice for those whose first-born is a daughter and will be their only-born. But Deng knows that without addressing the population variable, economic growth will be forever chasing a moving target.

By the late 1970's, it is becoming apparent that fully-communist, centrally-planned industrial economies are unable to perform as well as capitalist, market-based ones. So Deng begins to experiment with capitalism in controlled settings that he calls Special Economic Zones (SEZ's).

SEZ's are limited areas where foreign-owned companies can operate. They are not only free from Chinese government restriction; they receive tax incentives, as well.

The first of four SEZ's established in 1980 is Shenzhen, a primarily agricultural area just over the border from Hong Kong. As of this time, there are still a couple decades to go on Britain's 98-year lease of Hong Kong, which was made official in 1898. Deng would like his own country to emulate the dynamic growth that Hong Kong has seen while China has stagnated.

This is how Shenzen looked in 2019, when its annual growth rate exceeded Hong Kong's

(15)

223

So SEZ's were obviously an enormous success. This was evident quite soon after their start, so Deng created more. By the start of the next millennium, China would still retain some central control of the economy, yet in other ways they would be even more laissez-faire capitalist than the US, and more akin to the US of the 1890's, where there were yet no reform laws to protect workers.

In the mid-1980's, halfway through their war in Afghanistan, the Soviet economy will also begin to change, but it will be too late. In 1980, Americans elect a new president, Ronald Reagan. He campaigned on a promise to slash government spending, but in office, he does the opposite. Despite signing two Strategic Arms Limitation Talks, the USA and the USSR continue their nuclear arms race. It is an extraordinarily expensive undertaking. Whether it is shrewdness on the part of Reagan or just his hawkish nature, he puts the pedal to the metal on military spending, and the Soviet economy will be unable to keep pace.

Mikhail Gorbachev becomes the new Soviet leader in 1985. He inherits an empire with a weakening foundation, and he knows there will have to be change. Á la Deng in China, he decides to back away from pure communism and privatize a number of government-run factories. But whereas Deng has been able to take advantage of a Chinese workforce that was buoyed by Mao's positive propaganda, Gorbachev can see that Soviet communism has robbed Russian workers of their motivation. So he gets laws passed that give the workers better conditions and more time off.

Gorbachev also tries to improve the lives of Soviet people generally by ending much of the country's oppressive censorship. Taking a page from Mao's playbook, he begins to invite constructive criticism under an initiative called *glasnost*.

Things do not work out as planned. Economically, the cutover to privatization does not go smoothly. Politically, too much dissatisfaction has been kept under a lid. It is going to be impossible for Gorbachev to put the genie back in the bottle.

Freedom seems to be in the air everywhere in 1989. In April, a student protest begins in Beijing's Tiananmen Square. Protests calling for more Western-style freedoms in China have occurred a couple of times before and dwindled of their own accord over time, but, as the spring wears on, this one only grows.

By May, the square is continually packed with college-aged youth. Some of them have created a plaster-of-Paris sculpture they call the Goddess of Democracy.

These are the early days of cable news. A new station called CNN broadcasts images from the square 'round the clock. It is heartening for Americans to see

224

this new generation of Chinese looking up to American ideals, after witnessing the hatred of their parents' generation 20-plus years before.

This is a real problem for the Communist Party, and we can only imagine the behind-the-scenes discussions between Deng and the other leadership. Army units are called in, and soon columns of tanks are rolling in the streets.

There is a very famous photograph of an unidentified man standing alone in the middle of an avenue that is at least seven lanes wide. He stands before a line of four tanks, facing them down. To the watching world, he is known only as "Tank Man."

The fate of Tank Man will remain unknown. On the night of June 3, embarrassed by the escalating spectacle and infuriated by how journalism's latest technology has drawn back the curtain on the Communist Party's controlled messaging, Deng gives the order to pull the plug. The CNN cameras go dark.

By morning, the square is cleared.

Melinda Liu, reporting for *Newsweek*, records it this way:

> A convoy of about 50 military vehicles came roaring down Changan Avenue, smashing through barricades while civilians shouted....
> The tanks rumbled over everything: tents, corpses, debris from the 33-foot "Goddess of Democracy" statue.... Eventually loudspeakers began booming. All civilians were to remain in their homes:
> "The rebellion has been suppressed."... At the square's north end I saw a row of troops on their bellies, pointing machine guns toward the Beijing Hotel. I was sure they would never fire into a crowd of civilians. Then they did.

> ... The protests had been crushed by the time I returned to the Beijing Hotel with my colleague... to settle the room bill. The area had been cordoned off for several days, I reminded the clerk, so he shouldn't bill me for the days when the hotel was inaccessible "due to the situation in Tiananmen Square." [He] stared at me and asked stonily: "What situation in Tiananmen Square?"

No one knows how many were killed that night. In the moment that has just passed, if you had gone to Baidu (the Chinese equivalent of Google) and typed in "Tiananmen Square," all you would have found was distant history and tips for visitors, as if the demonstrations, and the ensuing massacre, never occurred.

But in Europe later that year, freedom would fare better.

Pressures on the Soviet Union abound. Having recently pulled out of Afghanistan after suffering heavy losses, it is struggling to maintain the expense of the arms race, and now is faced with the failed experiment with privatization. To sustain the teetering economy, Gorbachev pulls the army out of the Eastern European nations. Without being propped up by Moscow, those governments start to fall.

Poland is the first to become free. A union movement called Solidarity, which began early in the decade, has become a political party. In August, it fares well enough to form a coalition government with another noncommunist party.

In October, Hungary declares itself a multi-party republic. In November, West and East Berliners together tear down the hated Berlin Wall. Czechoslovakia and Romania become free in December; in Romania, a hated dictator is quickly tried and executed. Bulgaria will follow in the new year. All of the above will ultimately become members of NATO.

As freedom slips from the grasp of the Chinese people, it is not the only flaw that keeps 1989 from becoming a watershed year in world history. Something else slips from the whole world's grasp: a chance to nip climate change in the bud.

It was mentioned in the prologue that science warned humanity about global warming way back in 1896. In 1965, there was a warning from a politician when American president Lyndon Johnson told Congress that humans had "altered the composition of the atmosphere on a global scale through... a steady increase in carbon dioxide from the burning of fossil fuels."

In the 1970's, ExxonMobil's own senior scientist, James F. Black, cautioned upper management in no uncertain terms,

> There is general scientific agreement that the most likely manner in which
> mankind is influencing the global climate is through carbon dioxide
> released from the burning of fossil fuels.... Man has a time window of
> five to ten years before the need for hard decisions regarding changes in
> energy strategies might become critical.... Once the effects are measurable,
> they might not be reversible.

In 1988, the UN establishes the Intergovernmental Panel on Climate Change (IPCC). A presentation that climate scientist James Hansen gives before Congress gains the attention of President Reagan, and Reagan and Gorbachev sign a joint pledge stating that the two superpowers will cooperate to address global warming. The National Coal Association (yeah, that coal) goes on record acknowledging that the greenhouse effect is here, and we'll be "hearing more and more about it."

It is the final year of Reagan's term. The Republican nominee to succeed him, George H.W. Bush, campaigns as "the environmental candidate." But once in office, Bush delegates the climate issue to his Chief of Staff, John Sununu. Sununu, himself, does not believe that climate change should be a priority. Under his oversight, therefore, it will languish.

The next meeting of the IPCC's working group is scheduled for May in Geneva. James Hansen prepares testimony he hopes to deliver at the meeting, submitting it, as required, to the Office of Management and Budget (OMB). It comes back full of context-altering edits, changing reports of hard data into "estimates" that are "evolving" and therefore unreliable. A recommendation is even added that Congress should not pass climate legislation that does not show a near-term benefit for the economy.

It seems beyond the purview of the OMB to make these kinds of edits. Hansen suspects the Bush administration is involved.

In November, a meeting of environmental ministers is to take place in the Netherlands. Throughout the summer, President Bush remains hands-off on the topic, and Sununu does everything he can to keep it back-burnered. Nevertheless, a week before the meeting, Bush pronounces that the US "will play a leadership role in global warming."

The Dutch hosts and other concerned nations hope at the very least to come away from the meeting with a binding target, perhaps freezing greenhouse gas emissions by the year 2000. But after hours of negotiations, Sununu's hand-picked negotiator persuades the environmental ministers from the USSR, Britain, and Japan to hold firm on a final flimsy statement that only notes that "many" nations were in favor of stabilizing emissions. No target figures are established.

And so there is no great news to bring home to the general public, no real sense of urgency conveyed. Global warming is this invisible thing. It is not visual like smog. It does not sound like something broken, like a hole in the ozone layer. Its consequences do not capture the public imagination yet. So those Coal Association folks are like, *Hey, maybe we aren't going to be hearing more and more about it. What were we worried about? Our business is going to be fine.*

And fine it is. From 1989 to 2009, more carbon is released into the atmosphere than in all of history prior to 1989. Fossil fuel executives do not misjudge the public again. They have them where they want them, and they know what it will take to keep them there: a steady flow of propaganda and a little influence money sprinkled in the right pockets.

On Christmas Day 1991, the USSR ceases to exist. The former SSRs have been bailing on Gorbachev, one after another. With no empire left to oversee and a Russian president already in place, he steps down. A Commonwealth of Independent States is formed, in which Russia will be joined by 11 of the former SSR's, this time as sovereign nations. The Baltic States of Estonia, Latvia, and Lithuania say thanks but no thanks and, from this point on, migrate politically toward the West.

The Cold War has been won. All of the West's capitalists can feel that their way of life has come out on top. Americans have it one better: They are now the world's lone superpower.

The rest of the decade continues the good news and is something of a reprieve from international challenges. It is relatively free from war, with two exceptions.

First, Yugoslavia disassembles into all its constituent nationalist divisions: Slovenia, Croatia, Montenegro, Macedonia, Serbia, and Bosnia-Herzegovina. The phrase "ethnic cleansing" enters the world's vocabulary, and Serbian leaders in Bosnia are convicted of war crimes.

Second, multiple African nations continue to struggle with poverty and internal divisions, the worst being the genocide of Rwandan Tutsis by Rwandan Hutus (old enemies from the days of the imperialists' divide and rule strategy). Eight hundred thousand are killed in a six-month period.

But there is good news from Africa, too. South Africa's Black activist Nelson Mandela is finally freed from prison in 1990 and the chains of apartheid begin to break. By 1993, they are gone entirely, and elections with universal suffrage are scheduled for the following year. Mandela and President Frederick Willem de Klerk jointly win the Nobel Peace Prize. Mandela wins the election and takes over the presidency.

Also in 1993, the Oslo Accords, brokered by American president Bill Clinton, bring Jews and Palestinians to the brink of a peace agreement acceptable to both sides. The PLO for the first time recognizes Israel's right to exist, and the two sides come up with a Declaration of Principles around a two-state division of the lands now held by Israel.

Israel returned the Sinai to Egypt in the 1970's but retains the small Gaza Strip, which extends up the Mediterranean coast. They also still occupy Jordan's West Bank. The plan is for these two areas to become the nation of Palestine. A Palestinian Authority is created to be the new country's government.

They are so close, but there are sticking points. Israel had allowed Jewish settlements to be built in the West Bank, where residents have become established. There is contention about what to do with the city of Jerusalem. Sadly, the original 1948 proposal of making it a free international zone is not taken up again.

228

Throughout the decade, the world economy hums along, powered by global trade. "Free trade" is the catchphrase of the era. The European Union binds 15 Western European countries together as a trading bloc. The IMF and World Bank dangle loans before those in need, with strings attached so developing countries cannot undercut the big players with sweatshop labor or lack of environmental controls.

Even within the developed countries, the wealth being generated is less evenly distributed than in the past, as the division between rich and poor keeps expanding. A class of ultra-rich begins to pull away from the only-rich, many buoyed by success in tech ventures.

The personal computers of the 1980's gain graphical interfaces and are connected, at first on Local Area Networks, and, by 1998, on the Internet. In an amazingly short period of time, much of the world's knowledge will transition online. Soon everyone will be "Googling it."

Behind the calm '90's veneer, the components of another future are coming together in Afghanistan. Americans have one more debt to pay on that later chapter of the Cold War. In 1994, former members of the American-backed Mujahideen form a new group called the Taliban.

The Taliban adhere strictly to a radically conservative interpretation of a branch of Islamic law called *sharia*. Punishment for the most minor transgressions may involve beatings. Crimes like thievery can result in amputation. For more serious offenses, there are public executions.

The Taliban do not allow girls to be educated and forbid women from working. They force women to cover themselves at all times in public. The burqa, a gown that covers them from the top of their head to the ground, leaves nothing visible, not even the eyes. A woman's view of the outside world is perpetually covered in mesh. (Obviously, the Taliban know nothing of the true history of the Prophet Muhammad, or else choose to ignore it.)

Burqa-clad Afghan women

The Mujahideen had not depended exclusively on the USA for support in their war against the Russians. They had been financially backed by a wealthy Saudi by the name of Osama bin Laden. In 1996, bin Laden comes to Afghanistan just as the Taliban are gaining full control of the country.

Bin Laden has formed a terrorist organization called al-Qaeda. His main target is the USA, which he sees as the primary driver of Westernization, the expansion of the West's liberal consumer culture across the developing world. He wants to wall off the Islamic Middle East from what he views as sinful influences. He is fine with killing innocent civilians in order to achieve this goal. In 1998, he orchestrates dual truck bombings of two US embassies in East Africa. The bombs kill more than 200 Kenyans and Tanzanians, but only 12 Americans. The US retaliates by bombing a city in Afghanistan. A handful of terrorists are killed. "Collateral" casualties are unknown.

On September 11, 2001, a perfectly clear late summer's day, a commercial airliner flies directly into an upper floor of one of the two World Trade Center towers, at that time the tallest buildings in New York City. Americans tuning in on their televisions are unsure of what has happened until, only minutes later, a second plane crashes into the other tower. From that point, viewers are transfixed as—incredibly—both 110-story towers collapse.

It all occurs in just an hour and 45 minutes. Within the same span of time, a third plane had crashed into the Pentagon, the massive building just outside Washington, D.C., that houses the Defense Department, and a fourth had gone down in a field in Pennsylvania.

The latter plane had been flying westward over Ohio when it made an unexpected U-turn and began to head southeastward, directly toward Washington. The heroics of civilian passengers who overwhelmed the terrorists at the controls likely saved the nation's Capitol Building from destruction.

For Americans, it is a sudden end to a decade of relative calm on the international front. The skies over the country go quiet for a number of days while tightened security measures go into place that will lengthen airport security lines until and beyond the moment that just passed.

President George W. Bush (son of the earlier President Bush) gives an address to the nation in which he introduces Americans to al-Qaeda and to Osama bin Laden as the mastermind behind the attack. He gives a short lesson on the Taliban and how their beliefs are unrelated to those of mainstream Muslims. He declares a War on Terror that might extend indefinitely into the future (which basically allows the president to roll any number of wars underneath the one heading without further authorization from Congress).

Although bin Laden and al-Qaeda are separate from the Taliban, the Taliban are hiding them in Afghanistan. So it is to Afghanistan that American bombers return four weeks after the attack. By December, the Taliban are on the run and a new interim Afghan president is named. A NATO-led international security force is put into place. Though democratic elections will not be held until 2004, moderate Afghans can breathe a sigh of relief, and women can begin to emerge from their virtual imprisonment.

Of course it would be the height of naïveté to assume things are at a happy ending. Both the Taliban and al-Qaeda have only been dispersed, most likely to hiding places in the mountains toward the border with Pakistan. And Osama bin Laden is somewhere among them.

But ensuing American policy toward the Middle East is about to make things much worse...

Certain leading members of the Bush administration, referred to as neo-conservatives—particularly Vice President Dick Cheney and Defense Secretary Donald Rumsfeld—are high on "nation building." The idea is to use the American military to bring down bad actors who are in power in the Middle East and establish democratically elected governments.

To critics this seems like a repetition of the mandates set up after World War One in the Middle East that led to imperialist-dependent economic relationships based on oil. It is especially suspicious that Vice President Cheney just recently had a stint as CEO of an oil company.

The first place the neo-cons direct their focus is on Iraq. Recall that when the US assassinated OPEC co-founder Abdel Karim Qasim, it put the Ba'ath Party in power in Iraq. It remains so. The current leader, Saddam Hussein, has already caused problems for the US, first nationalizing Iraq's oil industry and then invading US ally Kuwait (for which the Americans under the first President Bush made his people pay dearly by thoroughly bombing Baghdad and Basra in the First Gulf War back in 1991, but let Hussein, himself, off the hook). Hussein went on to use chemical weapons to subdue an insurrection by Kurdish Iraqis in the north of the country.

The power of confirmation bias should never be underestimated. When we believe something to be true, our brains skew our perception of factual data to support that belief. By late 2002, the Bush administration suspects Hussein has moved on from chemical weapons to dabble in developing nuclear weapons. It looks at some sketchy field data provided by the CIA, which, to them, confirms their suspicion. (By this time, nuclear weapons are held not only by the US and Russia, but also by Britain, France, Israel, Pakistan, India, China, and probably North Korea, too.) The neo-cons look at this concern as an opportunity to finish the job the earlier President Bush chose not to pursue: Remove Hussein and establish democracy in Iraq.

231

In February, Secretary of State Colin Powell delivers a presentation at the UN that goes through all of the evidence the US is privy to. The intention is to get the Security Council to pass a resolution backing an invasion of Iraq. To skeptical eyes, the presentation lacks hard evidence. Even Powell seems unsure of it when probed later.

So there is no UN resolution. No matter. The US says it will go it alone, backed by a "coalition of the willing." Those "willing" turn out to be Britain, Spain, Poland, and Australia. Quite the motley group. For their part, both Spain (in 2004) and Britain (in 2005) will suffer al-Qaeda-inspired terrorist attacks on their commuter train systems.

The US begins an invasion in March 2003. The Hussein government is toppled, and by May, President Bush is doing a photo op on an aircraft carrier below a grand banner that says "MISSION ACCOMPLISHED." Hussein, himself, goes into hiding, but is rooted out in December. In January, the Bush administration publicly admits that its suspicion that Hussein had begun to develop nuclear weapons was incorrect.

Here is what the war has actually accomplished: It has taken out a government that, although not democratic, was at least secular (unlike the conservative theocracy in Iran and the ultra-conservative one that had existed in Afghanistan). A simple visual metaphor for what the war has done is this: It has shaken up a hornet's nest.

Recall that ever since the death of the prophet Muhammad, Muslims have been split into two sects: the Sunnis and the Shi'ites. Over the 14-plus centuries since, the bad blood between the two has only accumulated.

Worldwide, the majority of Muslims are Sunnis. Shi'ites tend to be more conservative. They follow the word of a supreme religious leader. The biggest center of Shi'ism is Iran.

Iraq is more divided but is also majority Shi'ite. Saddam Hussein, however, is a Sunni. With Hussein removed from power and occupying forces imposing democracy, the Iraqi Shi'ites rapidly take control of the provisional government.

Many Sunnis are angry with the way things are going and some begin to take this out on the American occupiers, whom they view as taking sides in a religious feud. They take control of the city of Fallujah. American troops are unable to take it back, but they do take prisoners. Their cause is severely compromised when photos are leaked from Abu Ghraib Prison showing prisoner abuse by US forces.

In May 2004, the Shi'ite head of the Iraqi governing council is assassinated by a group led by Sunni Abu Masab al-Zarqawi, and the country dissolves into civil war. Later in the year, al-Zarqawi's group pledges allegiance to Osama bin Laden. They become known as al-Qaeda in Iraq (AQI), the first of multiple incarnations of the terrorist group.

By the spring of 2005, Iraq is suffering as many as 135 car bombings per month. The Sunni insurgency controls the entire western third of the country. American troops have been fighting house-to-house to retake Fallujah, with casualties mounting among both troops and Iraqi civilians.

It takes until October 2008(!) for the Iraqi government to finally gain control in the west. A new American president, Barack Obama, is elected the following month. In February, he announces that the US combat mission will end by August 2010. Although terrorist actions remain frequent over the next year and a half, Obama keeps his promise. But American troops remain in Afghanistan, where the Taliban have regrouped and begun to incur again on the southern part of the country.

Obama, the first Black American president, had rapidly risen in popularity to snatch the Democratic nomination from Hilary Clinton, who had hoped to become the first woman president. His campaign took advantage of two recent technologies in order to gain support from many small donors: the cell phone and social media.

Fossil fuel company executives are also quick to put social media to use. Since 1998, propagandists have been spreading "alternative facts" on the Internet. Social media now becomes the amplifier to spread them virally.

By 2009, the amount of facts piling up about the threat of global warming is climbing toward a tipping point of undeniability. The first commitment period of the Kyoto Protocol began in 2008. It binds developed countries to individual agreed-upon targets for limited or reduced greenhouse gas emissions by the end of 2012. Coal and oil companies need to make one last push for a few more years free from regulation, taxation, and carbon markets...

They call it "Climategate." (The "-gate" suffix is supposed to identify it as a scandal, á la Watergate, the election-cheating scandal that brought down American president Nixon in 1974.) Thousands of emails between climate scientists are stolen from a university server in England. Someone on the denier side takes the time to pore over the stash, select certain clips, edit them to distort their original meaning, and present them out of context. They put the end product up on the Internet and crow on social media (amplified by FOX News) that they have found the smoking gun that proves once and for all that climate change is "a hoax."

Right-wing politicians call for the investigation of more than a dozen climate scientists. It takes two years and multiple investigations in the US and the UK to exonerate them. It is finally established that the scientists are not the ones who misled the public; the people who stole and manipulated the emails are the ones who did that.

But does it matter? Socio-technologically, it is a new world now. No doubt, many who were exposed to the news about Climategate in the intervening two years still form their worldview from that alternate reality.

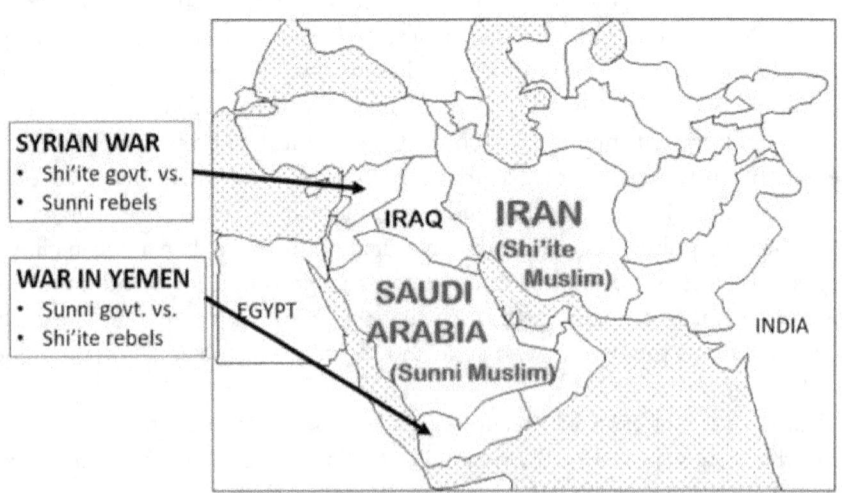

As the neo-cons are failing in their plans to plant the seeds of democracy in the Arab world, a poor Tunisian street vendor uses another approach to push for it. He sits on the sidewalk by his market stand, and he lights himself on fire.

Due to his sacrifice, the spring of 2011 becomes known as the Arab Spring. It leads to the fall of Tunisia's autocratic government and the establishment of a constituent assembly tasked with drafting a new constitution for a representative democracy. From there, empowered by young Arab voices on the Internet, calls for freedom spread across North Africa and the Middle East.

Similar to the drive for republicanism that spread across 19th-century Europe in the wake of the French Revolution, immediate successes are rare or limited. In Morocco, constitutional changes put limits on the powers of the monarchy. In Libya, a despotic dictator is taken down and dragged through the streets to his execution, but there is no stable government to replace him. In Egypt, a powerful autocrat is toppled and democratic elections held, but when a conservative Islamist is elected, fear that the nation will become a theocracy causes secular interests to align behind a military coup.

Divisions between the two Islamic sects intensify rebellions in Yemen and in Syria. The two biggest power brokers in the Middle East are the Shi'ite government of Iran and the Sunni government of Saudi Arabia. When Shi'ite rebels in Yemen known as Houthis mount a rebellion against Yemen's minority Sunni leadership, Iran is only too happy to provide them with arms. The Saudis, meanwhile, prop up the Yemeni government.

SYRIAN WAR
- Shi'ite govt. vs.
- Sunni rebels

WAR IN YEMEN
- Sunni govt. vs.
- Shi'ite rebels

IRAQ   **IRAN**
       (Shi'ite
       Muslim)

EGYPT   **SAUDI
        ARABIA**
        (Sunni Muslim)   INDIA

In Syria, the roles are reversed, with a majority Sunni population rising up against the despotic dictator Bashar al-Assad, a Shi'ite. Assad uses chemical weapons against the rebels. He repeatedly bombs hospitals and schools, and his regime is accused of torture and extrajudicial executions of civilians. The rebels are supported by Saudi Arabia and the USA, while Assad receives support from Iran and Russia.

While all these rebellions are in progress, Americans receive some good news. Special Ops, having located Osama bin Laden in an urban complex in Pakistan, kill him in a nighttime raid and dump his body in the Arabian Sea.

By November 2012, there is enough stamina left in the winds of change for Palestinians to achieve a milestone: Palestine is admitted to the UN as an observer state of the General Assembly. Israel, the United States, Canada, the Czech Republic, Panama, and four tiny South Pacific island states cast the only opposition votes.

But by the two-year anniversary of the Arab Spring, things are looking bleak for the Syrian rebels, the threat of famine is growing in Yemen, and things are about to take a major turn for the worse. Some former members of AQI resurface in remote eastern Syria under a new name: the Islamic State of Iraq and Syria (ISIS). It is the most heinous group of terrorists yet to come on the scene. Its members generate fear by using the Internet to publicize images of beheadings and by employing even more inhumane executions, like cramming multiple captives into a tiny cage and lighting them on fire. Even al-Qaeda puts out a statement disavowing any connection to them.

Flying black flags, ISIS fighters storm their jeeps into towns and take them over, raping women and killing indiscriminately. They attack Abu Ghraib Prison, setting nearly 1,000 militant prisoners free. They eventually carve out a swath of territory as large as Jordan in eastern Syria and northern Iraq. In doing this, they say that they have taken down the colonial borders drawn by the British and French. They declare a caliphate and establish their capital at the Syrian city of Raqqa.

ISIS is nominally Sunni, although normal Sunnis oppose it due to its extremism. Because ISIS is Sunni and because its fighters have captured territory in Shi'ite-governed Syria, Iran raises its own troops to fight them. The US, already making airstrikes in Syria, now turns its focus on ISIS as well, so the Americans find themselves in an unfamiliar position: fighting on the same side as the Iranians against a common enemy.

In September 2014, President Obama announces the creation of a broad coalition of nations formed to defeat ISIS. It includes all of the Middle Eastern nations. Some will contribute planes for airstrikes, others weaponry, training, or intelligence. The US adds some Special Ops boots on the ground.

Finally, in October, more than a year after the creation of the coalition, some of the ISIS-held territory begins to be chipped away. Even so, the war against it rages on until December 2017 in Iraq and May 2018 in Syria, where the land held by the Sunni insurgency also continues to shrink and the dictator Assad remains firmly in power.

In 2017, the US had acquired a new president. Donald Trump, a second-generation New York City real estate mogul, had used his popularity as a figure on "reality TV" to gain a political following. Russia had left its fingerprints on the previous fall's election, so Trump—who had business dealings inside Russia—wound up being investigated by his own Justice Department to see if there was any connection. Though they were unable to connect the dots, the department did find clear evidence that the Russians had carried out a highly sophisticated social media campaign that fabricated online personalities, intended to erode support for Trump's opponent.[1] Advancements in technology had already created a new world of mass influence. Now the ripples of that seismic change had extended its reach into the world of geopolitics.

Russia had created a democratic government after the split-up of the USSR, but it hadn't lasted very long. Under Vladimir Putin, it has once again become an autocracy. It has a capitalist economy, yet retains the same corruption at the highest levels of power as in its communist days. Putin, an old KGB hand (the Russian equivalent of the CIA), is a pro at stealthily eliminating his political opponents, and he has firm control of the press, so he wins all elections in a landslide.

Putin's foreign interference had not been limited to Syria and the American presidential election. In 2013, when Ukraine's president rejected an overture from the European Union and instead tried to tie the country's economy more closely to Russia, Ukrainians rebelled and sent him packing. Soon, military men in unidentified uniforms were coming over the border into the Crimean Peninsula. No surprise, these turned out to be Russians coming to swipe that part of the country. After claiming that the people of the Crimea had *asked* to become part of Russia and staging a fake election, Russia annexes the peninsula. With only slap-on-the-wrist economic sanctions leveled at Putin, it is vaguely reminiscent of something that went down in Czechoslovakia 65 years before.

---

[1]Though the department was unable to find evidence of complicity with the Trump campaign, they had enough evidence to charge them with obstruction of justice pertaining to the investigation. In the US, it is up to the legislature to prosecute members of the executive branch of government. They chose not to do so.

The Crimean annexation happened when Obama was the American president. Now, with Trump, Putin has the man in office that his team of cyber-spies "campaigned" for. It is easy to see why he favors Trump. Trump is antagonistic toward NATO, calling out other members of the organization for expecting the US to foot too much of its costs.

The respect between the two leaders flows both directions; Trump also speaks positively about Putin. As he struggles to fulfill his campaign promise to build a wall along the entire Mexican border in order to cut off Latin American immigration, he seems to envy the autocratic leader's freedom from government restriction, expressing frustration with the checks on presidential power that have been essential to the American way of governing ever since its creation.

The pressure of northward immigration is a natural outgrowth of the crushing poverty left in the wake of the Age of Imperialism, from Latin America over the Mexican land border to the US and from Africa and the Middle East across the Mediterranean to Europe. In Hungary, Viktor Orban had ridden a wave of anti-immigrant demagoguery to power early in the millennium and remains the country's leader, having instituted policies that hamper the operations of opposition groups, journalists, universities, and others.

Trump, himself, is a master demagogue. He knows how to apply the Joseph Goebbels principle of loudly accusing your opponents of being guilty of whatever you, yourself, are doing. Since dedicated fact-checkers have existed, no other American politician comes close to Trump in the number of pants-on-fire lies recorded, yet it is he who early on appropriates the term "fake news" and applies it to mainstream media, where, for many, it has stuck.

In Turkey, the increasingly autocratic Recep Erdoğan employs the same strategy, spreading copious disinformation while simultaneouly creating his Disinformation Law, which he uses to imprison anyone spreading information he deems to be false.

Trump's most fervent supporters, too, seem frustrated by constitutional and democratic restrictions. They see themselves as a shrinking minority in an electorate that is rapidly shifting demographically away from them. They fear ending up on the wrong side of democracy, with no way to forward their personal beliefs. Many think those beliefs represent the true America, a misunderstanding of history leading them to think that America's founders were as sure and united as they, themselves, are.

Similar to Trump's core supporters, India's Hindu nationalists are a large faction who feel that their personal beliefs represent the true India (quite counter to India's Axial Age emphasis on religious tolerance), and so do everything they can to impose their belief system on the country as a whole. The head of the Hindu nationalist BJP party, Prime Minister Narendra Modi, has presided over policies deemed discriminatory toward Muslims, and the country has experienced an uptick in incidents of religious violence.

Across the world, there seems less appetite for bridging differences and crafting middle-ground solutions to problems. The pull of the populist autocrat is finding favor seemingly more and more as we approach the moment that just passed.

In February 2020, Trump makes a deal with the Taliban, agreeing to pull all US troops and support personnel out of Afghanistan within 14 months. In exchange, the Taliban pledges to prevent al-Qaeda or any other outside actor from using the country as a base to threaten the security of the US or its allies. It makes no official pledge about what it will do for other Afghans.

News of the deal will soon be eclipsed by a much wider-ranging problem that strikes closer to home. In late 2019—a century after a great flu pandemic swept around the world—a second worldwide pandemic begins in the city of Wuhan, China. By March 1, it is spreading widely in the US. By the end of the month, the economy is shutting down.

COVID-19 strikes right at the start of Trump's 2020 re-election campaign. He badly misjudges the virus in its early days, trying to downplay it in the news cycle. As the US climbs steadily up the charts toward most per-capita COVID deaths worldwide, he loses the support of a key constituency that had come out strong for him in 2016: old people, the demographic in which most of the deaths are occurring. In November, they vote for Joe Biden instead, who had done most of his campaigning socially-distanced in his basement.

Back before the 2016 election, supporters close to Trump had been preparing a website called StopTheSteal. In hindsight, it is clear that Trump was preparing to dispute the results of an election he expected to lose. Four years later, he actually *does* lose, and the words "Stop the Steal" become a mantra that is repeated unceasingly by the Trump campaign, through every media channel, over the course of the two months between the election and its certification.

In American presidential elections, each state is given a number of votes to cast that is equal to its number of Congresspeople. All but two states cast *all* of their votes for whichever candidate wins the state. Because of the predomination of this winner-take-all system, elections are won or lost in only those few states with a relatively equal split between the only two competitive political parties.

So Trump gets his lawyers busy challenging the election results in those few states, which is, of course, entirely his right. Upwards of 60 individual suits are filed. Some are tossed without consideration due to lack of evidence. All but one of the others are lost due to having no convincing evidence of fraud. In the one case that finds a valid discrepancy, it is less than 100 votes out of over 6.7 million cast and a 1 million-vote margin of victory for Biden.

Despite the clear evidence of a valid election, Trump refuses to concede. When his own previously loyal Attorney General tells him the claims of fraud are "bullshit" and offers his resignation, Trump turns to other high-powered lawyers to see if there are loopholes in the complex American election system that can be exploited.

Those votes allotted to each state? They actually become an equal number of real people called "electors" (who are separate from the state's elected Congresspeople). These electors are appointed to something called the Electoral College. If a Democrat wins the state, the state appoints all Democrats; if a Republican wins, they appoint all Republicans. When the Electoral College convenes in December 2020, the elector's votes are tallied, and Joe Biden wins the presidency by a count of 306 to 232, exactly as reported by all major news outlets in early November.

But there is one more step in the process —a rubber stamp-like certification of the Electoral College vote in front of Congress as the state-by-state count is read off by the sitting Vice President. Trump's new team of lawyers convinces him that, even after the vote, they can form their own slate of bogus Republican electors for each of the states where the vote was reasonably close. Then, on January 6, when the certification is to occur, Republican members of Congress can point to the competing groups of electors and cry foul. Since it is Trump's vice president chairing the session, he could *throw out* the "disputed" votes.

On January 6, 2021, with a huge crowd of Trump supporters waving "Stop the Steal" signs gathering near the Capitol Building, Trump is on the phone with Vice President Mike Pence, who is telling Trump he does not feel he can legally do what he is being asked. Trump berates him and fumes before heading out to greet his supporters, telling them, "We're going to walk down to the Capitol..." And that is exactly what they do, en masse, overcoming the meager Capitol police barricade, smashing windows and stampeding their way into the building. (Trump, himself, is driven back to the White House by his security detail.)

The scene goes on for hours. At one point, Trump posts on social media that his VP has let them down, which leads some in the crowd to begin chanting, "Hang Mike Pence!" Pence and the members of Congress have taken shelter on- and off-site but are eventually able to reconvene. Quite late in the evening, the vote is eventually certified. Outside, one insurgent has been shot dead. One Capitol police officer will later die of heart failure.

The USA was the nation that first implemented the lofty Enlightenment ideals. Despite its imperfections, it had been a model of peaceful transfer of power for over two centuries. No more. Thanks to Trump, it can never have that perfect record back.

◇◇◇

In August 2021, four months behind the Trump-negotiated timetable, President Biden calls for a rapid exit of US troops from Afghanistan. The hope is that an American-trained Afghan resistance can keep the resurgent Taliban at least away from the capital, but even as the last Americans are being withdrawn, it is already being overrun. Before long—no surprise—Afghan girls are once again being refused an education, and women have lost their right to work.

The COVID-19 virus peaks in January 2022, having killed upwards of seven million people worldwide. In the period prior to the peak, China, despite being the origination point, experiences far fewer cases than elsewhere. This is due to the infrastructure of public monitoring that the government already had in place. Chinese people are used to sharing much of their private details and history with the government. If their private data is positive, that is a good thing, for it qualifies them for the best jobs, apartments, and public services like healthcare. Therefore, it is nothing new to have their cell phones tapped for COVID contact tracing.

China, by this time, has steadily risen to become the world's second-largest economy. Since 1971, it has been the China that fills a permanent seat on the UN Security Council. It has the world's largest military, measured by active personnel. Its current leader, Xi ("She") Jinping, has consolidated the most power over the country since Mao. His goal is to make China into the world's other superpower to counterbalance the United States, and he is almost there.

Nearly one-third of the world's 30 largest cities, measured by greater metropolitan population, are in China. In the 1980's and '90's, movement of Chinese people from rural to urban locations broke the record for the largest human migration in history.

The Chinese Communist Party is still the only legal political party. Censorship of the press and the Internet remains a fact of life. Despite this, many Chinese people are satisfied with their leadership. The One Child Policy was terminated in 2016. Almost everyone is better off than their parents were. They feel like they have nearly become equal rivals of the United States, that goal that Mao had their ancestors envision nearly 75 years ago.

Much less happy are those ethnicities who do not fit the government's mold. In the far west, Tibet was a strong, independent empire during the time of the Tang Dynasty, but it was overrun by China in 1950, soon after the communist victory in the civil war. Still, it remained a center of its own variant of secular Buddhism. Today, with their spiritual leader, the Dalai Lama, in exile in India, Buddhist Tibetans try to hang on to their traditions while Xi's government encourages the emigration of Han Chinese peoples in an effort to forcibly export Confucianist Chinese culture to the province.

To the north of Tibet is the even larger province of Xinjiang ("Shin-jiahng"), where the Muslim Uyghur ("Weeger") people live. Here, the government has taken a more direct approach to eradicating the local culture by forcibly sending the people to reeducation centers.

(16)

Since its handover from the British to the Chinese in 1997, Hong Kong has been considered a Special Administrative Region by the Chinese government. As part of the handover, it was promised 50 years of autonomy. Just how much autonomy was left open to interpretation. Hong Kong activists who took to the streets in 2014's Umbrella Revolution are still being tried and imprisoned.

Taiwan is another area where interpretations differ. The Taiwanese, themselves, along with their Western supporters, including the Americans, would like to think they are a sovereign nation. But they don't come out and say so, in deference to their much more militarily-powerful neighbor. China considers Taiwan a breakaway province. President Xi has said that its reunification with the mainland "must be fulfilled," but has said nothing about when. If the Chinese *were* to forcefully "fulfill" reunification, the US would come to the aid of its ally, bringing the world to the brink of an international crisis. As in Cold War days, the world's two most powerful—and nuclear-armed—militaries would be facing each other down.

As the West keeps watch on the situation in Taiwan, 5,000 miles away, a different nation is invaded instead. In February 2022, Vladimir Putin blatantly mobilizes troops along Russia's border with Ukraine. As the world looks on, wondering, "Is he really going to do this?", he does it. The troops pour in and bombs start raining on Kharkiv, near the Russian border, and on the capital, Kyiv.

But the Ukrainian people are not about to roll over and give up their sovereignty. Despite the bombs that obliterate hospitals and apartment blocks, despite the torturing of members of civilian resistance groups and other war crimes committed by the invaders, the country stands firm. As the winter of 2022–2023 begins to thaw, the Ukrainian army mounts its own counterattacks to reclaim areas in the east that have been occupied by the Russians.

Russia is also beginning to return to the old Cold War competition ground of Africa, where small numbers of American troops have been stationed ever since an African branch of al-Qaeda arose in the lands of the old Malian Empire, at the southern edge of the Sahara. Nigerian schoolchildren have been the victims of kidnappings, and six countries, stretching from the Atlantic Coast to the Red Sea, have been rattled by coups. It is not clear whether those new regimes will be as accommodating of the Americans. At the least, they will be able to shop for the best deal between two nuclear powers, just as newly independent African nations did in the 1960's. But whatever deals they procure are unlikely to have any immediate impact on their suffering populations, as longstanding divisions remain and a surfeit of weapons still effects the resolution of all disputes.

Since their mutual support for the Syrian war, Russia has grown closer to Iran. While the US and its allies slap sanctions on Russia for the Ukrainian invasion and US companies like Starbucks and McDonalds shutter their Russian branches, Iran joins China in keeping the Russian economy afloat.

Iran's influence has deepened in Iraq, where it is welcomed by much of the majority Shi'ite population. In addition to its influence there and in Syria, Iran's longtime proxy, Hezbollah, considered a terrorist group by Israel and the US, is embedded in Lebanon. The Iranian-supported Houthis now control one-third of Yemen and the majority of its population.

But in Iran itself, a protest movement is gaining strength. In September 2022, a 22-year-old woman had died while in the custody of Iran's "morality police." She was arrested for not wearing her hijab (the scarf that covers the hair) in public. Since that time, many women have begun pulling off their hijabs in public. As their anger spreads, young men, too, begin to join them in solidarity. In response, Iranian security carries out beatings and fires into crowds.

The Iranian regime has not yet teetered, but neither have the aftershocks begun so long ago by that simple Tunisian street vendor ceased to rattle this unstable region of our world.

CHAPTER SEVENTEEN

A 30,000 Foot Reflection as the Moment Nears
(up to 2024)

That is how we got to the point, in the late summer of 2023, when the words "how we got ourselves to this point in time" were first typed into this manuscript. So it is time to review, from 30,000 feet, the path that has taken us here:

1.   Because of the good fortune of their geography, Eurasians and North Africans get off to a much faster start with writing and sharing ideas, leaving other regions (sub-Saharan Africa, Australia, and the Americas) well behind.

2.   Distinct regional cultures develop across Eurasia. The first monotheist religions (Judaism, Zoroastrianism) develop in the Middle East, while mysticism (Hinduism, Buddhism, Taoism) becomes established in South and Central Asia and western China. Sophist Greeks in the West and Confucianist Chinese in the East establish strong secular philosophies.

3.   In the Classical Era, vast empires of relatively equal power stretch across Eurasia, connected by trade routes. In Rome, the Catholic Church is established with its severe orthodoxy—a Greco-Romanized interpretation of the teachings of Jesus, a spiritual leader executed by the Romans in occupied Judea, where thwarted revolts result in the Jewish "diaspora."

4.   After the destruction of the classical empires by pastoral peoples of the north, the center of power retreats to the shore of the Indian Ocean, where trade survives and advancement in knowledge is kept alive in India. From there, it spreads northward to China and to a new Arab empire that arises in West Asia, a theocracy begun by the spiritual leader Muhammad, based on an extension of Judeo-Christianity called Islam. Europe remains a backwater until a series of religious wars brings it into contact with the more advanced Arabs.

243

5. When the Mongols create a continent-spanning empire,
- China is little changed, as the Mongols, absorbed into its strong culture, become yet another dynasty. (Chinese belief in the "Mandate of Heaven" leads them to accept the authority of any new ruler who can maintain a harmonious society.)
- Because its ruler tries to resist the Mongols, the Arab capital is thoroughly destroyed, setting Arab culture far back.
- Europe makes rapid gains as continent-spanning trade reopened under the "Mongol Peace" brings it the knowledge of the Chinese.

6. China begins an ambitious program of ocean exploration decades before Europe and with much more capable ships. But a perfect storm of petty feuding between palace groups, the emperor's hubris, and a fateful lightning strike causes the voyages to be suspended and all records of them destroyed.

7. So it is Europeans that instead become the masters of the oceans, with great effects on three regions:
- Europe: Grows rich from sugar and cotton produced using African slave labor. This, along with other benefits from exploration, will help them become the first to industrialize.
- The Americas: The vast majority of people are wiped out by disease germs brought by the Europeans, who had acquired them centuries before from their farm animals.
- Africa: Its once-diverse economy is sacrificed for one dependent entirely on trade in human beings, and neighboring kingdoms turn against each other, causing the continent to descend into a state of endemic poverty and internecine warfare.

8. English thinkers reframe the monarch–citizen relationship as a contract between equal parties, and the English become the first people to overthrow a king for not protecting their rights. This "Enlightenment" thinking spreads to France and to Britain's 13 American colonies, which revolt after a later king threatens to take away their self-government and free their slaves. After winning their independence and struggling for some years as a confederation of nation-states, a new constitution using a French thinker's design for a separation of powers creates the United States of America.

9. Benefits reaped from ocean exploration plus fortunate geography lead Britain to begin the Industrial Revolution. This leads to rapid urbanization and the beginning of a large middle class, and makes it the world's most powerful nation.

10. Through a bloody social revolution, France gains social equality and temporarily conquers most of Europe, spreading ideas of republicanism and nationalism. As the war shakes up Spain, Spanish colonies in the Americas gain independence but remain socially unequal.

11. As ideas of social equality spread in tandem with industrialization across Europe, the modern political spectrum forms:
- Upper-middle-class factory owners stand for republican government with limited representation and embrace laissez-faire capitalism.
- Middle-class reformers stand for full democracy and reform laws to help workers.
- Marxist Communists wait for downtrodden workers to revolt and create a classless society.

12. Industrialization spreads only to continental Europe, the US, and Japan, and these few nations begin to use their industrial power to subjugate the rest of the world in the so-called Age of New Imperialism. Their objective is to plunder everyone's natural resources and turn them into captive markets for their manufactured goods. This sets Africa back even further, solidifies Latin America's class divisions, and leads to the collapse of the 3,500-year-old Chinese Empire.

13. Nationalism and competition for colonies lead to World War One. As the European nations batter themselves, the USA becomes the world's leading power by staying out of the war until its final year, then bailing out the British, French, and Italians. Japan, too, remains unscathed. Meanwhile, Russia pulls out of the war to suffer its own social revolution, from which the communist and authoritarian-ruled USSR emerges.

14. After witnessing the horrors of industrial warfare, many pin their hopes for everlasting world peace on American president Wilson's proposal for a League of Nations and promises of self-determination for imperialized peoples. But:
- No colonies are set free.
- European nationalities within the defeated Austro-Hungarian Empire get their own nations, while Asian ones within the defeated Turkish Empire become European possessions, beginning bad blood between the West and the Middle East.
- Despite Chinese assistance winning the war, only the defeated Germans are kicked out of China, and they are replaced by the Japanese, leading China to turn toward Russia and embrace communism.
- The US does not join the League of Nations, helping to render it ineffective.

- Germany is forced to pay for damages and sign a statement saying the war was all its fault, causing resentment that will lead to the rise of Hitler.

15. A booming postwar economy collapses into depression, shaking faith in capitalism and leading to interest in nationalistic fascism. In Japan, the military takes power. In Germany and Italy, democracy is dismantled by dictators. Aggressive expansion by those three nations leads to World War Two. The US, Britain, and the USSR unite to oppose them. Civilians are directly targeted in bombing campaigns, culminating with two atomic bombs dropped by the US on Japan. The Japanese military commits countless war crimes in other Asian nations, while Germany's Nazis are responsible for genocide of the Jewish population and other "undesirables."

16. The defeated Japanese, Germans, and Italians become Western allies, but the USSR establishes puppet communist governments across Eastern Europe, leading to a "Cold War," involving a nuclear arms race and "proxy wars." Communism spreads to China, North Korea, North Vietnam, and Cuba.

17. The League of Nations is replaced by the UN, which everyone joins. It intervenes in the decolonization of Palestine, splitting it into Jewish and Arab halves, which creates ongoing tension. Over the next couple decades, 50-plus former colonies gain sovereignty as new nations, but the former imperialists try to shift from political control of colonies to dependent economic control of the new nations. The US often opposes freedom where its business interests are threatened.

18. Capitalist economies fare better than communist ones. The USSR collapses, and its European puppet governments are replaced with democracies. The other Soviet Republics regain independence from Russia. Russia and China both adopt capitalism. Russia is briefly a democracy, but reverts to autocracy. China remains autocratic as it rapidly urbanizes and modernizes, pulling most of the country out of poverty.

19. In the Middle East, debts begin coming due on the American support of bad actors:
- In Iran, the US-backed shah is deposed and replaced by a theocracy.
- In Afghanistan, the US-backed Taliban shelters al-Qaeda terrorists, who orchestrate the 9/11 attack.
- In Iraq, the US removes a leader it was responsible for bringing to power, stirring up religious warfare between the two major sects of Islam and leading to the proliferation of even more dangerous terrorist groups.

20. For the past 60 years, scientists have warned that emission of greenhouse gases that power industry will lead to catastrophic, potentially irreversible, destruction of the planet's ecosystems if drastic worldwide action is not soon taken to change course. But fossil fuel companies launch a successful propaganda campaign to generate doubt about the findings, so little is done to address the problem until decades later, by which time industrialization of the developing world (home to most of the world's population) begins to make the problem much worse.

By the time these 247 pages are completed, it is December 2023. Somewhere in Ukraine, a broken family hunkers down for another wartime winter, the optimism of the nation's warm weather counter-offensive set aside, awaiting spring.

In the Middle East, since the early fall, a concurrent war against humanity has been raging...

Thirty years after the Oslo Accords, Palestine's two segments have followed separate paths, neither bringing them any closer to full sovereignty. The influence of the Palestinian Authority is confined to the West Bank, where countless more Jewish settlements have sprung up and real power belongs to the occupying Israeli government. The Israelis have constructed a wall along their entire border with the Gaza Strip. Gaza has been ruled independently by Hamas, a terrorist organization, for the past 17 years without holding elections.

Late on a night in early October, in a highly coordinated attack, Hamas fighters breech the wall. Their attack is directed at civilians, not the Israeli military. They storm into villages near the border and start murdering people. They snatch hostages of every age, from octogenarians to infants, and carry them back to underground tunnels in Gaza. Younger women are victims of rape and sexual torture.

Benjamin Netanyahu, the conservative hardliner at the head of the coalition government in Israel, vows revenge, and Israeli bombers start striking back. Soon, the number of civilian deaths in Gaza eclipses the number killed in Israel. Since World War Two made civilians fair game—especially since Vietnam, where enemy troops were embedded with civilians—their targeting has steadily increased. The American invasion of Iraq, where Saddam Hussein popularized the term "human shields," broke the record for the rate of civilian deaths (average deaths per day of war). The Israeli attack on Gaza has broken that record again.

Meanwhile, as the humanitarian crisis in Gaza steals the world's attention from the defense of Ukraine, nearly a million more are on the brink of famine due to a brutal civil war in Sudan. Ten million have been displaced and 25 million suffer acute hunger. As always since the back-to-back decimation of slavery and imperialism, Africa's perils are the last to gain attention.

The year 2023 is the hottest year on record for the planet. Just before Christmas, the world's climate bureaucrats wrap up the 28th UN-sponsored Conference of the Parties. COP28 is being held in Dubai, at the epicenter of the world's largest reserves of oil. Delegates from 200-plus countries wrangle with the language of a simple statement into the wee morning hours of the final day of the conference, settling on pledging "to transition away from fossil fuels." (The OPEC nations refused to allow the phrase "to phase out fossil fuels."). Glass half empty, it is far too little too late. Glass half full, it is at least progress.

A single economy-class passenger who flies one-way from San Francisco to New York (or from Mumbai to Hong Kong) will create a larger carbon footprint for that one action than a person who lives in the Central African Republic will create over the course of one year. While the wider world speeds into a future that is unlike its past, those harmed most by history still struggle to escape its shackles. As the effect of rapid development in China, India, and elsewhere drives the planet past warming milestones sooner than science had predicted, the poorest of the world's countries still can hardly be termed "developing."

Carbon emitted decades ago by the imperialists continues to make up the majority of the invisible blanket driving global warming, yet the worst effects of that warming occur in the tropics, where the poorest—and least responsible—of the world's people live. The COP28 attendees debated how much developed countries should pay for their past misdeeds' ongoing effects in order to help poor countries suffering from those effects. The question remains unanswered.

As these pages head off to be typeset, the indigenous Guna people are abandoning the island of Gardi Sugdub off Panama's coast, soon to become uninhabitable due to rising seawater. Panama expects to spend 1.2 billion American dollars over the next several months relocating the Guna and 62 other small communities that inhabit low-lying islands off both of the country's coasts.

Rising sea level is just one effect of climate change that is expected to increase immigration in developed countries in the years ahead. The economic impact of crops destroyed by hot weather pests, heretofore limited to lower latitudes, is another.

As the 2024 American presidential election heats up, surveys put Latin American immigration near the top of the list of voter's concerns. Climate change is consistently near the bottom. In the recently completed elections for seats in the European Union's legislature, parties that are for immigration restriction and against fossil fuel restriction made significant inroads. The American Republican party hopes to ride the same sentiment to victory in November.

For a short while in early 2021 after the January 6 attack on the Capitol, Republican Congresspeople and even some FOX News commentators (as learned from internal records that came to light in a libel suit) seemed ready to wash their hands of Donald Trump. But his vast pool of supporters had been conditioned to mistrust mainstream news sources, so instead they believed his "Big Lie" of election fraud and remained loyal. Trump handily won the Republican nomination for president quite early in the multi-month state primary process. Since that time, despite full knowledge of his 2020 defeat, most seated party members have declared themselves back on board. There were several Republicans who refused to back a man who is accused of the felony of defrauding the United States for his attempt to overturn the results of the previous election. Almost all of them have either walked away from politics or been voted out.

It is still uncertain how Donald Trump will be noted in the history recorded in the decades ahead. Will he be despised as having done lasting harm to the American nation by besmirching its once-shining reputation, by attacking its institutions and permanently brainwashing a significant minority of the population? Or will there be new writers of history who praise him for tearing down those institutions and changing the nation to be truer to their beliefs?

The online world of the moment seems to be split between those intent on the latest memes and celebrity gossip and those rushing to judgment on the conflict in Gaza. Few seem to be thinking too deeply.

But now that moment has passed.

EPILOGUE

The Next Chapter
(2024-)

So what's going to happen next?

You tell me. You have more clues than I, being any number of moments farther along by the time you read this.

You know now, if you didn't before, that history continues beyond the horizon. It isn't a still photo of the past. So what is changing? What direction are we headed? If history is an arc into the future, then –like trying to see beyond the curvature of the Earth—you must elevate your viewpoint.

Let's pull up beyond the 30,000-foot level, to where the only thing we can make out in our view of the past is this:

> Due primarily to fortunate geography and history, our world was divided between an elite group of industrialized nations and those whose development was held back by economic imperialism. The recent extension of sovereignty to the latter has begun an acceleration of worldwide industrial development. Emission of the greenhouse gases that drive industrialism has led to the existential threat of global warming, which this accelerated development will hasten.

Though the most developed countries of the Global North have experienced stronger storms and increased wildfires due to drought, the effects of warming are initially most acute in those developing nations that are located in the warmer latitudes. But, from this height, it is clear that these effects will not remain in those nations. Straining to peer over the arc of the present moment, at least two impressions can be glimpsed:

Nearest and most clear: The impact of climate change on the developing nations raises immigration to a level where it begins to overwhelm the elite nations and meet resistance.

Not far beyond: The climate crisis worsens. Certainly, rapid reduction in tropical forest due to cattle ranching and palm oil production reduces Earth's natural carbon storage capacity, even as it releases carbon stored in prior years. Probably increased polar ice melt releases natural stores of methane into the atmosphere, creating a vicious cycle of increased melting and sea level rise. The issues that first struck the tropical and semi-tropical developing nations now move rapidly north...

And then what? Isolationism is impossible when every nation's internal actions affect every other nation. Will the former imperialists agree to be held accountable for carbon they long ago emitted yet still constitutes the majority of the current threat? Will poverty-stricken nations agree to refrain from using coal, though it may be the cheapest alternative for driving their development? Will they refrain from destroying forests that the rest of the world depends on for carbon capture? What will happen when there is no more time for civil discussion over phrasing of shared intentions? What will happen if it becomes clear that voluntary emissions reductions aren't going to cut it? Are the needed solutions beyond what a free market and a world of sovereign nations are able to achieve?

The first step in addressing any problem is coming face to face with it –in all its present and future forms. What other negative patterns of change require our attention?

War has changed. Our reaction to its industrialization has been the opposite of what we thought it would be. Instead of fleeing from its horrors, we have embraced and strategically employed them. The time when only armies went to war is long behind us. Can that direction be changed? As bombs rain down on Gaza and US president Biden beseeches Israeli leaders to back off, to try to min-imize the "collateral damage" of civilian lives, there is a growing chorus asking, "Why not zero? Why accept any civilian lives?" But their task is so much greater now than it was for those who sat down at the table in Paris in 1919.

What of politics? A couple of decades ago, most would have forecasted continuing expansion of democracy. But zooming out on history shows that true democracy is a recent development. Like anything in its infancy, continued survival is perilous. From the Axial Age Athenians to the Enlightenment-inspired American founders, and for some time afterward, suffrage was limited to a minority of the population. There have always been those who opposed its spread—first the conservative royalists, then the bourgeoisie liberals (including most of those American founders). Recently, there is not only the threat of a new Cold War in which autocrats like Xi Jinping feel their form of government can better meet the world's challenges; there is also a populist-fueled movement within democracies where large minorities feel autocracy can better meet their *nation's* challenges.

The rise of autocracy may be attributable in part to the perfecting of a key piece of its infrastructure: the delivery of disinformation. The technology employed by its purveyors is evolving –each medium an order of magnitude more powerful than the last. Goebbels used radio and film. We have rocketed past television to the Internet, made it portable, layered on social media. Artificial intelligence is up next. Social media has allowed those who wish to sway an election to enter a new dimension –to go beyond the passive presentation of propaganda, to reach through the screen and cause those in the audience to engage in specific actions. Imagine how much more powerful this ability will become as the rapidly accelerating capability of artificial intelligence makes it impossible for the casual information consumer to distinguish reality from AI-generated fakery.

Then again, what might unexpectedly arise that is powerful enough to knock the arc of history totally off course—something as significant as the Agricultural or Industrial Revolutions? Each had such subtle beginnings. Would anyone have seen *those* coming? What if we are like those hunter-gatherers who had settled but hadn't yet learned to farm? Or like a weaver in a Midlands county who has just received a knock on the door from a stranger with a business proposition? How would we know that the world of humankind was about to radically change?

In asking this, I do not mean to be fatalistic. Just the opposite. I ask in an attempt to stimulate thoughts of something larger—something far more important than social media frivolity and far more nuanced than polarized knee-jerk reactions to the situation in Gaza (or whatever other divisive issue is at the top of the news cycle in the moment you read this).

Armed with a high-level knowledge of the full scope of human history, you can cast your insular lens aside and rise above both the propaganda and the groupthink.

Even more importantly, if you know that what we seem to have evolved to is actually only what we have recently tried, it can open your mind to a wider range of what's possible. And maybe you'll glimpse a way to bend history's arc toward something more positive, something that has *never happened before*.

If you enjoyed the book and found its lessons important, please consider leaving a review here:

AFTERWORD

Without a time machine we will never know the full story of our past. All authors of history are interpreters, constantly making choices to flesh out the gaps between hard evidence.

I would love to have that time machine –and an invisibility cloak—to be able to drop in on key occurrences to acquire first-hand knowledge of those big moments in history that have been variously interpreted. I would sit in on a session with Jesus, on a discussion between Zhu Di and his advisors, on a side meeting between delegates with their own pet interests at the Constitutional Convention.

So often in the telling, in the absence of a full picture, true history is lost. Sometimes, as with Jesus (or with several other religious figures), an orthodoxy develops. And it is the nature of orthodoxy to make things fit, even when new evidence should make one question the original framework. Sometimes, as with Zhu Di and the Treasure Ships, new evidence surfaces much too late to free people from the anchor of their existing biases. Sometimes, as with the "Founders" of the USA, the weight of the task elevates it to the realm of mythology, and the human fallibility of ordinary men is erased.

I am confident that, in making the choices I have made to flesh out the gaps, I have provided a history that is far closer to a time machine version than what the vast majority of people have in their heads. Here's why:

My metaphorical use of the word "anchor" above derives from a technical term. Anchor bias is something we all form from the start of our learning lives. Early learning is the most effective learning (as anyone who has struggled to learn a second language at a later age knows). Every time we learn something the first time –even if it isn't true—it puts an anchor down in our brain. To re-learn something correctly when it was wrong the first time is a much harder task. It is what makes dis-information so hard to shake. When blatant evidence to the contrary is put right in a person's face, it is more often than not discounted or even unrecognized. They cannot free themselves from the anchor.

All of us begin to learn history in elementary school, almost always from a teacher who specializes in early childhood education but knows little about history. All those "anchors" being dragged around by students makes the high school history teacher's task difficult. And, in adulthood, when asked to remember a historical detail and you reach into your memory bank to find it, often your earliest exposure to that detail is the first to bob to the surface.

One needs to train oneself to be as critical of their stored information as they are of new, contrasting versions. Information about the past does keep improving as we find more evidence and make use of new technology to better identify, analyze and interpret it.

Many of the sources I have used to inform my most recent teaching were not available in decades past, though they have been around long enough to be critically reviewed by other scholars. A few examples are Jared Diamond's study of the effects of geography and biology on early agriculture; the work of Elaine Pagels and her fellow graduate students at Harvard in close study of writings about Jesus, both collected in and withheld from the Bible; the work of Lynda Shaffer, who first coined the term "Southernization"; and Nikole Hannah-Jones' uncovering of certain American colonial attitudes on the eve of the Revolution.

My thanks to them, and to all those who continue to look anew at this fascinating journey we all share.

ILLUSTRATIONS

The arc of history depicted on the cover of the book represents the following turning points:

Using large tamable animals for plowing – detail from Limbourg brothers and Barthélemy d'Eyck. Trés Riches Heures du duc de Berry Folio 3, verso: March {PD-US}, Wikimedia Commons, 14 April 2005, commons.wikimedia.org/wiki/File:Les_Tr%C3%A8s_Riches_Heures_du_duc_de_Berry_mars.jpg

A Mongol warrior (orig.)

Lightning strikes the Forbidden City (orig.)

Slaves on a cotton plantation – William Aiken Walker. Cotton Pickers, Wikimedia Commons, n.d., commons.wikimedia.org/wiki/File:'Cotton_Pickers',_oil_painting_on_panel_by_William_Aiken_Walker.jpg

An early coal-powered factory – William Gauci. East view of the Yniscedwyn crane anthracite iron works, near Swansea, Wikimedia Commons, c. 1845, commons.wikimedia.org/wiki/File:East_view_of_the_Yniscedwyn_crane_anthracite_iron_works,_near_Swansea.jpeg

Humanoid head representing generative AI – Adobe Stock license, https://stock.adobe.com/images/side-view-of-a-humanoid-head-with-blue-and-yellow-eyes-and-vibrant-neon-neural-network-representing-futuristic-technology-and-artificial-intelligence-generative-ai/574937307

Internal Illustrations:

(1)
Unk. Eulogized by Shen Tu. Ch'i-lin (Giraffe) {PD-US}, Wikimedia Commons, Ming Dynasty, commons.wikimedia.org/wiki/File:ShenDuGiraffePainting.jpg

(2)
George Walker. Spinning and Carding Wool - The Costume of Yorkshire, plate XXIX, opposite 69, licensed through creativecommons.org/publicdomain/mark/1.0, Wikimedia Commons, 1814, commons.wikimedia.org/wiki/File:Spinning_and_carding_wool_-_The_costume_of_Yorkshire_(1814),_plate_XXIX,_opposite_69_-_BL.jpg

(3)

Jean-Pol Grandmont. Waterwheel of Braine le-Chateau, Belgium, 12th century, Wikimedia Commons, 11 June 2005, en.m.wikipedia.org/wiki/File:Braine-le-Ch%C3%A2teau_JPG02.jpg

(4)

Egbert van Heemskerck I. The Quaker's Meeting {PD-US}, Wikimedia Commons, c. 1680, commons.wikimedia.org/wiki/File:L%27Assembl%C3%A8e_des_Couacres_ (BM_2000,0930.63).jpg

(5)

Grady Klein (illustrator) and Yoram Bauman, ph.D. (author). From *The Cartoon Introduction to Economics – Volume One: Microeconomics*, Hill & Wang, a division of Farrar, Straus & Giroux, Macmillan Publishing Company (NY), 2010. Reproduced by permission. All rights reserved.

(6)

John Jabez Edwin Mayal. A Portrait of Karl Marx {PD-US}, Wikimedia Commons, 1875, commons.wikimedia.org/wiki/File:Karl_Marx.jpg

(7)

Eugene Delacroix. Liberty Leading the People, licensed through creativecommons.org/ licenses/by-sa/2.0/deed.en, Wikimedia Commons, 1830, commons.wikimedia.org/wiki/ File:France-003348_-_Liberty_Leading_the_People_(16238458795).jpg

(8)

Unk. The Miriam and Ira D. Wallach Division of Art, Prints and Photographs: Print Collection, The New York Public Library. Yuanyingguan zhengmian, main façade of Observatory of Distant Waters, 1786, digitalcollections.nypl.org/items/ 510d47d9-8408-a3d9-e040-e00a18064a99

(9)

Antony Ongayo. Boundaries of Historical Ethnicities Before Colonization and National Boundaries, 30 June 2018, researchgate.net/figure/ Ethnic-boundaries-in-Africa-before-colonisation_fig2_332028834

(10)

Toshikata Mizuno. Hurrah! Hurrah! For the Great Japanese Empire! Great Victory for Our Troops in the Assault on Songhwan {PD-US}, Wikimedia Commons, 1894, commons. wikimedia.org/wiki/File:Battle_of_Songhwan.jpg

(11)

Unk. A Fire Waiting to be Lit: The Origins of World War 1, Bill of Rights in Action, Constitutional Rights Foundation, Vol. 30 no. 1, Fall 2014

(12)

Unk. from Narodowe Archiwum Cyfrowe, the national archive of Poland. Munich Agreement, Chamberlain: Peace for Our Time, licensed through creativecommons.org/licenses/by-sa/4.0/deed.en, Wikimedia Commons, 30 September 1938, commons.wikimedia.org/wiki/File:Munich_Agreement_(M%C3%BCnchener_Abkommen)_1938-09-30_Neville_Chamberlaine_showing_the_Anlo-German_declaration_(%22Peace_for_our_time%22)._Heston_Aerodrome,_west_of_London,_England._Narodowe_Archiwum_Cyfrowe_3_1_0_5_268_3_1_111334_No_known_cop.jpg

(13)

Unk. from German Federal Archives. Dresden, partial view of the destroyed city centre on the Elbe to the New Town. In the center of Neumarkt and the ruins of the Frauenkirche, licensed through creativecommons.org/licenses/by-sa/3.0/de/deed.en, Wikimedia Commons, 1945, commons.wikimedia.org/wiki/File:Bundesarchiv_Bild_146-1994-041-07,_Dresden,_zerst%C3%B6rtes_Stadtzentrum.jpg

(14)

Unk. Protect the Great Results of the Cultural Revolution, 1974, World History Commons, worldhistorycommons.org/protect-great-results-cultural-revolution-1974

(15)

KPF. China's latest supertall skyscraper hailed world's fourth-tallest, 21 March 2017, New Atlas, newatlas.com/kpf-pkng-an-finance-centre/48698/

(16)

Unk. Internment Camps, 1 August 2017, World Uyghur Congress, uyghurcongress.org/en/political-indoctrination-camps/

Illustrations not listed here are either original, purchased, credited within the text, or unrestricted public domain

www.ingramcontent.com/pod-product-compliance
Lightning Source LLC
Chambersburg PA
CBHW071718120626
46550CB00001B/292